AF386535

CORRUPTED KINGDOM

CORRUPTED KINGDOM

BRITAIN'S DISAPPEARING INTEGRITY – AND HOW WE CAN GET IT BACK

ROBERT BARRINGTON

First published in Great Britain in 2026 by
Profile Books Ltd
29 Cloth Fair
London
ECIA 7JQ
www.profilebooks.com

1 3 5 7 9 10 8 6 4 2

Typeset in Garamond by MacGuru Ltd
Printed and bound in Great Britain by
CPI Group (UK) Ltd, Croydon CRO 4YY

A CIP catalogue record for this book is available from the British Library.

Our product safety representative in the EU is BGC Sustainability & Compliance, 7 avenue du Général Leclerc, Paris, 75014, France https://baldwinglobalconsulting.com

ISBN 978 1 80522 315 3
eISBN 978 1 80522 317 7

To all whistleblowers, investigative journalists and anti-corruption campaigners whose courage and persistence help protect the rest of us against corruption

CONTENTS

LIST OF ACRONYMS

ABC anti-bribery and corruption
ACA anti-corruption agency
ACCA Association of Chartered Certified Accountants
AML anti-money laundering
BOT beneficial ownership transparency
CCP Chinese Communist Party
CCU Counter-Corruption Unit (of HMPPS and Police
    Scotland)
CSPL Committee on Standards in Public Life
EIC Ethics and Integrity Commission
FATF Financial Action Task Force
FDI foreign direct investment
HMICFRS His Majesty's Inspectorate of Constabulary and
    Fire and Rescue Services
HMP His Majesty's Prison
HMPPS His Majesty's Prison and Probation Service
HMRC His Majesty's Revenue and Customs
HMSO His Majesty's Stationery Office
ICAC Independent Commission Against Corruption
ICIJ Independent Consortium of Investigative Journalists
IICSA Independent Inquiry into Child Sexual Abuse
IPCC Independent Police Complaints Commission
MPS/Met Metropolitan Police

NCA National Crime Agency
NDA non-disclosure agreement
NGO non-governmental organisation
OCCRP Organized Crime and Corruption Reporting Project
OCG organised crime group
OECD Organisation for Economic Co-operation and
    Development
PPE personal protective equipment
PSC Parliamentary Standards Committee
RUSI Royal United Services Institute
SFO Serious Fraud Office
SLAPP strategic lawsuit (or litigation) against public
    participation
SNP Scottish National Party
SOC serious and organised crime
SpAd special adviser
TBIJ The Bureau of Investigative Journalism
TI Transparency International
ToRs terms of reference
UNCAC United Nations Convention Against Corruption
UWO Unexplained Wealth Order

NOTE ON REFERENCING

With the use of modern search engines and AI tools, most facts, quotations and documents mentioned in this book can be located with ease, as can individual quotations within documents. To avoid excessive referencing, citations have been limited to academic works that are explicitly discussed, sources of direct quotations unless already widely quoted and easily traceable, and information that is less straightforward to track down. Where facts or quotations are widely available in the public domain, references have therefore not been included; instead, the main text aims to provide sufficient detail to allow readers to locate them quickly. Long URLs have been avoided as they are unsuitable for printed works, but adequate information has been included to allow websites to be easily found. One area that is harder to reference is social media commentary, which is most usually cited when an incident or individual is accused of being corrupt; in such cases, the text specifies that there are social media commentary or allegations, which can be verified through searches on the relevant platforms.

PREFACE

In 1962, the American ecologist Rachel Carson published a book called *Silent Spring*, a chilling warning which predicted that if mankind did not stop destroying the natural world it would soon fall silent, with devastating consequences for human life. Carson's work led to legislation to control pesticides and spurred an environmental movement that continues today. She expressed it like this: 'What we have to face is not an occasional dose of poison which has accidentally got into some article of food, but a persistent and continuous poisoning of the whole human environment.'

Having studied corruption in this country for more than two decades, it is clear to me that at some point – possibly soon – we may as a society be facing our own '*Silent Spring*' moment. And this one will be linked not with environmental problems, but with corruption.

The process of a country being taken over by corruption is known as state capture. This has happened in many countries around the world: places like Russia and Afghanistan may spring to mind as examples where a small and corrupt elite gain an iron grip on power, but it can also happen in places closer to home. Democracies and developed economies are not immune. Hungary – an EU country – is often described as having been in a situation of state capture, and all the indications are that what we are seeing under the Trump presidency is that the United States is moving in the same direction. In a situation of state capture, the country is run by a self-interested elite, dedicated not to the public interest but to maintaining power – and using that power for personal benefit. That does not just happen at the level of the national government; it rapidly permeates all aspects of society, because those in power depend on corrupt patron–client relationships to support their cause and eliminate opposition. And the example set by those at the top encourages corruption throughout the system of government, public services and the private sector.

Imagine a town in which the local council is run by a single party, re-elected regularly because it runs slick campaigns and is dominated by big well-known local personalities. When elections come round, the party promises the world: plenty of houses and good schools, while efficiently taking care of the elderly and collecting the rubbish. Low crime rates on the streets, a thriving high street and excellent parking. And enough of this is achieved for the party to sound convincing when the next election comes round. What's not to like?

For the councillors, however, office-holding is a chance to make money. Developers pay backhanders in order to be allowed to build whatever they want, wherever they want. Refuse collectors make hidden payments to the councillors for unspecified 'services', dumping the waste they collect in illegal sites. Schools and care homes have their budgets skimmed, and therefore are badly maintained and lacking basic equipment, even though they seem to be doing well on paper by managing to tick boxes for 'key performance indicators'. Green spaces are turned into car parks by private contractors that are secretly owned by council members, who make a fortune through parking fees and fines. The local police and inspectors for things like the environment, standards in care homes and health and safety all turn a blind eye; they are also part of the local scheme of cronyism and patronage, sharing the rewards of power. Opponents and whistleblowers are harassed and intimidated; they might be left unable to find local employment.

It does not take much imagination to see how corruption can thrive, and the damage that can be done as a result. The aim of this book is to present a picture of what is known about corruption in Britain since 1950, and to test the country against different forms of corruption identified in the academic literature. It will focus particularly on developments since 1990, when the modern anti-corruption movement came into being.

We will see that, in general, the national response to corruption has been founded on a conviction that corruption happens abroad and we therefore do not need to look for it at home. At the same time, despite this complacency, the UK is interpreted by some commentators as being fundamentally corrupt, run by a political and business establishment that systematically and consistently rigs society, the economy and politics in its own self-interest. We will test such claims. As we assess various aspects of British life, we will find examples of how bad things are in some areas, but also considerable grounds for optimism – for Britain does some things very well.

My own professional journey into the murky world of corruption started when I left a job as head of an environmental NGO to work in the City. And when I got there, my boss tasked me with looking at the long-term risks that corruption might pose to companies, in case recent international anti-corruption treaties – and the national laws that followed them – looked likely to have a negative financial impact on the companies in which we invested. This brought me into contact with the emerging case of BAE Systems and its contracts with Saudi

Arabia – since the company I worked for was a major shareholder in BAE.

It also introduced me to Transparency International (TI), an NGO that was less than ten years old but had already established a reputation both for being a think-tank producing high-quality research on corruption, and for intelligent campaigning about this complex issue. TI was strongly critical of the UK government's handling of the BAE case. I had always thought of myself as working undercover in the City – doing a job in plain sight, while trying to work out how capitalism operated from the inside. So when I was contemplating my next career change, going back into the non-profit sector and working at the London office of Transparency International felt like a natural step.

My experiences of more than a decade at TI, as head of its division in the UK and latterly chair of its International Council, permeate many of the chapters in this book.

Like everyone else, I could already see that all over the world – from Lebanon to Venezuela and from South Africa to Indonesia – there were popular protests that seemed increasingly to be focused on corruption. At the same time, populist politicians were harnessing this anger and using it to gain power – a false dawn when they proved to be corrupt themselves. Meanwhile, eye-catching sums were being looted by politicians and public officials, while the lives of millions of ordinary people were being blighted by having to pay petty bribes and being deprived of basic public services.

Being inside TI and seeing this happen every day, I was struck by a few other things. First, the courage that was required to work as an anti-corruption activist around the world. My colleagues risked intimidation, imprisonment and even death; one of my TI colleagues in Sri Lanka, a respected human rights lawyer, had his house firebombed. By comparison, the worst I faced in London was the threat of lawsuits delivered on behalf of thuggish oligarchs, having my communications 'compromised' and being told that if I carried on giving the government a hard time I was less likely to make the honours list.

London felt like a privileged place to be an anti-corruption campaigner, but working at TI made me aware of how the world's global financial centres are involved with other countries' corruption problems. Centres like London can provide a transit hub and a destination for money stolen from a health budget in West Africa, the bribes paid by a British company in Malaysia or the vast profits made by an oligarch from a former state-owned enterprise privatised under opaque circumstances in the 1990s.

Anti-corruption campaigners need to be optimists, or they would simply give up in the face of such challenges. Corruption has a significant cost for society and the economy; and, once it takes hold, it is like an aggressive weed that can take over an entire garden – even when you think you have removed it at the roots, it keeps on coming back. But at TI I also saw what can be done to defend against corruption; there are some things that clearly work, and some countries are able to do them better than others. Naturally, as I saw these things happening across the world, my mind turned to Britain and the United Kingdom.* Where do we sit in this world of corruption?

I was surprised to find that relatively little is known about corruption within the British Isles – whether in the police, prisons, local government, social housing or immigration, all areas that in other countries are high-risk. What we do know has to be patched together from research, reports and scandals that are usually dealing with some other issue entirely. There has

---

* See further down for this distinction.

been no systematic study to date of this body of information, and it is that gap which this book seeks to help fill.

There is also a fundamental challenge of how to reconcile the conflicting views of Britain, which come from both home and abroad. It is simultaneously believed to be: a strong and stable democracy; subject to the malign influences of the Establishment and the City; a colonial corrupter unwilling to take responsibility for its legacy; a strong supporter of the international order; a cynical and complicit centre for illicit financial flows; a moral force for good. I hope that in the course of this book I can explain some of these contradictions.

Much of Britain's corruption is what we might describe as subcutaneous. As I will show, our body politic is in many places either infected or at risk of infection, but this lies beneath the surface. Our antibodies have until now been able to keep the infection in check, but the infection is getting worse – and the defences are getting weaker. It sounds pretty bad, and there is a risk that a book such as this will add to the doom and gloom of the nation. That is by no means my intention. On the contrary, I hope that by applying the lens of corruption analysis to institutions and events that are in many cases already well known, we will get closer to understanding the problem – and therefore be better placed to deal with it.

My underlying approach is that understanding and evidence are the basis of good policymaking. After all, if we have a sound analysis of the problem, we are more likely to find solutions that are fit for purpose. This brings to mind a saying from Einstein: 'If I had an hour to solve a problem, I'd spend fifty-five minutes thinking about the problem and five minutes thinking about solutions.' In this country, we do not spend enough time thinking about whether corruption is a problem. If we were more aware, we might appreciate that while corruption does not explain everything about contemporary Britain, it can explain a great deal about political leadership, economic growth and the decline of our key institutions.

While researching this book, I have often been asked what is going wrong with Britain – and whether corruption is the cause. Many people share a sense that things are out of kilter and are unsure where the country is heading. In fact, Britain may be experiencing what corruption analysts call a 'big bang' moment:[1] a point when a country can choose between two paths – one that leads to more corruption or another that brings it under control.

I often encounter deep-state conspiracy theories about the City and the Establishment. For example, that the outsourcing of so many public services to the private sector is driven by a small cabal of politicians, financiers and business leaders who want to feather their own nests irrespective of the quality of service provided, and that this is enabled by the fact that so many were at the same schools and universities together. The truth is both more complex and more worrying. As I will demonstrate, there are many pockets of corruption in the UK, sometimes barely kept in check by a set of weakened institutions. There is no single group pulling the strings, but corruption can be damaging without being coordinated. This comes against a background of some deep-rooted issues like increasing inequality, economic stagnation and political instability, constituting a series of social, economic and political threats to our national well-being. These are prime conditions for corruption to thrive, which gives rise to an uncomfortable reality: the corruption in this country may not yet have been as damaging as in other countries, but we should not believe the UK is immune, and there may be worse to come if corrective action is not taken.

Based on thousands of interviews and conversations with

everyone from ex-offenders to ex-prime ministers, this book explores the links between important contemporary ideas such as chumocracy and Londongrad, as well as high-profile issues like corruption in the Metropolitan Police and the monarchy. Britain is complacent about corruption, but the threats are rising and the defences are weakened. The rotten apples are starting to look like a rotting barrel.

As a country, we can avoid waking up to the silent spring. If we do not act, we may move into illiberal democracy, state capture or systemic corruption. But there is an alternative. We could use integrity and standards to refuel Britain's national well-being and international reputation. The choice is ours to make.

INTRODUCTION

In 2018, David Cameron agreed to deliver the annual Transparency International lecture – his first public speech after stepping down as Prime Minister. Cameron's private office wanted to vet the possible press attendees. After some discussion, we allowed them to see the list, but not to decide who could come. They principally objected to the attendance of *Private Eye*, on the grounds that they did not see the connection to corruption. In a nutshell, this encapsulated much about the attitude of those in power in the UK: that corruption happens abroad but not at home; that if it is not straightforwardly illegal bribery, it isn't really corruption; and that exposing it is a niche occupation of a few conspiracist cranks, who have no place in a room of grown-ups. It was an excellent speech as far as it went – but some of those very same assumptions ran through it. In fact, when I asked Cameron in the Q&A about his own government's failed attempts to regulate lobbying, he neatly deflected the question, which he evidently had little inclination to answer.

The sense of complacency, denial and exceptionalism will be a key theme in this book. To borrow a term used by political scientists, we will look at how Britain is locked into a 'path dependence', a subject I will explore further in Chapter Three. The consequence is that we are inclined to spot rotten apples rather than look for a rotting barrel – and as a result we are not properly facing up to the problem.

There are lots of terms that can be used instead of corruption: misconduct, wrongdoing or fraud are just three examples. We will look in the next chapter at the definition being used in this book. But why should it matter at all whether we use the term corruption? I think there are three good reasons.

First, you need a proper understanding of the problem if you are to find a workable solution. If something fits the definition of corruption, we should be unafraid to apply the label rather than a more comfortable synonym. Second, corruption is self-evidently rotten. Some associated terms such as chumocracy can be helpful in giving a sense of what is happening, but there is almost universal agreement that corruption is not a good thing. So if you apply the label correctly, you are also implying that action needs to be taken. And third, corruption is serious, with deep and lasting consequences – not something that you can leave alone and only turn to when other problems have been dealt with. In fact, it may well be a cause of or key contributor to those other problems, so it needs addressing sooner rather than later.

The theme of protecting democracy runs through this book, but that means much more than simply having a well-functioning electoral system. It also refers to the necessity of protecting democratic values, which include the rule of law, fair allocation of the nation's resources, and rights that are equally available to all citizens. In a well-functioning democracy, people trust that the institutions of the state will safeguard these values and provide security, stability and prosperity. High standards of public life by individuals in public positions – from council officers and police constables to judges and cabinet members – help to maintain the health of those institutions of the state, which in turn both keeps corruption at bay and reinforces society's confidence that democratic values are worthwhile.

By contrast, corruption undermines trust in the institutions that protect democratic values – and also the trust that democracy will provide security, stability and prosperity. This can lead voters to look for illiberal leaders who promise to achieve these things by other means. History tells us that those illiberal leaders are themselves likely to be corrupt – and in order to keep themselves in power may seek to progress towards state capture, along the way neutering the kind of institutions and constitutional checks and balances that are meant to prevent this from happening.

We should, therefore, be in no doubt that corruption matters – its existence or mere perception can cause liberal democracy to slide into illiberal democracy, a phrase proudly adopted by Hungary's Viktor Orbán to describe his regime, but which corruption analysts see as a pathway towards the all-out corruption of state capture. Even being in an illiberal democracy is a rescuable situation because people still have a functioning voting system, albeit one that can be distorted by media ownership, electoral gymnastics and government inducements. But the corruption of the ruling group, supported by an oligarchy, leads almost inexorably towards state capture. There are plenty of recent examples: Georgia, Serbia, Thailand and Turkey, to name but a few. And one of the most worrying lessons of state capture is that recovering from it seems to be next to impossible.

However, just because state capture represents an undesirable end point, we should not be misled into thinking that liberal democracies are havens of integrity. As the coming chapters will illustrate, the UK has its own problems. Plenty of things, from cronyism to political influence by companies, hover on the verge of corruption; while they may not always be individually corrupt, they can collectively add up to a system that is.

Correctly labelling something or someone as corrupt in a liberal democracy is therefore important. The label is not to be used lightly, but we should not shy away from applying it when the situation requires. In the next chapter we will look at the baseline definition of corruption I intend to use to analyse the UK.

As an aside, we must be wary of characterising corruption with a simplistic 'problem–solution' approach. Certainly, we should not think it is possible to 'solve' or eliminate corruption. I prefer to use terms such as 'address', 'tackle' or even 'deter' or 'prevent' to describe the approach that must be taken. And while I think it is fair to characterise corruption as a 'problem', that does not mean it is a simple one.

Moreover, using the problem–solution terminology might suggest a transactional rather than structural type of corruption – an important distinction. Transactional corruption refers to a relationship in which someone gives something and gets something else in return – often described as a 'quid pro quo'. An example is a company paying a bribe to a public official. They pay the bribe, and gain a reward such as planning permission or a contract. Although the corruption is usually deliberately concealed, such transactions can be more recognisable than structural corruption. For example, if a public service has been diverted over time towards the enrichment of a handful of employees rather than delivering a good service, that kind of corruption is system-wide – deep-rooted, harder to spot and far more damaging.

In this book we will find plenty of transactional corruption in the UK. But if structural corruption is more damaging, how far does it permeate our institutions? This question gets us into tricky territory. Some scholars – and many polemicists

– argue that the very basis of our society is corrupt: it enriches an elite while leaving most people poor. While I believe that such inequality is bad for society, I am more hesitant to term it as intrinsically corrupt. That is in part because arguments over whether a country like the UK is structurally corrupt are highly subjective. They often reflect pre-existing ideologies. Those with a left-wing predisposition eagerly cite capitalism and neoliberalism as being fundamentally corrupt. Populists on both right and left argue that a corrupt elite has taken hold of 'the system' and must be thrown out root and branch. They assume that you can't have *a bit* of structural corruption: either the structure is corrupt or it is not. But a more nuanced view might be that a country can be on a journey towards structural corruption, and before reaching that fundamental point there are staging points like failures of integrity by politicians and public officials, widespread transactional corruption, and structural corruption within some but not all institutions.

Corrupted Kingdom aims to give readers the tools to form a judgement about structural corruption in the UK, in part by pointing out where some of the arguments do and don't stack up.

I am most interested in working out what we actually know and can agree on: where we see corruption in its more conventional form. We might still conclude that there is structural corruption, but we will have taken a bottom-up approach to forming that judgement. Fundamentally, I am arguing that even without entering philosophical debates, we can discern that there is more widespread corruption in Britain than has been previously recognised. Our situation seems to be the classic syndrome of the frog in boiling water – when the temperature gradually increases, the change is not noticed until it is too late.

* * *

Finding out how well a country is doing, and how things compare to the past, often comes down to measurement. We do that in many areas, from the economy and health to education and the environment, so it seems obvious that we should do the same for corruption. After all, it would be useful to know how well Britain is doing and whether there is more or less corruption than in the past. But even working out what corruption means can be difficult. To complicate things further, some parts of a country might have higher levels of corruption than others. There might be a relatively clean sector, such as the leisure industry, and another, such as the construction sector, where bribe-paying is much more common. There might also be some areas of the public sector that are much less corrupt than others – for example, what is known as the supreme audit institution (in the UK's case the National Audit Office) may be clean, while the police are highly corrupt.

The best-known and most frequently used measure of corruption is the Corruption Perceptions Index (CPI), produced annually by Transparency International. This is based on a series of surveys of experts, asking them to score the levels of public sector corruption in countries around the world. The CPI was regularly launched in London when I was heading up TI, and I became familiar with the arguments of both its critics and its supporters. There was always plenty of media coverage, as well as inevitable criticism from academics about the methodology. Other well-known indices try to measure so-called proxy factors, the idea being that if other building blocks of the political economy are healthy, then corruption will be less likely. These indices include the World Bank's Worldwide Governance Indicators, the Index of Public Integrity, the Rule of Law Index and the Quality of Government Index. Although there are fierce academic debates about which of these is best, they all tend to tell a broadly similar story.

The UK usually performs well on these indices. The countries that do best are small, rich and democratic – typically the Scandinavian countries, Switzerland, Singapore and New Zealand. The standard of living in those countries tells us something in itself about how pleasant it would be to live in a corruption-free environment. After these countries, there's a cluster of larger rich democracies, including most of the G7. The UK jostles for position among this group, along with others that are moving up the tables thanks to a period of stable and effective government – these periodically include countries like Barbados and Uruguay, both of which have performed well in recent years.

But although the UK is usually in the top quartile of these tables, we should note that our position on every one of them has declined in recent years. The position on the Corruption Perceptions Index is particularly instructive. In 2017 the UK was in eighth place with a score of 82 per cent; by 2025 it had sunk to twentieth place with a score of 70 per cent. There are real-world consequences to a country being seen to perform worse on issues like governance and corruption. In 2020, for example, the credit agency Moody's downgraded the UK's credit rating, due principally to the impact of the Covid pandemic, but also – and unusually – citing 'The weakening in the UK's institutions and governance' and noting that 'While still high, the quality of the UK's legislative and executive institutions has diminished in recent years.'[1]

These things matter to governments, and I remember being summoned to the Home Office one year to explain to the relevant minister why the UK's score had declined on the index that TI had produced. He was very irate and rather loud, spelling out with a red face all the things he had done to address the UK's role in international money laundering. I had to explain that despite some progress in that area, the UK was being judged on a basket of issues, including domestic corruption and integrity in politics; the perception was that the UK was not doing well – and in politics in particular.

I should concede that the minister did have a point. The UK's role as a global financial centre is not generally reflected in those indices, and therefore the role played by London, the Overseas Territories (like the British Virgin Islands) and the Crown Dependencies (like Jersey and the Isle of Man) in the flows of corrupt capital does not cause the UK's position to be pushed downwards, just as his passing of new laws to combat money laundering had not caused the UK's position to improve.

Some critics of these indices claim that they let the UK off the hook – that the nation's greatest contribution to global corruption is allowing people from overseas to launder the proceeds of their corruption through our system. A further criticism comes from those who feel that the UK has an under-lying level of hard-wired corruption that such indices fail to capture – that it has been going on for so long that people have forgotten it is corrupt. That critique comes from people who see chumocracy and the public-school, Oxbridge elite as exercising a disproportionate and unhealthy control over the country; and from people who are suspicious of untrammelled capitalism and deregulated markets, believing that the pursuit of profit is fundamentally incompatible with the public interest. We will look in more detail at those debates in Chapters Five and Six.

So what do we actually know about corruption in the UK? Getting involved in debates over definitions and measurement risks overcomplicating an already complex subject. Even without concluding that the UK has underlying structural corruption linked to the establishment or capitalism, enough corruption is happening in plain sight for a worrying picture to emerge. Several chapters in the book try to piece together what we concretely know about corruption in the UK, while setting aside more subjective discussions.

One simple illustration of this concerns the bribery that takes place in this country. There is universal agreement that bribery is a form of corruption. And looking at patterns of it here can help fill out the wider picture of corruption in the UK. For example, even though there are those who still believe that bribery and other forms of corruption happen overseas but not here, the evidence from the Bribery Act of 2010 tells a different story. This new law had been expected to be applied to UK companies paying bribes overseas, so it was surprising when the first three cases turned out to involve bribes paid by individuals within the UK.

The first case was Munir Yakub Patel,[2] a clerk working at Redbridge Magistrates' Court in Essex. In August 2011, he was convicted of accepting a bribe of £500 to help a driver avoid being placed on the court record system for a speeding offence. Patel was said in court to have repeated this action at least fifty times, assisting those guilty of road traffic offences to avoid fines, disqualifications from driving or having penalty points put on their driving licences. Patel was arrested after the *Sun* newspaper filmed him arranging the bribe, acting on a tip-off from a member of the public to whom Patel had offered his services. Patel received a sentence of six years in prison, which was reduced to four years on appeal.

The judge's remarks illustrate the seriousness with which the crime was regarded, because Patel was a public official in a position responsible for upholding the rule of law: 'A justice system in which officials are prepared to take bribes in order to allow offenders to escape the proper consequences of their offending is inherently corrupt and is one which deserves no public respect and which will attract none.' Moreover, there was the further cost to society of letting dozens of potentially dangerous drivers back onto the road.

In addition to Patel, more than twenty of those people who paid him a bribe were convicted, many for perverting the course of justice. The court was read a text message from Patel in which he said: 'I only do this for Asian bruvs. I do this all day long.'[3] Media coverage at the time speculated that he had repeated this offence several hundred times.

The second case was Mawia Mushtaq.[4] He was hoping to qualify as a taxi driver in Oldham, Lancashire, for which he needed to take a driving test accompanied by a council licensing official to qualify for a private hire licence. When Mushtaq was told he had failed the test, he offered the official a bribe of £200, which he subsequently increased to £300, to record that he had passed the test and to issue the licence he required. The official reported the attempted bribery to his manager, who in turn reported it to the police. Mushtaq was convicted in December 2012 and sentenced to two months in prison, suspended for twelve months.

The third prosecution under the Bribery Act, in April 2013, concerned Yang Li,[5] the son of a wealthy Chinese businessman and a student at the University of Bath. He had received a mark of 37 per cent for his dissertation, fractionally below the 40 per cent pass mark. At a meeting with two tutors, Li was given three standard options for how to proceed. He proposed a fourth: producing £5,000, he proposed, 'You can keep the money if you give me a pass mark.' His offer was declined, and he caused further alarm when he dropped a gun – later found to be an air pistol – on the floor, before leaving with the cash and gun. His tutor reported the incident, and on conviction Li received a twelve-month prison sentence.

You will notice that in all of these cases someone refused a bribe and reported it to the relevant authorities. In the case of Munir Yakub Patel and the speeding tickets, hundreds of others had apparently already paid the bribe before someone refused and sounded the alarm. But in how many such instances do the bribes go unreported? Should we infer that for each reported case, hundreds are never uncovered? This is a question that we will face throughout this book: are cases of corruption the exception or part of a repeated pattern? Rotten apples, or rotting barrel?

To help build up a picture, we might ask how much it costs to pay a bribe in the UK. Prices of goods and services are usually established by the market, in which there is transparency about what other people are charging for the same thing. For example, we can easily find out the price of a pint of milk, and with a bit more effort how much to pay for an ounce of cannabis. So if we can establish what the market price is for a bribe, it may give a sense of how common such transactions are. In a study from 1999, Vannucci and Della Porta observed: 'Where corruption is systemic, bribery not only extends to "everything" but precise rates of payment tend to emerge, reducing the risk of endless negotiation between corrupter and corrupted.'[6] But how much one needs to pay for a bribe in the UK is actually quite hard to establish. One further twist is that where people are paying bribes, and how much, can be affected by other factors, and can fluctuate according to how those external factors change. For example, in 2025 I first became aware that bribery in driving tests was becoming more frequent – not just to pass the test, but also to get a booking for a test. It seems likely that this was a response to the lack of availability of such test bookings, and the long waiting times for them.

The easiest place to find data is from cases that have come to court. There were 327 bribery prosecutions between 1989 and 2017,[7] for offences prosecuted under at least seven different laws including the Bribery Act, misconduct in public office, the Anti-Terrorism, Crime and Security Act and the Public Bodies Corrupt Practices Act.[8] We can add to this picture a recent data source on bribery in business from the Home Office's Economic Crime Survey, which forms the most extensive study of UK bribery in the past decade.[9]

Putting all this together, what does it tell us about the market for bribes in the UK? Companies – as you might expect – pay larger bribes, and are looking for larger rewards. The sums here can be in the tens of thousands of pounds upwards, depending on how much benefit they are receiving – and, in cases of British companies bribing overseas, the bribes can be in the tens of millions. For companies of all sizes, the average bribe paid or received in the UK is £2,640 (according to the Home Office research).

Public officials in the UK, by contrast, are relatively cheap: a notable feature of many of the cases in this book. A few hundred pounds will suffice as a bribe, if you can find an official willing to take it. For a police officer, whose career may be on the line, we are in the realm of thousands of pounds, often paid through long-term relationships with regular payments. And there are some areas where it is harder to discern the trend or market price because there are few known cases, like jury-bribing. In one well-known Scottish case, the jury member Catherine Leahy was bribed £2,830 to let off a drug dealer in a Glasgow court. She was caught and prosecuted after a tip-off. The only other recent case of bribing a juror involved a much smaller sum: in a case in Leeds, seven defendants tried to bribe five jurors by offering them £500 each. The jurors reported the attempt to the judge.[10] These cases offer a fascinating glimpse into what can go on, but, based on just these two cases alone, we cannot confidently state that £2,830 is sufficient to bribe a juror but £500 is not enough, let alone have any sense of how widespread the practice is.

Bribery is easy to focus on – it is against the law and everyone agrees it is corrupt – but it is just one form of corruption. The key message from these cases is that corruption, in its most blatant form, does indeed happen in the UK. In the course of this book we will encounter other types of corruption, such as embezzlement, trading of influence, abuse of function and illicit enrichment (all offences in UNCAC, the UN Convention Against Corruption), as well as other areas like cronyism and nepotism. For newcomers to the subject, it is important to remember that there are many more forms of corruption at play in the UK than simple bribery – some of which operate entirely legally.

So there is plenty of variety to explore. We will look at public sector corruption (ranging from bribery of politicians to the prisons crisis), private sector corruption (whether cronyism in planning decisions and abusive lobbying or overseas bribery by firms like Rolls-Royce and BAE Systems) and political corruption (like access capitalism and handing contracts to party donors in non-competitive bidding processes). But it does not stop there. We will also look at corrupt capital flows as well as strategic corruption, through which hostile powers and organised crime groups weaponise corruption to undermine the state. Inevitably, some areas are missing; the fact that I will not analyse corruption in education, trade unions or the NHS, for instance, does not mean they are free of it.

Some of this story will be familiar from popular culture,

in which corruption seems widespread: police and prison corruption are endemic, with close links to organised crime, in *Line of Duty*; we see it in the prison drama *Time*, along with money laundering and organised crime in *McMafia*. How far do these reflect reality? Popular dramas accentuate the worst and imply that it is the norm. We may enjoy *Inspector Morse* without assuming that Oxford has a higher murder rate than Bogotá. But popular fiction is not entirely divorced from reality, and the sheer number of books, plays and dramas that identify a plausible or recognisable form of corruption in the UK should at least cause us to ask how much truth lies behind them.

One of the themes we will explore is whether there is a 'peculiarly British' form of corruption. A strand of polemical writing on the UK seems to take this as a starting point, and in the next chapter we will explore what that means. What about the arguments that the establishment, the monarchy or capitalism are inherently corrupt? We will also examine definitions that we can apply, such as structural and institutional corruption, to give greater analytical focus to such claims.

Like most analyses of the UK, it is easy to be London-centric – the City, Whitehall and Westminster are dominant forces in all our lives, after all. To build a map of corruption in the UK we need to look beyond London – to the countryside, our major cities, and each of the UK's four nations. Later chapters deal with that geographical diversity. Unless otherwise identified, I am taking the whole of the UK as the book's territory; however, I have used the terms 'Britain' and 'British' as shorthand to refer to things nationwide (although it is not technically correct – the United Kingdom consists of Great Britain plus Northern Ireland, though the term British Isles encompasses all of the above).

While I do not believe that the UK needs to be humbled

into apologism about corruption, we do need to know how close we are to waking up to that silent spring. We may not share the levels of corruption of Russia or Afghanistan, but that should not allow us the luxury of complacency.

1

PECULIARLY BRITISH: THE SMALL PRINT ON WHAT WE MEAN BY CORRUPTION

This chapter will look at definitions and methodology. They are important in order to explain my approach in collecting and analysing the information that is examined in this book. But they are the small print of a work like this, and you may want to come back to this chapter later if you prefer to get more quickly to the tangible examples of corruption in the UK that support the book's overall argument.

We should first look at the four common approaches to describing corruption in liberal democracies, and work out which of these is most applicable to the UK. The term 'transactional corruption' refers to individual one-off actions such as bribe-paying, where there is an element of quid pro quo; while 'systematic corruption' and 'systemic corruption' are used to describe situations in which there is lots of that transactional corruption, though the latter is also sometimes used interchangeably with 'structural corruption'. This refers to corruption that is embedded within structures and institutions, describing the situation when rules, incentives and power relations encourage or normalise corrupt practices but individuals often do not feel themselves to be acting corruptly. 'Institutional corruption' means that an institution has become so captured by groups advocating for their own interests that it is diverted from its original purpose. Confused? You should be. It has taken scholars decades to work out these fine differences, and many of them are still argued over today. But help is at hand in the form of a handy four-step test that allows us to determine whether something or someone is corrupt, and that is the starting point for much of my analysis. More of that in a moment.

If you read the scant literature on corruption in the UK, you will often find the suggestion that there is a 'peculiarly British' form of corruption. The phrase tends to be used to suggest that an elite educational system, a dominant financial services sector, rigid class structure and colonial legacy have combined to create something that is not seen elsewhere. Well, a core theme of this book is that the corruption that can be found in the UK is not peculiarly British, but rather the opposite. It is, in fact, depressingly similar to the corruption that can be seen elsewhere in the world. By calling it 'peculiarly British', we are claiming an exceptionalism that it does not deserve. We do not have a special form of corruption – we have the same dirty, selfish, secretive abuses of power in Britain that we delight in condemning abroad.

Recent scholarship has tended to argue that local context is vital to understanding corruption, particularly when designing solutions to tackle it.[1] From this we might infer that every country does have its own peculiar form of corruption. In some cases that is true, but I think we might more accurately say that all countries are choosing from the same menu, but mixing up their order in different ways and delivering it with some national variance. So even if British corruption is not exceptional, we need to understand what corruption means in the British context, and how it operates, if we are to address it.

There is a methodological conundrum at the core of any study of corruption in liberal democracies. How can we find a language and an approach that allows us both to describe the particular forms of corruption that take place in liberal democracies, and to assess the extent of corruption in the absence of data? In an age of evidence-led policymaking and the primacy given to arguments based on quantitative analysis, any examination of corruption in the UK will point towards the findings of the various indices of corruption as the most obvious data source. Such quantitative measures have therefore been the basis of much UK policymaking, including our national anti-corruption strategies. Yet the favourable portrayals of the UK from such indices are at odds with more qualitative analyses of corruption in the UK. For example: historians, who seldom have the luxury of quantitative evidence, tend to sense an underlying level of corruption that periodic scandals reveal; while theorists in political science and economics detect levels of corruption risk that are not matched by measurable levels of corruption; and polemicists see such high levels of inequality and injustice that they believe corruption must be a cause.

To unpick this conundrum, we must start by examining what the term 'corruption' actually means. Thousands of academic papers on the subject have been published in the past thirty years. One recent study[2] found 5,417 published between 1990 and 2020, up from 914 that an earlier study had found in the decades up to 1990.[3] Many of these papers have been excellent, but there remains considerable academic debate around how to define corruption.

Throughout this book, I will use as a starting point a four-step test to determine whether to apply the label. This baseline definition of corruption is:

'The abuse of entrusted power for private gain that harms the

public interest, typically breaching laws, regulations and/or integrity standards.'[4]

This definition suggests a sequential four-step process in order to determine whether something or someone is corrupt. Do they have entrusted power? Have they abused it? Is there private gain? And does this harm the public interest? This is sometimes described as a 'principal–agent' approach because it assumes that the person or body with entrusted power (the agent) has obligations to do something on behalf of the public (the principal); corruption can occur when they have divergent interests and the principal does not have enough information to check that the agent is really acting on their behalf.[5]

There are long-standing academic debates on how to define corruption, but to my mind this definition is applicable in most practical circumstances. In fact, a review of 117 definitions by Rebecca Dobson Phillips at the Centre for the Study of Corruption settled on this as the best short-form combination that incorporates all the essential elements while also being easily interpretable.[6]

However, no single definition seems to apply satisfactorily to corruption in liberal democracies. So there now follows a brief exploration of other well-used definitions that can be used alongside this four-step test. We will start with a brief excursion into the definition of 'political corruption', the area of corruption that has exercised many scholars in the field from the mid-twentieth century onwards.

Corruption has been the subject of serious academic study since the 1960s, when the Harvard political scientist Joseph Nye called it 'behaviour which deviates from the formal duties of a public role' – in other words, there is an assumption that someone in a public role with formal duties should be acting in the public interest.[7] It places the responsibility on an individual or group of individuals for acting wrongly, and this represents one key school of thought in corruption definitions. The other main school of thought is that we live within a system that is corrupt: the body politic is in a state of decay, which both explains and causes the actions of individuals.[8] Both schools of thought assume there is a 'right' way of doing things, which political scientists would describe as a normative view. In my opinion, these two approaches to defining corruption are not mutually exclusive: they are symbiotic. The more individuals abuse their entrusted power, the closer we come to structural corruption; and where there is a prevalence of structural corruption, individuals are more likely to abuse their power. Moreover, in the situation of there being a corrupted system of politics and society, individuals do still have responsibility for doing things in the right way, even if that is harder because they are fighting the system to do so.

The issue of corruption in politics moved from theory to reality in the US with Watergate in the 1970s, and the study of political corruption was given further impetus with the fall of the Soviet Union. Fledgling democracies then faced the challenge of reconciling deep-seated societal corruption with a new democratic political system, while at the same time absorbing the rise of influential oligarchs who were growing exorbitantly rich through the acquisition of resources such as privatised state-owned companies.

Those events of the 1990s opened the door to a new generation of discussions about the nature of political corruption. The leading British academics Paul Heywood and Mark Philp,[9] for example, wrestled with the idea of whether corruption always involves law-breaking, and how to tell the difference between the cut-and-thrust of democratic politics and political corruption. Former World Bank economist Daniel Kaufmann has been a prime exponent of the notion that corruption does not always mean breaking the law;[10] while Harvard professors Dennis Thompson and Lawrence Lessig have taken this a stage further,[11] arguing that parliaments and governments can themselves be institutionally corrupt when they have been so captured by outside interests that they are diverted from their original purpose of serving the people. They cite the US Congress as the prime suspect, because – they argue – the dependency of all US politicians on campaign donations skews law-making away from the public interest and towards the interests of their financial backers.

The debate among US academics has been hotting up since Donald Trump's first election victory in 2016; his critics feel both that he is personally corrupt and that the pandering of the Republican Party to his corruption exemplifies institutional corruption. His supporters argue that Trump is the defender of the constitution, and that it is his opponents who are corrupt. Meanwhile, through widely circulated conspiracy theories and disinformation, the term 'corruption' has become a general form of abuse, increasingly deployed by politicians of all colours. Trump declared that his opponent Hillary Clinton 'may be the most corrupt person ever to seek the presidency.' She returned the favour, calling him a 'corrupt human tornado.' By 2024, Trump was claiming, 'Joe Biden is a corrupt politician who has done nothing but betray the American people.' Trump seems to have revelled in this. Like many other populists, he fought the presidential elections in 2016, 2020 and 2024 on an anti-corruption ticket, applying the label to a wide but vague array of social, political and economic ills such as the 'swamp' of Washington.

This is not unusual. Everyone can point at things they do not like about how people in power operate – from the apparently unmerited wealth of City traders to the profits of the water companies or a local planning decision. The label 'corruption' is often applied to such activities – particularly on social media. At the same time, broad-brush labels such as 'institutionally racist' or 'institutionally transphobic' are freely applied to institutions that hold power in the UK – sometimes followed by the charge that they are also 'institutionally corrupt'.

With so many accusations flying around, it becomes ever more important to understand what we mean by the term: if people dismiss everything they don't like as corrupt, the term becomes meaningless. We also need to be wary of working back from an undesirable outcome or consequence and assuming that corruption was the cause. For instance, if we take abuse of power as a starting point for what is meant by corruption and we see blatant harm caused by some entity with power, it is tempting to conclude that the harm must have been caused by corruption.

Take the Windrush scandal as an example. You do not have to look far on social media to find general allegations that officials have been corrupt, or that the decisions made were symptomatic of institutional corruption at the Home Office. Thousands of people of Caribbean origin who had come to the UK before the 1970s were told in 2015 they had no legal right to be here, even though they had lived here entirely legally for decades. One hundred and sixty-four people were detained or deported before the scandal reached the media, and the scheme was put on hold. Many more had received threatening official letters. This looks like a misuse of power, with racist overtones, to meet immigration performance targets and implement a 'hostile environment' policy. A subsequent inquiry found that Home Office officials were guilty of 'institutional ignorance and thoughtlessness.'[12] But as far as I can see, there is no evidence for corruption being the cause of the scandal. The four-step test can help here: we can see entrusted power, abuse and harm to the public interest, but what is missing is evidence of private gain. The abuse – or misuse – of power therefore does not always indicate that corruption is involved. In other words, although we must be willing to use the label when it is merited, we should avoid it when it is not.

We can see from this example that the four-step test can help us to be more forensic in explaining when corruption does and does not apply. That is more complex than it sounds, because corruption comes in many different forms and depends a great deal on circumstances. While we can all agree that bribery and embezzlement are always corrupt, cronyism or nepotism, for instance, might be corrupt on some occasions but not others – for example, if doing a favour to a friend or relative does not involve an abuse of power or does not harm the public interest, that would be cronyism but not corruption. A good definition should be able to capture the variety of corruption, from a prison officer being slipped a few hundred pounds to turn a blind eye, to a politician who has helped to pass a law from which they benefit, and from a company that has damaged the environment but escaped prosecution after capturing the regulator to the appointment of a party donor to the House of Lords.

Let's have a brief recap of these various layers of the corruption onion. Our definition of corruption needs to encompass: the notion that it sometimes takes place entirely legally (you can be corrupt without breaking the law); institutional corruption, in which an organisation is itself corrupt or corrupted; and both petty (low-level) corruption and grand corruption. The definition also needs to cope with the difference between transactional corruption – a one-off act in which there is a quid pro quo – and the more deep-seated corruption that may variously be described as systemic or structural. The four-step test is good at capturing transactional corruption, but has to work harder to capture more deep-seated corruption because it is difficult to describe an abuse of power when it is so hard-wired into the system that it no longer seems to be an abuse. To explore definitions that capture this, I will turn to the American scholars Lawrence Lessig and Michael Johnston, whose work we can consider alongside the four-step test.

As I have already mentioned, Lessig describes 'institutional corruption' as a scenario when an institution has been diverted from its original purpose by vested interests.[13] He sees this as being

> when there is a systemic and strategic influence which is legal, or even currently ethical, that undermines the institution's effectiveness by diverting it from its purpose or weakening its ability to achieve its purpose, including, to the extent relevant to its purpose, weakening either the public's trust in that institution or the institution's inherent trustworthiness.

This might allow people to label the US Congress as corrupt, but on the other hand it is so broad a definition that many institutions are brought within its reach even if they are not recognisably corrupt by other criteria. We will, however, find those concepts of lawful influence and diversion of purpose helpful for interpreting corruption in the UK context because much of the corruption explored falls within the law and is about the subtle but damaging exercise of power.

Professor Johnston, meanwhile, has identified 'four syndromes of corruption' into which every country in the world can be categorised.[14] He classes the UK as an 'influence market',[15] which relates to 'the use of wealth to seek influence within strong political and administrative institutions'.[16] Johnston is exploring whether the huge influence of the private sector on policymaking, government and institutions should be considered corrupt; he coins the term 'influence markets' to explain that, while this might not be corrupt according to standard definitions, the outcome for democracy and society is far from good. According to Johnston's reasoning, corruption may not look the same in the UK as in Russia or Afghanistan, for example – it may be less extreme, violent or harmful, and less blatant in terms of distributing the spoils – but nevertheless, a liberal democracy like the UK also has a syndrome of corruption which is damaging to society.

Scholars like Johnston are pointing out that liberal democracies can possess a level of underlying corruption in which the political economy evolves through the interaction between the wealthy and the powerful, to produce unequal outcomes that favour an elite few. In a more recent book,[17] the term he uses for this underlying corruption is 'structural corruption'. This is such an intuitively descriptive term that I will adopt it here to convey a sense of a society that is fundamentally rotten: an entrenched, systematic misdirection of politics and society away from the public interest even when the individuals within the system are acting lawfully (although that does not mean I am adopting wholesale all of the other assumptions behind this term that come with Johnston's long career of insightful scholarship).

The most plausible alternative term to structural corruption would be 'systemic corruption'. In much of the academic literature, this has been taken to refer to widespread petty or transactional corruption – where systematic bribe-paying is the norm. Over the past few years, the term has also been used to mean a society – usually a liberal democracy – in which a loose oligarchy holds the reins of power, with government diverging from the interests of the common people.[18] To avoid confusion between these two definitions of underlying corruption, I am opting to use 'structural corruption' to describe underlying embedded corruption, and 'systemic corruption' in the usage that refers to lots of transactional corruption. Two further terms – 'systematic corruption' and 'institutionalised corruption' – are also used by some scholars, often synonymously with systemic corruption.

Johnston – alongside other leading researchers in the field such as Alina Mungiu-Pippidi – also outlines the key role played by good institutions.[19] This theme of institutionalism is a dominant strand in much research on corruption, and one I wholeheartedly endorse. Well-governed institutions, with a strong culture of integrity, are critical in the defence against corruption. Conversely, poorly designed or dysfunctional institutions can create an environment in which corruption thrives, sometimes irrespective of the personal integrity of the individuals involved – and in this case we might blame the institution and not the individuals. A simple example in the UK is the MPs' expenses scandal: 373 MPs were required to repay expenses following an official audit in 2010, representing over half of all MPs. Did they all lack personal integrity – or were they locked into a system that shaped their behaviour?

However we choose to describe it, the increasing number of scholars who warn about structural corruption in liberal democracies have not been able to come up with firm rules to tell for sure when a country is suffering from it. Does the inequality in the UK, the US, South Korea or France mean that there is structural corruption in all those countries? If we were to take such a position, we might conclude that every country in the world is structurally corrupt, which does not seem to correlate with other indicators. And if we brand all countries in the world as structurally corrupt, do we lose any chance of defining the problem in a manner that allows us to find a way forward?

So while I think the label structural corruption can be useful, I have four caveats about how and when to apply it to a country like the UK. First, it is something of a nuclear option – it implies that society has such fundamental problems that truly massive change is needed. That may be the case, but I would want to see reliable evidence for the problem being that bad. Second, it can sound a bit black and white, as though a country is either structurally corrupt or not: in reality, a country could simply be showing some signs of being so. It may therefore be more useful to talk about being on a path towards structural corruption, rather having fully arrived. Third, a country like the UK may have had a history of structural corruption from which it has partly or fully emerged. While there may still be strong echoes of the past – such as the class system – that does not mean the structural corruption persists today except in these echoes. Finally, some parts of the body politic may be corrupt, and others not. If, for example, we feel that our politics is structurally corrupt, that does not mean that every part of the political system – civil service, public broadcasters, Electoral Commission, etc – is structurally corrupt, and we should be very clear what we are really talking about.

I think what we can sensibly say about the UK and similar countries is that, even if we cannot finally determine whether they are structurally corrupt, we can for each country identify specific characteristics and weaknesses that make them vulnerable to corruption. We can also identify many cases of corruption, even without knowing definitively how representative they are. This means that we are sometimes examining the risk of corruption rather than corruption itself. But that is still worthwhile; it shines a light on loopholes to close so that we can head off widespread corruption, and means we can be on the lookout for corruption risk that is morphing into actual corruption. History clearly demonstrates that every type of country is vulnerable to structural corruption, and so even if the UK is not at present structurally corrupt, we must assume that it may not be too far away.

It is worth bearing in mind that even blatant corruption is usually only spotted quite a few years after it starts to take over the system. Talk of Putin's Russia and Erdoğan's Turkey as being structurally corrupt is now commonplace, but that was not the case during their early years in power. Donald Trump may provide an exception to the rule: from his first day in power, he was being called out as personally corrupt and criticised for introducing structural corruption, perhaps a result of the blatancy with which he was operating. Relating this back to the UK, it is therefore a matter of personal judgement as to whether our country is structurally corrupt, heading that way or doing well. The aim of this book is to allow such a judgement to be made.

To summarise, while I will take into account the views of Lessig and Johnston to evaluate the question of structural corruption in the UK, my definition places the four-step test at the core of my analysis. But whenever I apply it, remember that there is a second stage, which is to check whether there is some kind of underlying structural corruption that has not been detected. In this, the key determinant is still the question of the public interest. Is an institution, organisation or system intended to serve the public interest – and is it doing so? And if it is not, has it been diverted to serve private interests? Ultimately, I emphasise the four-step test first and foremost because it is a little less subjective. Rather than getting distracted by debates on whether capitalism or neoliberalism or chumocracy are structurally corrupt, I believe we can find common ground in things that the vast majority of people will agree are corrupt – and that in itself reveals a surprising picture of life in the UK.

Having established these core definitions, the question remains of how to apply these concepts. What is the best way to go about gathering evidence and material so that these definitions can be best applied to the UK? In academic jargon, this is the methodology.

My academic background is as a historian of the Renaissance. Until the late 1980s, the historical method consisted largely of using primary and secondary sources to develop a narrative of what happened in the past. It was unusual – but not unheard of – at that time to apply a theoretical framework to explain what had happened; Marxist historians, for example, felt able to explain any event through their particular lens. In many ways, historians are journalists of the past, constructing a narrative from the available resources. Historian Simon Schama describes this as 'the retrieval of evidence in pursuit of the truth'.[20]

Historians' techniques include contextual analysis (looking at the broader context to understand something), comparative analysis (looking at all sides of a story) and source criticism (evaluating the reliability of sources). A narrative or analysis is constructed using archival and biographical sources and – for recent history – interviews. These techniques are all deployed in this book. The core of my narrative is archival material, traced back to source where possible (for example, where a politician is quoted, I will aim to have gone back to the original speech or the parliamentary records in Hansard), but otherwise drawing on contemporary media reports.

One skill in which historians tend to be well schooled is how to make sense of a situation when the evidence is incomplete

– and the further back you go, of course, the less complete the evidence. This means that, in terms borrowed from the legal world, historians are not often trying to prove 'beyond reasonable doubt' but rather are assessing 'the balance of probability'. As corruption analysts, like historians, we need to assess how far individual cases are representative of a wider problem, and whether they highlight holes in the system that could be allowing more corruption to happen. Even individual cases can be ambiguous: it might be tricky to point to proof that Putin is corrupt, but does anyone seriously doubt that he is?

Historians assimilate the available evidence and evaluate it using the techniques outlined above to reach a conclusion – and that is the essential approach of this book. But it also draws on other disciplines. The field of corruption analysis more typically uses the tools of economics and political science; I will borrow from those approaches, which can be useful in helping to understand what is happening. For example, the question of when a parliament becomes institutionally corrupt can help answer whether the UK parliament has merely suffered a series of rotten apples or has itself become a rotting barrel. Legal studies, meanwhile, can help determine where corruption is a crime, as well as lending the criminologist's analysis of victimology to discern whether corruption has caused harm.

Finally, the book borrows loosely from the field of anthropology by using an approach similar to ethnographic interviews and participant observation. It distils thousands of conversations and interviews into a picture of corruption in the UK. I can state with some confidence, for example, that people in the country feel that our planning system is tainted by high levels of corruption – but the evidence base for this statement might not satisfy many political scientists.

The formal research interviews used here were part of

research projects at Transparency International and the University of Sussex. The informal interviews and conversations – some documented, others not – occurred during my time at those two institutions, as well as while working in the City. I have also had the advantage of being a protagonist in some of the events – such as the campaign for the new Bribery Act and the organising of the 2016 Anti-Corruption Summit – and in such cases there is a trade-off between inside knowledge and objectivity. In essence, I have spoken about corruption in the UK with a vast array of people from all parts of the country, in all sorts of jobs and at every level of seniority, for over two decades. For this book, that has been supplemented by archival work on a wide range of documents and transcripts.

To some academics, the effort to draw on five different disciplines will inevitably seem muddle-headed. That is the risk of an interdisciplinary study. Putting all this together, the book's broad approach is perhaps something akin to that taken by the contemporary historian Peter Hennessy, who describes his methodology as 'a journalistic approach, mixed with an archival approach, lubricated by gossip'.[21]

Where does that leave us on the common claim that there is a peculiarly British form of corruption – a claim that I realise I had also made myself in 2015? A decade on, I have changed my view. It is clearly important to understand national context – and to that extent, the corruption that happens in the UK is distinctively British, just as it would be distinctively French in France. However, the corruption in Britain is not especially peculiar – on the contrary, it is recognisably global. The definitions I apply to the UK – the four-step test, plus institutional and structural corruption – can be applied to many other countries.

This is not just a semantic issue. With the phrase 'peculiarly British' comes the danger of exceptionalism, of believing ourselves to be an exception to the rule. That might be used to downplay or even to excuse corruption. It certainly helps to explain our national complacency: if there is a peculiarly British form of corruption, perhaps it is just part of our long history, and rather than being harmful sits alongside our success as a nation. We may be technically corrupt, but not in the way that causes such harm elsewhere. The rules and consequences of corruption do not really apply here.

As long as we think that we are some kind of special case, we are failing to diagnose the problem properly. And if we think that foreigners do things worse and regard ourselves as different and better, we are not far from thinking that what happens elsewhere could not happen here.

TWO BARONESSES AND OTHER STORIES: APPLYING THE THEORY TO REAL-LIFE CASES

In this chapter, to road-test our definitions, we will look at some real-life cases and examine whether they should have the label 'corruption' attached to them. We start with an example of how the four-step test can be applied, using it to make a distinction between the activities of two Tory baronesses during the Covid-19 pandemic. Both Dido Harding and Michelle Mone faced widespread allegations of corruption on social media. Remember the four steps: entrusted power, abuse, private gain and harm to the public interest; and that in the background we will also be alert to evidence of structural and institutional corruption, where the four-step test has not given a clear answer.

Dido Harding was put in charge of the 'test and trace' system during the Covid crisis. It had a budget of £37 billion, of which £29.5 billion was spent, but was widely condemned as being hopeless. She was a well-known business leader but was directly appointed to the role, thus avoiding a lengthy public appointments process. The appointment was made by the Health Secretary, Matt Hancock, and like lots of government decisions during Covid bypassed the usual systems because there was an emergency situation. Hancock and Harding had mutual connections in the world of horse racing and, moreover, her husband was a Conservative MP. She had no expertise in the health sector but had run a large company, the telecoms firm TalkTalk, and chaired an NHS board. This looks like a classic example of chumocracy, a term examined in a later chapter. In slightly old-fashioned terms: it's not what you know, it's who you know.

However, the facts as we have them (and we should remember that this can always change as more information comes to light) suggest that Harding was not personally corrupt, and the scheme itself was in parts expensive and ineffective, but not fundamentally corrupt. The 'trace' component aimed to trace all the contacts of someone who had tested positive for Covid-19 and was a badly run scheme, as Harding herself later partially admitted to the Covid Inquiry; but the majority of the funds were spent on the 'test' component by which individuals across the country received free Covid tests and which seems to have worked better, though it was costly to the government. Overall, a vast use of public funds on a scheme with many flaws and poor delivery. But was it corrupt?

Harding possessed entrusted power, but she was not abusing it or making any private gain; indeed, her post was unremunerated and there seem to have been no other benefits typical of a corrupt approach, such as the ability to award contracts to cronies. We might also consider whether there was an element of institutional or structural corruption in her appointment – and the way in which private companies were able to influence the design of the test and trace scheme for their own benefit. Yet there does not seem to be any evidence that either the intent in creating the scheme or its operation was what Lessig would describe as a 'diversion of purpose' from delivering a test and trace scheme; it was a genuine attempt to help tackle Covid-19.

Large sums of the money were indeed spent on expensive consultants, including a senior consultant from Deloitte who charged £6,624 per day, but this seems to have been poor management rather than a deliberate attempt at rent-seeking, the term used to describe a situation where someone in power gouges public funds for excess profits.

Michelle Mone and her husband, Doug Barrowman, did, by contrast, make a fortune as a result of the pandemic: they personally gained at least £60 million from over £220 million of government contracts awarded to their company PPE Medpro. The private gain is clear. We might consider that she possessed entrusted power as a lawmaker in the House of Lords, although she did not have any direct power over the allocation of funds – but she was by virtue of her position able to influence decisions. And what about abuse? Well, Mone lied about her association with the company and actively used her contacts in government to secure the contracts – indeed, her behaviour was described by Hancock as 'extraordinarily aggressive.' Ironically, in one email to him she accused the government itself of corruption when it at first refused to grant her company a contract.*

When Mone's companies did get contracts and supplied equipment, much of it was alleged to have been unusable by the NHS because they did not meet sterility standards, an allegation later proven in court. So was this behaviour corrupt? The investigation by the National Crime Agency, which has frozen £75 million of their assets, might provide evidence to support the widespread allegations. Mone and Barrowman continue to deny any wrongdoing. This seems much closer to ticking the four boxes than the behaviour of Baroness Harding.

---

* Whether the government's own role in setting up such a scheme might be considered corrupt is examined in a later chapter.

Having compared the cases of Harding and Mone, we can see that two instances where the label of corruption has been applied are actually quite different. While the outcome was bad in each case – unnecessary cost to the public purse – there seems to be a discernible difference between a well-intentioned and well-connected person doing a poor job and someone seeing an opportunity to take advantage of their position of power to make a quick buck.

It all comes back to how we classify corruption. And the crux of the definition I am applying is simple: who has entrusted power – and are they abusing it for private gain? Most importantly, does this harm the public interest? You will notice that power is central to understanding corruption – look for who holds it, and whether it is being abused. This harks back to what might be the best-known description of corruption, used by the historian Lord Acton to describe the papacy in 1887: 'Power tends to corrupt, and absolute power corrupts absolutely.'

Sixty years after Acton coined the phrase, the philosopher Bertrand Russell was linking the dangers of accumulating power to the rise of fascism in Europe.[1] He argued that in a well-governed country, where there are good checks and balances, the 'desires for power and glory' common to most of us can be held in check, and that those who wield power do so with the consent of those they govern; but this can all too easily descend into 'naked' power. In other words, power is something to be wary of – and we should be careful who gains it and what we allow them to do with it.

Across the UK, we can see the concentration of power in many places: prisons, police and politics, but also local government, the private sector and sport. We need mechanisms to prevent power from being abused for private gain – which does not just mean money; it can be to gain influence or sexual favours, or to benefit an institution such as a political party.

We cannot take for granted that power will be exercised fairly and in the public interest – but who in any case determines what 'public interest' means? The term is notoriously hard to define and, in an age of populism, the question is at the heart of many political debates. Politicians on both the right and the left claim to speak on behalf of 'the people', while those who oppose them are described as an unrepresentative 'elite'. So it is not always clear either what the public interest is, or who is representing it.

Despite this lack of clarity, many scholars agree that public interest is a useful concept to capture a key point about corruption. Should people in power service their own interests, or the wider interests of society? While this may be open to debate when it comes to the managers of multinational businesses, there is an overwhelming assumption in the UK that public office and public servants are there to serve the public. Moreover, even without defining what the public interest is, we can still apply the part of the four-step test that says corruption 'harms the public interest'; and that is because we can often easily tell when something is *not* in the public interest – like sewage leaks or overcharging for personal protective equipment (PPE) – without defining it.

Being as precise as we can about definitions has a further advantage: it means we can rule some things out. That is useful because it helps us spot where the label of corruption is being misapplied. For instance, writers and commentators about the UK's social inequalities and economic malaise have often tried to widen the definition of corruption so that it encompasses a basket of things they feel are bad for society. They would broadly argue that actions and inequalities that favour those who are in power are more or less the same as corruption, and so it is reasonable to describe these things as such. In some cases this may be right, but in others it can lead to the label being mistakenly applied, as in the Windrush case mentioned in the previous chapter.

So what else can we rule out? One clear area is fraud, which can seem superficially similar to corruption, but unless it is carried out by someone with 'entrusted power' and 'harms the public interest' it does not qualify. A simple example is a bank employee who steals from a customer's account. They have undoubtedly harmed the customer and the bank, but not the public interest. They may have held sufficient authority to be able to authorise a payment from the customer's account into their own, but this is not really 'entrusted power'. Although one could probably make a case that a bank official does have entrusted power and that breaking the law always harms the public interest, that would push the definition to its limits. It is a good reminder that even the four-step test has some subjectivity built into it. A more clear-cut example would be an online scammer from Nigeria: if you hand over some money, they make a private gain and are abusing your trust – but they are not abusing any entrusted power.

Just as the definition needs to avoid being too wide, nor should it be too narrow. A long-standing difficulty with the UK government's approach to tackling corruption has been its classification of corruption as an 'economic crime'. This narrow categorisation implies both that the actions are criminal and that they are economic. There are some significant consequences of such a definition in that some varieties of corruption would not be covered. The UK's recent anti-corruption strategy does actually incorporate a definition that is much closer to the four-step test, which is a welcome advance; but in practical terms, it may be a long while until that is rolled out across the public sector.

It is time for some further examples to illustrate how the four-step test can help rule some things out from the label of corruption.

First, a case in which a company applied for Covid furlough compensation for twenty employees, despite having placed only ten employees on furlough. This is a case of simple fraud. There is both abuse and private gain, but the company was not in a position of entrusted power.

How about the matter of Boris Johnson lying to parliament as Prime Minister? He had entrusted power, and was aiming for private gain through political advantage; and there can be little doubt that a prime minister who lies is likely to damage the public interest. But it is not clear that he would have been abusing his entrusted power, because he was not using the power of his office to tell the lie – was he simply lying while being PM? That might be considered bad, but not in itself corrupt.

Third, how about when Amazon has used schemes to avoid paying a fair share of corporation tax in the UK? This is damaging to the public interest, and there is private gain. But although it is an incredibly powerful company, Amazon is not in a position of entrusted power, and so is not abusing its position. Again, it is bad but it is not corrupt. Although if Amazon had managed to rig the tax laws in its favour, perhaps through extensively resourced lobbying, there might be a case for calling it a form of structural corruption.

The examples of Boris Johnson's lies and Amazon's tax policy highlight the fact that you sometimes need to think hard about whether the term corruption should apply. Sometimes, two apparently contradictory things are true: there may be some aspects of a situation that are corrupt, while others are not. In the Post Office Horizon scandal, the head office staff at the state-owned Post Office came to believe that a large number of sub-postmasters were committing fraud to steal money, when in fact the problem was caused by an error with the computer system that was being used. We can plausibly say that the managers at the Post Office HQ had entrusted power: they were state employees in senior positions delivering a public service, and they in turn had extensive powers over the sub-postmasters, both through the financial and contracting arrangements and because the Post Office had an internal investigations team to which those contracts granted extensive powers.

The original decision to prosecute sub-postmasters who were thought to have committed crimes, while mistaken and based on poor judgement, does not appear in itself to have been corrupt. It was a case of a reasonable policy (prosecuting people for suspected fraud) being pursued based on false information and executed in a vindictive and unfeeling manner, with a terrible human cost: small businesses forced into bankruptcy, families split apart and punitive jail sentences for people who turned out to be entirely innocent. But the Post Office managers who originally investigated and prosecuted were not apparently at first abusing their entrusted power for private gain, even though some seem to have carried out their task with a relish that bordered on being abusive.

As time went on, it does start to look like an abuse of power took hold. Information came to light that might clear those already convicted, and should have halted further investigations. Investigators instead ploughed on, deliberately denying the facts that were emerging and continuing to act like corporate bullies. They may have committed perjury through lying in court about Horizon's reliability, or even perverted the course of justice through knowingly pursuing false prosecutions. The Post Office HQ then moved into cover-up mode to protect both individual and corporate reputations – which in turn protected their own jobs, pensions and bonuses. Over more than a decade, what had started as a mistaken investigation became a corrupt abuse of power.

We have seen in this chapter that there are plenty of people and cases to whom the label corruption is loosely applied. The term is also used increasingly by populist politicians and their supporters about many things their opponents do, and about organisations that try to hold them accountable; a recent example is President Trump's description of the BBC as corrupt after the BBC broadcast – and later apologised for – a poorly edited documentary about his role in the 6 January 2021 storming of the Capitol. By applying the four-step test we can work out more easily whether the label is being correctly applied. And to reiterate why that is important, if you can diagnose the problem properly you are more likely to find a solution. In the next chapter we will look at the history of corruption in the UK and reflect on the trajectory of corruption and anti-corruption defences in this country over the past few hundred years.

HOW WE GOT HERE: A BRIEF RECAP OF THE PAST 600 YEARS

Where do you think the UK would have been listed on a world index of corruption in 1945?

The chances are that it would be doing well – perhaps in the top two or three countries, along with the USA and New Zealand. Almost every other country had been either invaded during the war or previously colonised, the conditions in which corruption thrives.

For the UK, the outcome of the Second World War confirmed in the national psyche the lessons of empire and the First World War: Britain is a winner. And this was not just by chance; as Churchill explained, Britain had a moral superiority over other nations.

One historian recently described this as 'the claim Britain was not fighting purely for national self-interest but was the embodiment of forces of good that would rescue all mankind from tyranny and barbarism'.[1] Churchill himself had told the electorate in 1924 that 'this famous island is the home of freedom and representative government. We have led the world along these paths.'

Victory in the Second World War gave Britain a ground zero, in which the overwhelming moral clarity of the war was able to erase other recent memories – from the UK's own anti-Semitism to the high levels of support for the fascist politician Oswald Mosley, to say nothing of the mixed legacy of empire. The political scientist Bo Rothstein has proposed a 'big bang' theory of how countries shift from significant corruption to significantly lower levels of corruption, overcoming the problem of people feeling unable to improve things even if they want to.[2] The end of the Second World War represented this sort of change in several areas of national life, such as the national drive to form the NHS. In terms of corruption, however, it was like a reverse big bang: it reinforced the nation's basic self-belief in its own integrity, rather than causing the national self-reflection seen in so many other countries at the time.

This sense of moral superiority did not come out of the blue; it had also characterised the British Empire. Lord Curzon, Viceroy of India, referred to the Empire as 'under Providence the greatest instrument for good that the world has seen'. Abuses of power may have been common in the vastness of the Empire but, like slavery in previous centuries, it was easy to discount what happened so far out of sight, and what took place overseas seemed to have little effect on the nation's self-perception as a moral force for good.

Looking at the past helps us to understand the roots of today's corruption, and attitudes towards it. Political scientists might call this approach 'path dependence'; by tracing a line back to the past, we can see that we may be locked into doing and thinking about things in a certain way by past decisions and structures. The UK is blessed with superb historians who have researched corruption as far back as the Tudors in the late fifteenth century.[3] The story they tell is as follows.

Some time in the late Middle Ages, the idea that there was a difference between the public interest and the private interest began to develop. There followed a centuries-long tussle between those who believed holding public office was for their personal gratification, and those who believed in a responsibility to operate on behalf of the wider body of citizens. This was decisively resolved in the nineteenth century, when the idea became dominant that public office came with an obligation to act in the public interest. After that time, it was rare for politicians and public officials to become conspicuously enriched during their time in public office.

That change in attitudes is the key point on which we should focus: the nation started to agree that public office should be exercised in the public interest.* Since then, a combination of laws, rules and cultural norms have embedded this concept in the national conscience and kept corruption in check. This has been supported by strong institutions, some of which were specifically designed to prevent corruption – like the merit-based and impartial civil service introduced by the Northcote–Trevelyan reforms of 1854. It is easy to forget that, before the mid-nineteenth century, the problem of corruption in this country was so widespread that specific defences needed to be put in place. Many of these, like the independence of the civil service, continue to this day. Others, like the Audit Commission, have been abolished by governments that thought they had served their purpose. And others, such as the Victorian anti-bribery laws, have been superseded by modern legislation.

Despite this change in attitude and the defences that were put in place, there have been periodic corruption scandals. Each has usually been regarded as an aberration from the norm, a one-off, and there was generally a response in the form of a Royal

---

* Although late-twentieth-century economists tend to describe this in terms of 'principal–agent' theory, it is not a term I use much as the debate was clearly going on for several hundred years before that term was coined.

Commission, or trial, or a new law. Examples of this are the Marconi scandal of 1912 and the Poulson affair of the 1960s, both of which are described below.

The reasonably thorough analysis by historians of British corruption prior to 1950 has been followed by a relative lack of interest in what has happened since the mid-twentieth century.[4] Alan Doig's 1984 book *Corruption and Misconduct in Contemporary British Politics*[5] was the most comprehensive attempt at an overview, while *Corrupt Britain* by Peter Jones[6] continued the theme of placing politics at the heart of the discussion on British corruption, as well as developing the concept that politicians have turned a blind eye. Many other books focus on politics and the establishment, with corruption playing an implicit role. Those that look explicitly at corruption have generally focused on the UK's role in assisting overseas kleptocracy, which we will examine in detail later.

That is a lightning summary of what historians have written about British corruption over the past few hundred years. They have traced a pattern of high levels of corruption in public office, declining in the Victorian era and levelling off at a much lower level in the twentieth century – while at the same time abuses of power in the colonies, though depressingly frequent, were thought of as somehow disconnected from the mother country's sense of its own moral authority. To bring the story of historical corruption up to date, we should look at a few more recent scandals – useful because some of them have been seminal either in what they reveal about what has been happening more generally, or in terms of national perceptions of corruption.

In fact, the UK has a history of grand scandals, some of which helped stimulate the reforms in the nineteenth century – for example, the case of Lord Melville, the First Lord of the

Admiralty during the Napoleonic Wars, and the last politician in this country to be impeached. He had used his position to embezzle funds designated for the Royal Navy. By the time of the Marconi scandal in 1912, there had been changes in the law, the electoral system and the meritocratic appointments to public office. Some of these, such as the Prevention of Corruption Act of 1889, were specifically corruption-related and others, such as the Reform Acts, were not specifically so, but collectively they created a set of anti-corruption defences. It seems to have been around that time that the nation's self-perception shifted from viewing the country's politicians and public servants as a rotting barrel towards a perception of there being a few rotten apples in an otherwise sound system.

The Marconi scandal, however, represented the last gasp of the old system. This case involved allegations of insider trading against senior members of the Asquith government, including the Chancellor of the Exchequer, David Lloyd George. It was prominently covered in the media, but the government denied impropriety. After an inquiry, and despite the evidence of wrongdoing if not actual law-breaking, ministers were cleared of all misconduct, and nobody faced criminal charges; the worst punishment was for the journalist Cecil Chesterton, editor of the *New Witness* and brother of G. K., who had relentlessly pursued the story and was fined £100 for libel. There was, at least, a public outcry: the scandal seemed to reinforce the sense of popular disenchantment against a self-interested political elite feathering their own nests, combined with the collusion of the private sector, a reaction that probably made politicians more cautious in the decades thereafter. If this all sounds eerily reminiscent of such scandals today, we should remember that this interplay between public and private benefit is long-running.

If we fast-forward to the 1970s, we will notice two or three major corruption scandals in each decade between then and now, starting with the notorious case of John Poulson.[7] An architect and property developer, Poulson paid bribes to council planning and property officials across the country to secure contracts, sometimes using T. Dan Smith as an intermediary, spanning 23 local authorities and more than 300 individuals at a time of extensive modernisation and public works. The value of these bribes was revealed at his trial in Leeds in 1972 to be over £500,000 – nearly £8 million in today's money. Smith was the well-connected leader of Newcastle City Council, and set up a PR firm that generated millions of pounds worth of business for Poulson via local councillors, for which Smith received £156,000. They were both convicted and imprisoned, and both continued to declare their innocence – admitting the payments but not that they were bribes. Poulson protested: 'I may have been a fool, but I will always maintain that I was innocent of corruption. I have never tried to bribe anybody. I have squandered money on people I thought were my friends. They conned me. I did not realise what an old twit I had been until I heard some of the evidence here.' The judge was less forgiving, remarking on 'the magnitude and evil nature' of their crimes and that 'To offer corrupt gifts strikes at the very foundation of our system. To accept them is a betrayal of trust.'

Since then, as well as the serial corruption cases in the Met Police, we have the gerrymandering of Shirley Porter at Westminster Council; cash-for-questions under John Major; the Jubilee Line extension; serial bribery by BAE Systems for defence contracts in Saudi Arabia and elsewhere; MPs' expenses; the many scandals of the Johnson government; and most recently PPE procurement during the Covid pandemic.

Let's take a brief look at some of those cases. The cash-for-questions affair under John Major's government in the 1990s was one of a series of 'Tory sleaze' scandals. Two MPs – most famously Neil Hamilton – were found to have taken cash from the businessman Mohamed Al-Fayed at the rate of £2,000 per question, in order to ask questions in parliament that would show him in a favourable light or advance his commercial interests. Subsequent inquiries lifted the lid on dubious lobbying practices that were widespread among MPs. Like the expenses scandal that would cause shockwaves when it emerged in 2009, when hundreds of MPs were found to have been manipulating their expenses to bolster their incomes, the cash-for-questions affair reinforced the widely held belief among the public that many MPs were out for themselves and had little sense of a moral compass.

The BAE Systems case was a story of bribery by Britain's largest defence company to secure contracts overseas. Allegations centred on bribes paid to Saudi Arabian officials during a £43 billion deal for fighter jets, called Al-Yamamah.[8] After forensic media reporting and increasing public pressure, the Serious Fraud Office opened an investigation – only for it to be dropped due to political interference from the Blair government, at the insistence of their Saudi customer. Critics felt that the case highlighted the links between the defence industry and the government, and a willingness by civil servants, politicians and business leaders to operate outside the law when considerations of foreign policy, domestic jobs and corporate profits were at stake.

Several of these scandals were examined in detail by commissions and inquiries that were set up to prevent them from recurring. Notable among these were the Redcliffe-Maud Committee looking into local government, whose report was published in 1969, the Salmon Commission into Poulson and standards of public life, which reported in 1976, and the Nolan

Committee into sleaze of 1995.[9] Their reports give a fascinating insight into the national state of corruption; the prevailing narrative is that, in the words of the Nolan Report, 'there is, and always will be, a minority who fall short'.[10] In other words, we should always expect there to be rotten apples – but there is no finding that there is currently any systemic corruption.

However, the Nolan Report does acknowledge that corruption is an inevitable end point if standards in public office are not adhered to, noting that 'experience elsewhere warns that, unless the strictest standards are maintained and where necessary restored, corruption and malpractice can become part of the way of life. The threat at the moment is not great. Action needs to be taken before it becomes so.'

One of the Nolan Committee's suggested changes to ensure that corruption did not take root was the establishment of a committee to oversee public standards: the Committee on Standards in Public Life (CSPL), which has recently been rebadged as the Ethics and Integrity Commission (EIC). A framework of related standards and accountability mechanisms were either introduced or strengthened in order to support the Nolan recommendations, including Commissioners for Standards in each house of parliament, the Ministerial Code and an independent Commissioner for Public Appointments. Each of these was given a part of the problem to look after. The approach to upholding integrity – a politer term for preventing corruption – changed at this point. Having previously relied on the unmonitored moral character of those in power, from now on politicians and public officials had set out for them what standards they were expected to live up to, along with mechanisms to check that the standards were being adhered to. However, the emphasis was still focused on Westminster, and strongly depended on the assumption that pretty much everyone covered by these regimes could be relied on to do the right thing. More-over, much of the system depended on the personal patronage of the Prime Minister, with the assumption that, failing all else, at least he or she could be relied on to act with integrity.

By 2021, and the administration of Boris Johnson, the chair of the CSPL had more reason to worry than his predecessors. Responding to the Owen Paterson affair, in which the government had tried to bypass the ethics procedures to help out a Brexiteer ally caught up in a lobbying scandal, the CSPL chair warned that the UK could 'slip into being a corrupt country'.[11] When his term in office ended in 2023, he noted that 'The priority that is given to this across government departments is low and this opens a door to opacity and potentially corruption.'[12]

So that is where we stand today. We went from being a country with high levels of corruption, with public office seen as an opportunity for private gain, to a country in which private interests were subordinate to the public interest. Victory in the Second World War seemed to give us a sense of moral purity, but this was gradually punctured by scandals. Various corrective mechanisms were put in place, but by the time Boris Johnson was Prime Minister it was becoming clear that they were dependent on convention, principle and personal values – and as a result were not able to function effectively.

What can we learn from this brief history of corruption in the UK, and the nation's response to it? Historians differ in view as to whether the periodic spikes in our awareness of corruption reflect the fact that corruption itself dips and surges, or whether it is more that the coverage of corruption is cyclical while the underlying level remains the same. However, despite this disagreement, we can discern four key themes in the writing on the subject.

First, the UK has clearly not been immune in the past to

the type of deep-rooted corruption that exists in many countries today,[13] though in this country it was subsequently tempered by Victorian notions of integrity and probity.[14] But our history tells us that, like any other country, if the circumstances are right, we can be prone to corruption happening on a large scale – and at all levels, from the people at the very top to those much further down the pecking order.

Second, lower levels of corruption are closely associated with greater accountability of those in public office, and higher standards in public life. Giving people the right to vote has increased accountability, since voters can ultimately decide who holds power. However, just granting someone the right to vote does not in itself guarantee accountability. It needs to go hand in hand with other things, like a free press and a properly functioning electoral system.

Third, the conflict between public and private interest is an enduring theme in UK public life. In previous times, the private interests who benefitted from entrusted power were a relatively narrow groups of individuals, whether the monarch and their extended patronage networks or a powerful aristocrat or Church leader. Nowadays such positions of entrusted power are held by a wider range of people and organisations. For example, due to the expansion of government services into so many areas of daily life, as well as privatisation and outsourcing, entrusted power might be held by managers in a care home or the executives of an arms company, as well as local councillors, teachers and police officers. Whereas in the past the prioritisation of a private interest over the public interest may have looked like Lord Melville embezzling the Navy funds, today the private interest might mean a privatised water company prioritising its shareholders, or G4S and Serco making a profit through running prisons or asylum hotels.

Fourth, we have the unresolved question of rotten apples. Many analyses of other liberal democracies with strong institutions have also identified this as a problem: when corruption is revealed, should we be satisfied that it is a one-off rotten apple, or should we be concerned that there is a rotting barrel? The historical response in Britain since the Second World War has been to blame problems on a few rotten individuals; by contrast, all writers on British corruption – without exception – conclude that there is more widespread corruption than the few rotten apples that are generally acknowledged by politicians and the establishment.

4

TONE FROM THE TOP:
POLITICAL CORRUPTION

'The fish rots from the head.' I've heard this phrase more times than I can count – and it is used so often because it summarises incredibly well the serious knock-on effects of political corruption, the subject of this chapter. Surveys show an inescapable correlation between high levels of political corruption and high levels of bribery throughout the public sector.* In the main, this chapter will not question too deeply whether there is structural corruption in our parliamentary system. The reason for that is that there are reasonable arguments for and against, so what you conclude is generally a matter of opinion – and often of ideology. What I want to show is that plenty of things go on that we can all agree are corrupt or present a high risk of corruption; if they continue, or happen on too grand a scale, we would unambiguously reach a point of institutional and structural corruption.

Inevitably, much of this chapter will focus on the mishaps and misdemeanours of Boris Johnson. He stretched to breaking point the checks and balances that were expected to restrain

---

* For example, Our World in Data charts correlation between the V-Dem Political Corruption Index and the Global Corruption Barometer: https://ourworldindata. org/grapher/bribery-prevalence-un

corruption, and in doing so has given corruption analysts more fuel to answer some basic questions: what does political corruption look like in this country? How effective are our anti-corruption defences in the face of concerted political pushback – and at what point do breaches of integrity and the dismantlement of anti-corruption defences become corruption? And most fundamentally, to what extent can we describe British politics as corrupt?

We are too close to the Johnson era for the full evidence of corruption to have emerged – for example on procurement of PPE during the Covid crisis. However, what is clear about the Johnson government is that there were multiple breaches of integrity, including certain cases that clearly fall within the four-step definition of corruption. While these may be described as cases of transactional corruption, suggesting that each of them is a separate and unrelated incident, an underlying question is whether the large number of such cases adds up to a systemic pattern, and therefore whether we can reasonably describe Johnson or his government as corrupt.

The scandals were many and well documented. There are, in fact, so many of them that several acquired familiar nicknames, such as Wallpaper-gate (when a party donor paid £52,802 to allow Johnson and his then-girlfriend Carrie to refurbish their Downing Street flat, once they had spent the official allowance, which had not stretched to the gold wallpaper or a £6,000 lamp). Some have been looked into by the relevant authorities, but many have not – Transparency International in 2022 identified forty potential breaches that had not been investigated.[1] A bit further on I have selected a few cases to examine in detail. The cases can be loosely categorised into four types:

Potentially corrupt activity within the wider government and party, which Johnson permitted, defended or supported. Examples:

the Jenrick–Westferry planning permission affair; the Towns Fund; Owen Paterson's lobbying; PPE procurement and the 'VIP lane'.

Potentially corrupt activity by Johnson personally. Examples: the Lebedev Lords appointment; the Richard Sharp BBC appointment and related personal loan facility to Johnson; support for the other individuals cited in the cases in this list.

Breaches of standards within the wider government and party, which Johnson permitted, defended or supported. Examples: the Priti Patel bullying; several backbench sex scandals, including the Chris Pincher case that precipitated Johnson's demise; Dominic Cummings' bizarre excursion to Barnard Castle during the Covid lockdown; appointment of party donors to the Lords; and appointment of cronies to senior public roles.

Personal breaches of standards by Johnson. Examples: Partygate; lying to the Commons; lying on other occasions, for instance over the Jennifer Arcuri affair; undermining the Privileges Committee; Wallpaper-gate; obfuscation over the Caribbean holiday freebie; accepting employment without consulting the Advisory Committee on Business Appointments (ACOBA).

Political corruption has a deeper impact on a country than any other form of corruption. This is because the small group of individuals who are in charge are responsible for allocating the huge resources of the state, for ensuring that justice is done and that public order and national security are maintained. Putting such power in the hands of corrupt individuals diverts the resources of the state towards their personal interests and away from the public interest.

Conversely, political leadership is critical to the control of corruption – infusing the ethos of public service into politics and the public sector, and ensuring that anti-corruption laws and enforcement make a difference. That does not mean that a country can only tackle corruption if it has favourable political leadership, but case studies around the world show it is much easier when there is political will to solve the problem. It is notable that the countries that make the biggest improvements on the Corruption Perceptions Index have usually shown strong political leadership on corruption or specifically sought to address political corruption. Over the period 2012–2024, for instance, both Greece and Hungary significantly changed their scores – by 13 and 14 per cent respectively. Hungary, which saw a marked increase in political corruption under the Orbán government, slid down the rankings, while Greece – which had new anti-corruption laws, international pressure and public procurement reforms – moved in the opposite direction.

The instinctive view of most people is that political corruption looks like autocracy, or the potent mixture of politics with organised crime: a narco-state like Mexico, or a captured state like South Africa under Jacob Zuma. Such extreme examples are, of course, very unlike what happens in Britain. But does that mean Britain is entirely free of political corruption? Of course not.

Campaigners often point to four key corruption vulnerabilities in UK politics that make up a dark quartet: the funding of political parties, particularly problematic due to the suggestion that rich people can buy political favours; the revolving door between senior positions in business, politics and the public sector; conflicts of interest; and lobbying. The partial release in 2026 of the Epstein files has given a glimpse into how concertedly such relationships between wealthy private individuals, business and politicians are developed, and then leveraged to influence political decision-making.

The four components of this dark quartet have been well examined by other writers,[2] so I will not re-tread that ground here, but they lie at the core of any analysis of political corruption in a liberal democracy. In many of the examples we will look at, a mixture of those issues is at play. Lobbying has long been a particular concern of campaigners, as it is at the same time both secretive and influential. It is not even known how many lobbyists there are in the UK, as there is no official list: it is credibly estimated as around 4,000 in an industry worth £2 billion per year.[3] A sense of their close relationships with our political class can be gained from the statistic that in the 2024 general election, 103 candidates were professional lobbyists.[4] Such concerns are common to many liberal democracies, and over time many of those countries have developed anti-corruption mechanisms to keep them in check. In the UK, each of these areas of concern has been the subject of recommendations from the Committee on Standards in Public Life, which have been ignored or passed over by successive governments. It is not that we have no idea what to do: the problem is that there has been no political will to do what's needed.

Has anything changed over the last few decades? To give some historical context to today's situation, we will test a hypothesis that 'there was more corruption and corruption risk in and around the Johnson government than any British government since 1945,'[5] a comment that received both enthusiastic support and disenchanted repudiation on social media when I floated it in an article in 2021. In this chapter, unlike the others in this book, most readers will probably be familiar with the examples. The key question, though, is to determine what behaviours we can reasonably describe as being corrupt. To reiterate my earlier assumption, if we believe that a good understanding of the problem is a prerequisite for finding good solutions, when trying to analyse political corruption in the UK we should aim for whatever precision and objectivity are possible.

A good starting point is to return to the question of who holds power and what they decide to do with it. When I meet people who hold political power, I often find myself recalling that dictum of Lord Acton that power tends to corrupt. As the head of Transparency International, I came into contact with dozens of high-profile political figures as part of my daily work – including heads of government and heads of state. There was a chance to size up in person some of the characters we mainly see on television or hear on the radio. So let me ask a question. Which recent British prime minister would you most like to go for a drink with? Perhaps none of them.

Being in a room with a major political figure like Tony Blair, David Cameron or Boris Johnson reinforces some of the stereotypes about those who rise to the top of politics. They are highly charismatic and persuasive, leaving you feeling that you want to support them. Boris Johnson was amusing, David Cameron was charming, Tony Blair magnetic. They exude self-confidence, usually thinly disguised by a veil of humility. There is typically an easy good humour, but they also have something else – a sense that they have been selected for their position by the people because they are the answer to the country's problems. They radiate self-assurance. And the combination that such politicians have of power, self-confidence and popular mandate could be used for the good of the country – or the good of themselves. We encounter that recurring issue of public interest vs private interest. It turns out that a key question in a country without a formal constitution is – as identified by historian Peter Hennessy – are they 'good chaps'? That has been one of our key defences against corruption.

Our democratic system relies on personal integrity and

people operating to a common set of assumed values, rather than a strict set of laws and rules. For example, we have a principle that politicians should act with 'honesty', but we do not have a law that makes it illegal to lie in parliament. Such principles are not the law: and they rest on what Hennessy characterises as a voluntary and inherited self-restraint that underpins this country's unwritten constitution. He explains:

'We have long assumed that those who rise to high office will be "good chaps", knowing what the unwritten rules are and wanting to adhere to them, even if doing so might frustrate the attainment of their policy objectives, party political goals, or personal ambitions – the argument being that "good chaps" (of different sexes) know where the undrawn lines lie and come nowhere near to crossing them.'*[6]

There is an underlying assumption that British leaders would act in the public interest.

During Boris Johnson's government, the reliance on 'good chaps' was left floundering. If you feel that you can do things without being punished, you might be inclined to do so. Johnson and his ministers found there were few, if any, penalties to breaking the rules, and that in any case they themselves were ultimately in charge of setting and policing most of them. It cannot have been hard for them to conclude that there were few actual limitations on their behaviour. This is what corruption scholars describe as 'rational choice theory' – the tendency to try to get away with things if you think you can.

A good example of the norms that were in place, and proved insufficient, is the expectation that prime ministers should not lie. Former *Spectator* journalist Peter Oborne describes how

---

*Chaps in this case is a gender-neutral term: it can apply to anyone in political power.

far this changed under Johnson's premiership in his book *The Assault on Truth*. As he recounts, 'I have been a political reporter for almost three decades. I have never encountered a senior British politician who lies and fabricates so regularly, so shamelessly and so systematically as Boris Johnson.'[7] The question of whether Johnson was acting in the public interest – for example, cutting constitutional corners to 'get Brexit done' – is put in context by the assessment of his former editor at the *Daily Telegraph*, Sir Max Hastings: 'he is unfit for national office, because it seems he cares for no interest save his own fame and gratification.'[8] Lord Patten described Boris Johnson as a 'moral vacuum'.

To give a balanced view, we must also ask whether the Johnson era was different from any other, and if so why it was different. There were in fact several discernible differences from other post-war governments: the number of breaches of integrity standards; the deliberate attitude of treating informal conventions and long-standing traditions as voluntary; the shamelessness, with no expectation of resignations or censure; and the fact that the Prime Minister himself was personally involved, time after time.

At the time, many neutral commentators were clear that these behaviours were worse than had been seen for quite a while. Peter Hennessy explained that we may be witnessing a significant and recent change: 'A key characteristic of the British constitution is the degree to which the good governance of the United Kingdom has relied on the self-restraint of those who carry it out ... Recent events suggest it is worth considering the implications of a decline in the viability of the "good chap" system in this country.'[9] In other words, the country's foremost historian of contemporary politics, who himself identified the 'good chaps' approach as an underlying principle that places personal integrity at the heart of the constitution, was questioning whether the country was still being run by good chaps.

John Major went further in a speech in June 2025: 'Standards have been undermined by being ignored, by being broken, by public figures who put personal or political interest before public virtue.'[10] After some searing comments in the subsequent audience discussion, the digital magazine *Politico* summarised his view as 'John Major reckons Britain is more corrupt than three decades ago.'[11] His predecessor, Gordon Brown, was equally uncompromising in 2022: 'I think it's possible to argue that the governments of the eighteenth century were perhaps more corrupt, but in terms of the scale of resources that appear to be wasted, or not properly used, I think it's very difficult to see that this government has not been the worst in living memory, at least … the worst for a century.'[12]

Is there a risk of overstating the differences between the Johnson regime and those of his predecessors? There were clearly echoes of what had gone on in previous governments. The patronage of the British honours system has for many decades been perhaps the most blatantly corrupt feature of British politics, though it is seldom acknowledged as such. The Blair government had its own scandals over party donors, and likewise appointed some of its supporters to public positions. And it is less than thirty years since the Tory 'sleaze' scandals under John Major, both within parliament and among his own ministers. Major's response was very different from those of his successors: it was both swift and thorough. This resulted in the seven Nolan Principles of standards in public life,* which themselves drew on a heritage of public standards stretching as far back as the Northcote–Trevelyan principles of the 1850s, and to

---

* Selflessness, integrity, objectivity, accountability, openness, honesty and leadership.

this day form the basis of the codes by which ministers, MPs and civil servants are meant to conduct themselves.

To avoid any suggestion of being anti-Conservative, I must point out how disappointing Keir Starmer's regime has been in this regard since his election in July 2024. To ordinary people, it seems blindingly obvious that taking free gifts from interested parties and failing to reveal them is not good practice. Yet Starmer did exactly that when he accepted £16,200 worth of clothes from a party donor, to whom he subsequently gave a security pass to Downing Street. Moreover, this only came out through being spotted by journalists. If you think this looks like someone was able to buy access to those in power, you are right.

Starmer's false start was reinforced when he accepted expensive football tickets from clubs about whom he was planning regulation, which they wanted to be diluted. It is well known that he likes the sport – but as Prime Minister he might reasonably be expected to show self-restraint in the face of such a clear conflict of interest. This misjudgement on ethical standards was also on show when his City Minister, Tulip Siddiq, was placed under investigation for corruption and money laundering by the authorities in Bangladesh. Effectively, she was in charge of regulating the apparatus that might be investigating her. This looming scandal was known before Labour won the election, yet Starmer still appointed her; she was further supported by him when the scandal broke in the press, until the pressure mounted too far and she resigned.

Clothing-gate, football freebies and the Tulip Siddiq affair were all ethical issues in which Starmer leaned the wrong way – a far cry from the moral high ground taken by the Labour Party when it criticised the Conservative government and promised it would appoint an Ethics and Integrity Commission to investigate such things. Campaigners were encouraged at the time, but it all went quiet after the election. As a senior former minister explained in private when the clothing scandal broke, 'It's easy to say when you are in opposition.' The Ethics and Integrity Commission was finally 'created' in October 2025, simply by rebadging the existing Committee on Standards in Public Life, but without giving it some of the key things experts had identified as being required. These included that the existence of the EIC should be enshrined in law; an independent process for appointing members, to avoid political patronage; and giving the EIC the power to investigate and punish wrongdoing.

The breaching of standards by all parties makes it hard for any of them to take a stance on the issue – and easy for ministers to divert attention from their own behaviours by pointing to their political opponents having done something similar or worse in the past. It can be no surprise that the levels of trust British citizens have in their politicians have fallen significantly in recent years, according to surveys conducted by bodies like the Institute for Government. This decline in trust may be bad for democracy, but does it tell us anything about political corruption?

* * *

It's time to have a look at some cases in a bit of depth, and we will start with the Owen Paterson affair. Our mode of analysis is applying the four-step test: *'The abuse of entrusted power for private gain that harms the public interest, typically breaching laws, regulations and/or integrity standards.'*

Paterson was a former government minister who, on becoming a backbench MP, used his position and contacts to lobby on behalf of companies that were paying him a retainer. In particular, a healthcare company called Randox paid him a monthly fee of £8,300, around £100,000 per year, and in return Paterson used his party contacts to lobby ministers and health officials. Although his monthly fee was declared, there was much less clarity about who he was meeting and what he was saying to them, and some of the meetings that came to light seemed to be in clear breach of the parliamentary rules against paid advocacy. Randox (which has always denied any wrongdoing) flourished: in the Covid crisis, it received £777 million of contracts from the Department of Health, which were directly awarded rather than going through standard procurement processes – and the company's profits increased a hundredfold. A report from the Public Accounts Committee in 2022 was strongly critical of Paterson, Randox and the Department of Health,[13] with six damning conclusions including that 'Woefully inadequate record-keeping by the Department makes it impossible to have confidence that all its contracts with Randox were awarded properly.'

When these arrangements with Paterson (a pro-Brexit ally of Johnson) were scrutinised by the Parliamentary Standards Committee, he was found to have committed an 'egregious' breach of lobbying rules, and the committee recommended his suspension from parliament. The response of the government was to go on the offensive: it defended Paterson publicly, and criticised the independent Parliamentary Commissioner for Standards for bias, while at the same time trying to change the rules to accommodate Paterson's behaviour. Instead of supporting the standard disciplinary motion to suspend him, senior ministers put forward proposals to create a new committee, with a Conservative majority, that would re-examine the case and could overturn the original independent investigation. The vote took place; the government won by 250 votes to 232, but tellingly 98 Conservative MPs abstained or missed the vote, and 13 voted against the government. On paper, Paterson and his ministerial allies had won, but the public and media outcry was such that the plan was shelved, and Paterson was forced to resign.

For the first time in living memory, a British government was facing widespread accusations of corruption – and with it there was a suggestion that one-off scandals had tipped into systemic corruption. Chris Bryant, chair of the Parliamentary Standards Committee, described Paterson's lobbying as 'a corrupt practice'. Former prime minister John Major took a broader view of the government's approach and said in an interview with the BBC that the UK was 'politically corrupt.' Lord Evans, the chair of the Committee on Standards in Public Life, warned that 'We could slip into being a corrupt country.' Keir Starmer, as might be expected from the Leader of the Opposition, was clear on what he was seeing: 'Government corruption. There is no other word for it.'

Before the Paterson affair, the word corruption had rarely been used in UK politics during the past fifty years. From that point onwards, and probably connected with the rise in social media, the term started to be heard much more frequently. There was so much furore about the Paterson affair, which was combined with a flare-up over the conflicts of interest when MPs hold second jobs, that Johnson felt compelled to respond. He announced at an international meeting, 'I genuinely believe that the UK is not remotely a corrupt country, and I genuinely think that our institutions are not corrupt.' What he was ignoring was the charge that he was personally corrupt – and that so was his government.

What does the four-step corruption test tell us in the Paterson case? The entrusted power (held by an MP) was abused (by his lobbying in breach of the rules) for private gain (Randox gained contracts, while Paterson gained money for his services).

This harmed the public interest by breaching the Nolan Principles, and by unfairly giving privileged treatment to one company, possibly to the detriment of its competitors. It certainly seems to fall within the definition of corruption. Furthermore, the support given to Paterson by his political chums in government, as they sought to change the rules so he would not be found to have breached them, demonstrates collusion. That may not in itself have been corrupt, but we might consider it does at least contribute to building evidence of systemic corruption.

Our next case is the Lebedev lordship. You may recall that Evgeny Lebedev, the oligarch son of a former KGB officer, newspaper owner and friend of Johnson, was awarded a seat in the House of Lords as Lord Lebedev of Siberia. Entrusted power (in Johnson as Prime Minister) was abused, as was subsequently revealed: Johnson personally overruled the advice of both the security services and the House of Lords Appointments Commission. But was there private gain? There has been media focus on Johnson's enjoyment of a reportedly hedonistic party in Lebedev's eighteenth-century palazzo in Italy, though this alone seems too trivial to support the charge of corruption. In fact, we need not be distracted by arguing what level of extravagance and nudity at a party qualifies as a private gain, because in the Lebedev case we also have the important fact that he owned two newspapers that were supportive of Johnson. More details may yet come out about the extent of Lebedev's hospitality, but we already know that for a politician the support of major newspapers is an important private gain. As for the final step in the four-step test, we do not know why the security services advised against this appointment, but we can reasonably assume they thought that it was not in the public interest. Lebedev said, 'I am not a security risk to this country, which I love' and that his father 'was a foreign intelligence agent of the KGB, but I am not some agent of Russia'.

Frustratingly, as so often when studying corruption, there are several cases from the Johnson era in which we can see there is a likelihood of corruption, but do not yet have sufficient detail to be able to state that definitively. A prime example is the Towns Fund, allegedly an example of what is known in the United States as 'pork-barrelling' – in which politicians use their positions to ensure government funds are channelled to their own favoured locations and projects, with the purpose of retaining the support of voters. In this instance, the Johnson government created the £3.6 billion Towns Fund to support the levelling up of disadvantaged areas. This was overseen by the Communities Secretary Robert Jenrick, who exercised 'disproportionate influence' over the selection of which places got the money, according to a report from the Public Accounts Committee. Several areas that were Tory marginal seats and rated by civil servants as low priority in terms of need were nevertheless awarded funds; whereas some highly deprived but safe Labour seats missed out. Robert Jenrick's own constituency of Newark was one of those to benefit (though Jenrick was apparently not involved in that particular decision). But there is a lack of transparency about precisely who made which decisions, and whether there was an abuse of power. This situation is crying out for thorough investigation so that facts can be proven and allegations substantiated; so far, there is no sign that will happen.

A second case involving Jenrick also remains in the realm of allegation due to lack of investigation. This was the Westferry development planning decision, which is examined in more detail in a later chapter. There are several other cases of alleged corruption about which we lack information, of which the biggest is around PPE procurement – though, for reasons also examined later, we can be fairly sure that the corruption around Covid will never be properly investigated.

Such cases are already beginning to fade into the past, and it's tempting to think we should just move on. However, it is in my view important to acknowledge these matters as corruption even if it is some time after the event: political corruption is so damaging, and recognising the heart of the problem may help to stop such things happening in future. One of the challenges of doing so is that nobody has any official responsibility for calling it out in the UK. The good chaps system was not meant to face such concerted challenge, and particularly not from several senior ministers simultaneously, let alone the PM himself. Under our present system, an unusually high degree of political will is needed even to launch an investigation, and then the process can take several years. Unless we find a mechanism to treat political corruption with the seriousness it deserves, we'll always be playing catch-up as the latest scandal breaks.

* * *

We have in this chapter so far seen multiple breaches of integrity by our political class, which few senior politicians seem too worried about – each of which is a step on the pathway towards corruption because they normalise rule-breaking. We have also seen instances that fall within the definition of corruption; and we have seen some gaping areas of corruption risk.

It's now time to address the question of whether UK politics is institutionally or structurally corrupt. Rotten to the core, as opposed to suffering from a few one-off unconnected incidents. In the absence of hard evidence, this is where theory can help us. As we saw in an earlier chapter, a swathe of American academics have developed theories allowing them to accuse the US Congress of being institutionally corrupt. In this framing of the problem, the purpose of parliament is no longer serving the people via democracy, but rather serving the vested interests who fund – and thereby distort – politics. In the jargon, ordinary citizens are subject not to empowered inclusion but to duplicitous exclusion.

There is plenty of evidence from elsewhere in the world that liberal democracies can be corrupt at their political core: for example, Italy (with close political links to the Mafia); the USA itself (President Trump – almost all serious scholars in this field agree his presidencies tick all the boxes, multiple times, for corruption); and France (which has convicted two successive presidents – Jacques Chirac and Nicolas Sarkozy – of corruption). Is Britain any better?

Academic research on this over several decades also tells us that political corruption need not involve law-breaking; it may be about how the institution behaves, and not just the individuals within it; and that before we use the term, we must understand that sometimes bad outcomes are produced by inefficiency and incompetence, not corruption.

Despite the instances of corruption outlined above, and the inexorable rise over recent decades of lobbying and other areas that are high in corruption risk, I am not persuaded that the UK parliament is institutionally corrupt. Lawrence Lessig would assert that this would require a diversion of purpose; in my view, our parliament is still passing laws, and the government is still governing, with the broad public interest in mind.

But at the same time, some things have been going badly wrong. We should certainly see breaches of the Nolan Principles and integrity standards, even if they are not directly related to corruption, as steps on the pathway towards structural corruption. The Owen Paterson affair demonstrated this starkly; when asked to support him, a majority of the House of Commons voted in favour of a corrupt act in not censuring Paterson and amending the rules so he could be let off. The institutional environment of voting along party lines allowed and even encouraged this.

Fundamentally, corruption is closely linked to maintaining standards of integrity. The distinguished Oxford academic Gillian Peele was one of the early British scholars to assert that if standards were not adhered to, at some indefinable point the door would be open to corruption, even if she was not quite ready to concede that the boundary had been crossed. Peele and her co-author David Hine wrote about the pre-Johnson era: 'For the most part the British political system has been seen as relatively free from corruption. Yet since the so-called "cash-for-questions" affair erupted over John Major's government in the early 1990s a number of question marks have appeared over the traditional assumptions about the ethics prevailing in the public sector. The problem of how to sustain high standards in British public life has become a fixture of the political agenda ... There has been a steady drip of scandal in British public life. While rarely suggesting systemic wrongdoing or formal corruption, they have been enough to cause recurrent political controversy.'[14]

The normalisation of such breaches of standards can in part be explained by complacency. British politicians, almost without exception, consider corruption to be a problem that happens overseas and only occasionally drifts over to pollute our shores. And if they acknowledge it might be a problem within the UK, they seldom consider that there might be political corruption. Even the most obvious areas of corruption risk in British politics – the dark quartet of party funding, lobbying, conflicts of interest and the revolving door – are routinely explained as marginal concerns, an inevitable part of our political system, and so low-risk that they can safely be deprioritised in the light of other pressing challenges. This reveals a notable lack of insight from people who do not seem able to conceive that British politics might ever be described as corrupt.

Why should that be the case? There is also something else at play. The most honest assessment of the problem came from a former Conservative Party chairman who has since become a grandee in the House of Lords. His response to my probing him over a cup of tea in Whitehall was that it would be political suicide for any party leader to try to tackle these areas of corruption risk; to do so would mean treading on the toes of too many people on whose support they depended. This starts to look as if the self-interest of politicians and political parties may be parting company from the public interest: dangerous territory.

A further explanation for the political complacency around corruption may lie in what commentators and journalists have termed the 'chumocracy'. This develops from long-standing critiques of the British establishment which theorise that people who were privately educated or attended the Oxbridge universities are self-serving, self-perpetuating and self-interested when in public office; the good chaps, in other words, were in fact never that good. Some statistics seem to bear out this argument: seated round the cabinet table in Downing Street in 2019 were three Old Etonians, while 64 per cent of cabinet members were privately educated, and half had been at Oxford or Cambridge. Going back over previous decades, that would have been a familiar picture – in fact, the Johnson cabinet of 2019 had an almost identical Oxbridge make-up to the Attlee cabinet of 1950. This dropped very markedly in the Blair years, and perhaps surprisingly the numbers were at their post-war lowest under Theresa May, though still with around a third of cabinet members from private schools and a third from Oxbridge. This small coterie of interconnected politicians have chums with similar back-grounds in business and other senior public roles, and at times allow a select and very rich few to join their circle – usually through funding political parties.

The *Financial Times* asked in 2021 'Is the UK's democracy for sale?', commenting that 'the whiff of chumocracy risks becoming overpowering'.[15] This was in an editorial about the number of Conservative Party donors linked to the property sector, just as the government was about to push through a set of reforms favourable to property developers. It is certainly possible that the chumocracy is distorting political decision-making in this way – and that would chime with Lessig's concept of 'diversion of purpose' if as a result of such donations the government or the Parliamentary Conservative Party or Labour Party were to start making decisions based on the interests of its donors rather than the public interest.

It is claimed by its critics that the chumocracy's reach extends beyond parliament: for example, in the appointment of political friends and allies to public positions, including Richard Sharp as chair of the BBC and Robbie Gibb (described by journalist Emily Maitlis as an 'active agent of the Conservative Party'[16]) as a BBC board member; the allocation of public funds and contracts, most notoriously during the Covid-19 pandemic; and rewarding political donors and friends in the media with honours. An extraordinary manifestation of the chumocracy in action was the Greensill affair. Lex Greensill, a financier with political connections, was given a desk in 10 Downing Street from which he could pursue his business interests of selling complex financing arrangements to government departments; he later employed former prime minister David Cameron to lobby his recent ministerial colleagues for a reported £8 million.[17] Greensill's company collapsed with billions of dollars of debts, and is now being investigated for fraud and breach of fiduciary duty.

Chumocracy has self-interested complacency at its heart. Even without making the argument that such an arrangement of our political economy is itself inherently corrupt, it should be evident that drawing political leaders and senior public office-holders from a narrow gene pool, expanded only to include those who can pay or are ideologically loyal, has an inbuilt flaw. They will be inclined to consider themselves, and their chums, to be good chaps. They also find it hard to conceive that what they are doing may be corrupt, or may be leading in that direction.

Returning for a moment to academic theory: rational choice theorists broadly think everyone is likely to be corrupt unless they are incentivised not to be; institutionalists by and large argue that the right institutional setting – comprising rules, norms and structure – will create the right behaviours. They both agree that strong defences against political corruption are necessary. In trying to assess the status of political corruption in the UK, one approach is therefore to look at the strength of those defences, but also – equally important – how far politicians are supporting them.

While this cannot tell us whether a government – or any individual within it – is corrupt, it can show how seriously they take the issue and also perhaps whether there may be something to hide. Politicians who weaken the defences may legitimately be subject to the suspicion that they have done so in order to permit or obscure corruption in the past, present or future. Those who knowingly permit inadequate defences without trying to strengthen them are creating elevated levels of corruption risk.

In the absence of a written constitution, the UK has four essential defences against political corruption. First, there is a set of ethical or integrity standards – formalised as the Nolan Principles, mentioned earlier – that politicians should adhere to. Second, there is the expectation, also mentioned earlier, that 'good chaps' will adhere to those standards. Third, there are formal mechanisms to ensure those standards are adhered to, such as investigations under the Ministerial Code and the Parliamentary Standards Committee. Fourth, there are informal mechanisms such as the traditional powers of the Speaker of the House of Commons, gathered into the parliamentary handbook known as Erskine May. Underpinning all of these is the principle of transparency. Finally, as a backstop, there are elections: if the voters do not like what they see, they can vote someone out of office.

Whatever scandals may have happened, this last defence = described by specialists as vertical accountability – is rolled out time and again by politicians the world over to explain why they are right and their critics are wrong. If this was so wrong, they say, people would not be voting for us. It is, however, a tarnished argument: voters around the world have, for a variety of reasons, regularly elected politicians they know to be corrupt – even when those same voters say in opinion surveys that they feel strongly about corruption. For example, voters may feel that the most important thing for the country is to 'get Brexit done' or to keep a left-wing activist out of power at all costs, and on those grounds would vote for a corrupt populist. In other words, success or failure at the ballot box is not a reliable indication of the electorate's attitude towards corruption.

On that measure of the strength of their support for anti-corruption defences, how well have recent governments been doing? At the time of writing, Keir Starmer has been frankly disappointing. In opposition, he promised strict adherence to standards and new institutions to police them. This did not happen. One MP, Rosie Duffield, who chose to give up the Labour whip for a variety of reasons, explained: 'the sleaze, nepotism and apparent avarice are off the scale ... I am so ashamed of what you and your inner circle have done to tarnish and humiliate our once proud party.'[18] That view is something of an outlier, but it captures some of the disappointment felt by those who felt change was badly needed – and that the new government was treading too similar a path to its predecessors. Instead, the reforms that have trickled out have been half-hearted at best, while uninspiring leadership has done little to reset the norms. There was barely a fuss, for example, when Reform UK leader Nigel Farage was found in January 2026 to have breached the parliamentary rules seventeen times through late declarations of income worth £380,000. Farage apologised and explained that his affairs were 'complicated and complex', but the incident demonstrated that such basic matters of transparency can all too easily be considered a low priority.

The publication of the UK's new 120-page anti-corruption strategy in December 2025 may yet improve things – but on the key area of political corruption it is muted at best. Spotlight on Corruption's evaluation was not favourable: 'Amidst all the announcements, those on political integrity are surprisingly weak, largely relying on existing announcements and containing some startling gaps, particularly on lobbying and ethics. This is despite the Prime Minister promising to *"clean up politics"*, *"restore standards in public life"*, and have a *"total crackdown on cronyism"*.'[19]

Of course, the reason why a substantial reset was so necessary was due to what had gone on immediately before under Johnson, Truss and Sunak. Their governments were notable not just for serial breaches of standards, but for the deliberate weakening of the defences.

As Professor Liz Dávid-Barrett, a world expert on state capture, said at the time in a speech to the Constitution Society, 'the Johnson government's attacks on the accountability institutions are numerous'.[20] She cited attacks on the judiciary, the media and parliament, as well as regulatory bodies, all of which are important checks and balances in the UK's institutional defences against corruption. One example of this was the Elections Act of 2022, which put the Electoral Commission, and its responsibility for regulating political party funding, under much tighter and more direct government control. Another example was the attempt to shoehorn a chosen candidate, the former *Daily Mail* editor Paul Dacre, into the job of chairman of Ofcom, in which he would be responsible for regulating the BBC, an organisation he had long criticised and which many senior Tory politicians felt needed to be brought to heel after its 'biased' coverage of Brexit.

Sometimes such changes are explained away as an attempt to create a more vigorous and effective culture in British bureaucracy. But attacking what some politicians and their special advisers describe as the 'Whitehall blob' does not simply indicate frustration about inefficiency; it is deliberately undermining some of the key checks to the improper exercise of ministerial power. Other checks and balances, such as the Committee on Standards in Public Life or the Independent Adviser on Ministerial Standards, were simply ignored or overruled during the three premierships that came after Theresa May. In the Owen Paterson case, the government even attempted to change the system so that he would not have to be held to account; when Johnson himself was later scrutinised by the Parliamentary Standards Committee for lying about Partygate, he and his allies declared it a 'kangaroo court'.

These attacks on the country's accountability institutions by

Johnson and his immediate successors may have been driven by short-term political expediency rather than a deliberate attempt to foster corruption; but at the same time, the post-Brexit Conservative governments were increasingly willing to maximise the political advantages that could be gained by disregarding the accountability regime.

* * *

Putting together all the pieces of this chapter, the picture that emerges is one of a newly exposed but fundamental weakness in Britain's defences against political corruption. The system of principles and norms has been gradually undermined over three decades, but in recent years breaches of integrity standards have snowballed into an avalanche, and the undermining of the defences has become more systematic and deliberate.

Let's return to the hypothesis that there was more corruption and corruption risk in and around the Johnson government than any other British government since 1945. This statement is slightly fudged; it does not distinguish between 'corruption' and 'corruption risk', and it refers to those as being 'around' the government as well as in it. However, although there was no shortage of shoddy behaviour and individual scandals in other decades since the Second World War, I cannot find evidence of anything equivalent to the Johnson era – either in the prevalence of breaches, the personal integrity of the PM or the willingness of the ruling party to put political advantage over the public interest. Certainly, there was no other premiership in which those three elements so obviously coincided.

What can we therefore conclude about corruption in British politics? I think there are six broad things we can confidently say.

1. Historically there has been a high level of complacency among politicians about political corruption in this country, but the scandals and approach of the Johnson government have provoked significantly more concern and comment about corruption.

2. Things were worse during the Johnson era than they have been in any decade since the end of the Second World War – individual scandals may have been no worse, but the sheer number and regularity of them increased, and this has already changed the norm of what is acceptable.

3. The defences against corruption have been not only bypassed, but actively undermined from within, by the very politicians who are meant to be prevented from acting corruptly by our system.

4. Corruption is never far away – it is there under the surface and waiting to break through when given the opportunity; the social norms – or reliance on good chaps – that made the system work can no longer be counted on.

5. There have been some clear cases of corruption, with the collusion or involvement of the government or the Prime Minister; in the UK system, it is both individual misconduct and structural weaknesses that allow corruption to flourish.

6. While the evidence is not yet there to make a compelling argument about systemic or structural corruption, the reverse is also true: there is insufficient evidence to combat the claim of systemic or structural corruption. In other words, the jury is out.

Precisely because political corruption in Britain does not

resemble the narco-state of Mexico or the historical corruption of Italy or South Korea, it is easy to understate – or to underestimate – the level and systemic nature of corruption in British politics. Equally, it would be a mistake to overstate the case, as those who claim a neoliberal takeover and establishment stitch-up are inclined to do. As in other mature democracies, two key questions are simply not possible to answer objectively: when does a breach of standards become corruption, and how many individual incidents add up to systemic corruption? Yet the fact that the boundary between structural corruption and poor behaviour cannot be neatly drawn does not mean that it will never be crossed. The UK has certainly come very close recently.

To remind ourselves why this matters, let's turn to the views of a couple of eminent professors. First, Gillian Peele: 'Confidence in the probity of a country's governing arrangements and personnel is a vital part of a healthy democracy.'[21] Or Liz Dávid-Barrett: 'I used to see democratisation as a journey from A to B, but I've come to realise that it's more like trying to climb a hill in a creaking carriage. You might make it to the top, but you're always at risk of sliding back down the hill. And once the carriage starts sliding, it is quite literally an uphill struggle to push it back. But it's critical that we stop it from gaining momentum.'[22] Both agree that corruption fundamentally undermines democracy, but also that the appearance of corruption does the same. Moreover, democracy is not just about having free and fair elections; it is about a set of values that lie at the heart of the kind of society we want to be.

The tone from the top sets the standards we expect as a nation. Corrupt leaders always go hand in hand with corruption elsewhere in society and the economy; the fish does indeed rot from the head. As we will see in the following chapters, there is plenty of corruption to be worried about in the UK. The good news is that there are remedies. We can strengthen our defences, incentivise improved behaviours and react more appropriately to proven cases. The tone from the top in the form of leadership, from the Prime Minister downwards, is an essential ingredient. But the Starmer government reminds us that we should not naïvely expect to wake up and find that good chaps have taken over government. If we are fortuitous, they may sometimes be in power, but sometimes they will not be. So we need anti-corruption systems that are fit for democracy and its challenges.

It would be a mistake to regard Boris Johnson as a one-off within a broadly sound system – he is part of a longer-term trend that has outrun the ability of the anti-corruption defences to do their job. In a perverse sense, Johnson's unruly approach to governing did the country a favour: he identified the weaknesses in the system that need to be addressed – but without successfully exploiting them either to downgrade democracy or embed himself in power. Next time, we may not be so lucky. If corruption were to be combined with competence or systematic venality, Britain would be much closer to becoming an illiberal democracy or even vulnerable to state capture by a malign ruler. What is at stake here is what kind of political system we want to live in. We Brits sometimes watch with a mixture of horror and smugness what happens elsewhere in the world; but no nation should ever believe that such things can happen to its neighbours but not to itself.

5

FORMER GLORIES: MONARCHY AND EMPIRE

The United Kingdom has a lot of historical baggage, and a central question in our analysis must be whether it carries some kind of structural corruption that results from its history and ancient institutions. This takes us back to the notion of path dependency, the idea that we might be locked into a certain course of action because of what happened in the past. When we are trying to interpret the corruption of today, we therefore need to know a bit about what the baggage is – and how it relates to corruption.

I have so far argued that there is not much peculiarly British about corruption, and that it has the same ingredients as corruption elsewhere. But on the other hand, corruption in this country does have a British flavour; it would be astonishing if the UK did not in some way carry the legacy of colonialism and of considering itself – with some justification – to have been a winner on the world stage.

In this chapter we will look at the monarchy and the British Empire. Other elements of our historical legacy – the class system, the City and religious institutions – will be examined in later chapters.

Monarchies are no strangers to corruption – and this does not just mean the Tudors, the Habsburgs or the Romanovs. Look around the world today and you will see allegations about the royal families of Spain, Sweden, Norway, Saudi Arabia, Thailand and Dubai, to name a few. So what should we make of recent scandals involving the British royal family? Does corruption lie at the heart of the British establishment, as some in the media claim, or have we seen isolated incidents of poor behaviour from individuals who are too cut off from the world to know better?

Republicans often argue that the very idea of monarchy is inherently corrupt. This reflects a view dating back to the Enlightenment, when it was aired both in France and Britain. These days, the argument that having an unelected monarch alongside an electoral democracy is a form of corruption hard-wired into the constitution is frequently rolled out by those who wish to discredit or abolish the monarchy. Perhaps there is a germ of truth to it: in recent years, several members of the British royal family have been accused of acting corruptly, leading to the inescapable allegation that the entire edifice is rotten and needs to be replaced. There have been clear cases of abuse of power, including several scandals examined below involving the then Prince Andrew, and the sale of honours by Prince (as he was) Charles. Prince Harry's memoir *Spare* paints an unflattering picture of a family that is entitled, self-preserving, closed in on itself and out of touch. There is by any measure a lack of transparency and accountability. But even though individuals may at times act badly or corruptly, this does not necessarily make the institution itself corrupt.

What is certainly true is that over the past decade some members of the royal family have behaved in ways that are verging on being corrupt – as well as potentially criminal. We have without doubt seen an absolute failure of integrity on a number of occasions. And if you think the monarchy matters to the UK, this failure of integrity is very important.

We will focus here on three recent cases: Prince Andrew (now known as Andrew Mountbatten-Windsor) and various misdemeanours, the involvement of Queen Camilla's nephew with Conservative Party donors, and favours granted to donors to Prince Charles's charities. In each of these cases we can apply our four-step definition to give a sense of whether there has been corruption, starting with the question of entrusted power. Although it is rarely used, there is certainly entrusted power within the monarchy – so we must probe the issues of abuse and private gain, and look at whether the entrusted power extends beyond the king to other members of the royal family.

The former Prince Andrew's arrest in 2026 for Misconduct in Public Office centres, like Peter Mandelson's case, on his passing of confidential government documents, while holding public office, to Jeffrey Epstein. As part of this relationship, Andrew and his ex-wife seem to have been able to advance their various money-making schemes. These are allegations at present, although given credence by the evidence published from the Epstein files, but if the allegations turn out to be true they can be unambiguously categorised as corrupt. In this example, Andrew's government-appointed position as a 'UK Special Representative for International Trade and Investment' is what allows us to say definitively that he would have been abusing entrusted power when passing on government documents.

The related Epstein case of Andrew allegedly having sex with a trafficked minor would, without doubt, qualify as abuse. And if you assume that private gain includes personal gratification, then you would seem to have a case of corruption – but the question hinges on the notion of entrusted power. If Andrew was having sex, as alleged, was this in his capacity as a person with entrusted power – if indeed we can consider the person who is eighth in line to the throne as having any residual entrusted power? On the one hand, a prince does not stop being a prince when he removes his clothes. What might not be corrupt in an ordinary citizen might become so when an office-holder does the same thing. But on the other hand, there must be some point at which even a very public figure is acting in a private capacity. Behaviour can still be wrong, and prosecutable, without being corrupt. Over and above breaking the law, an errant parliamentarian might be accused of 'bringing the House into disrepute' – and the sex abuse allegations relating to Prince Andrew's case are perhaps akin to 'bringing the monarchy into disrepute'. Whether or not it is corrupt, the sordid episode, compounded by his lies and sense of impunity, is a gross breach of integrity and trust. And if it is not in itself corrupt, we might view it as contributing to the evidence that the monarchy has become institutionally corrupt – in the sense of serving itself rather than serving the people.

A further scandal involving Andrew concerns his dealings with a Kazakh oligarch who was the nephew of the country's autocratic ruler President Nursultan Nazarbayev. Andrew was widely reported to act as the nephew's 'fixer' in generating high-level contacts. He was apparently rewarded for this through the sale of his former residence Sunninghill Park, which was acquired by the nephew for £15 million – £3 million above the asking price, despite having been on the market for five years. There were allegedly other business dealings between the two, generating further millions in income for Andrew. However, as so often with an untransparent royal family, little is known publicly. We can see entrusted power and private gain: whether or not there was abuse of power by Prince Andrew as a member of the monarchy, or in his other role as the government's trade envoy, remains for now a matter of allegation.

The present queen's nephew, Ben Elliot, was co-chairman of the Conservative Party, and runs a 'concierge' business that provides exclusive services to wealthy people. It is the combination of his business activities with his political position and relationship to the royal family that leads us to ask whether corruption is at play.[1] Did these different things mix, and can this be described as corruption?

Elliot seems to have used his proximity to the royal family – before Prince Charles became king – to introduce Conservative Party donors to his aunt Camilla and her husband. In some instances, donations were made to the prince's charity. It is not clear what Elliot's clients or Prince Charles expected from these encounters, but it is clear that Elliot was being paid. He was widely described in the press as 'peddling access': if you had enough money, you could get access to the royal family via Elliot – either by becoming a client of his company or by making a donation to the Conservative Party. Elliot insisted that his political role and charitable endeavours were kept separate from his business and that he did not 'sell access'.

Was this an act of corruption? Well, it was all within the rules. It is not quite clear who held the entrusted power – arguably Elliot, as a holder of political office – whether there was an improper offer of access or reward, or whether there was private gain by Elliot. Moreover, how might this harm the public interest? But still, it rings alarm bells for potential corruption with a British flavour: out-of-view establishment back-scratching that blurs the lines between business, politics and the royal family. It may not be provably corrupt, but there is clearly a corruption risk, and it therefore taints the royal family.

Let's now turn to the case of Prince Charles's charities (also in the period before he became King Charles), in which it is alleged that an honour was improperly granted to a Saudi businessman who was a donor. The key question is whether an honour was effectively sold; if it was, that would be an abuse. The entrusted power lay with Prince Charles, who was able to ensure an honour was granted. Was there private gain? For Prince Charles, the gain was for his charitable work. The Saudi businessman gained an honour, but it is hardly unusual for philanthropists to be so rewarded – and in any case, he was not the one abusing his entrusted power. The question of wrongdoing hinges on whether it was quid pro quo: was money paid to the charity specifically with the expectation of receiving an honour? We do not know. But like the Ben Elliot case, it smacks of behind-the-scenes cronyism, a self-serving establishment and the toxic mix of politics, money, honours and the royal family. We might not be able to call it corruption, but it's not a good look.

The conclusion in all these cases – apart from former Prince Andrew's yet-to-be-proven Misconduct in Public Office – is that there was at minimum a breach of integrity, but not necessarily corruption. There is also the common theme of impunity: rule-breaking and standards breached with no expectation of being held to account. However, just as with Boris Johnson's government, we must ask at what point serial wrongdoing, cronyism and abuses of power add up to institutional corruption – even if no individual act has been proven to be corrupt. Are the royal family really serving the nation – or are they serving themselves? There have been serial failures of integrity, and we seem perilously close to institutional corruption, in which an institution's purpose is diverted to serve the interests of others. I have never heard anyone propose that the Nolan Principles should be applied to the monarchy – and anyway, our unwritten constitution would probably make that difficult. But in light of these flirtations with corruption, some sense of what the monarchy itself regards as a reasonable expectation of its own behaviour would surely be a useful set of principles. At least, some enhanced mechanisms for transparency and accountability clearly need to be put in place.

You might not think this matters. The monarchy is, after all, one of this country's quaint former glories, and we tolerate and/or admire it for various reasons. But as we can see from the press coverage that they generate, what the royal family do still has weight. This is the case both within the UK and also overseas, where the head of state often commands greater respect than whichever government happens to be in power. By virtue of their position in the constitution, it is reasonable to expect that the monarch and his or her family should be free of corruption. If nothing else, there is self-interest at play: support for the monarchy cannot be taken for granted. Yet in recent decades, the former queen's children seem to have been balancing dangerously on the borderline of corruption, when they should be safely on the right side of it.

* * *

I approach the subject of the British Empire with trepidation. There is already a vast literature on colonialism and neo-colonialism, and a body of academics writing on corruption who argue that definitions and measurements have been skewed by the global north, unfairly portraying 'developing' countries as corrupt while 'developed' countries are not. I disagree with some of those characterisations, but, if we view corruption as abuses of entrusted power, it is beyond doubt that there were many cases throughout the British Empire – and in certain countries these were deeply embedded into the institutional structures.

Right from the earliest days of corruption studies, the subject of corruption in the colonies attracted attention. This was by no means in line with Lord Curzon's view that empire was an 'instrument for good.' The Yale anthropologist James C. Scott pointed out in the 1960s that 'Colonial office until the twentieth century was regarded more often than not as an investment in an exclusive franchise that was expected to yield a good return to the political entrepreneur who acquired it.'[2] For some British colonial officials, particularly in the eighteenth and nineteenth centuries, corruption was both a means of consolidating the rule of the Empire and a means of personal enrichment.

More recently, a group of eminent scholars have pointed out that it is important 'not to treat "colonial corruption" as only about – and taking place in – the colony.'[3] In other words, corruption in the imperial capitals like London and Paris, and the tolerance of corruption abroad, was an intrinsic part of the imperial model. This could both shape Britain's domestic policy – for example, when wealthy 'nabobs' like Robert Clive returned home and bought seats in parliament – and distort decision-making about the colonies. There is an increasingly rich literature on Britain's relationship with corruption through its role as a coloniser. Professor Mark Knights, the leading historian in this field, has traced some of the effects on Britain itself. These could be positive as well as negative, paving the way for some of the reforms of the nineteenth century. For example, he notes that 'The public discussion – in the press, in parliament, at East India House and in conversation and correspondence – of imperial corruption could not help but to focus domestic attention on the problem: the two spheres were thus inherently overlapping.'[4] Interestingly, Knights traces a divergence between the UK and its colonies from around the 1830s, when we started to clean up our act at home but corruption continued abroad. Perhaps this was the moment at which Britain's sense of moral superiority set in, along with an enduring and comforting thought: foreigners are corrupt, but we are not.

Such thoughts are able to endure, even today, because there has been little interest in examining whether this complacency is merited, except among a narrow group of scholars. Historians Ian Cawood and Tom Crook have recognised that our society lacks 'serious engagement with the British Empire, both as a site of corruption in itself and as a source of corruption in Britain'.[5] In other words, the UK has a blind spot, which has yet to be addressed, with regard to corruption in its own colonial history – and the modern-day effects on the nation.

It is worth giving a couple of examples that illustrate not only how individuals enriched themselves, but also how corruption was pervasive within the governance structures of much of the Empire.

We start with the largest colony, India, and Sir Edward Colebrooke, the head of the East India Company in Delhi. Colebrook was prosecuted for corruption in 1829, and this well-documented case gave a glimpse of how he was running his part of the colony. Claiming that gift-giving (and receiving) was respectful to local culture, he and his wife amassed large quantities of spoils, which they retained for their personal use, including gold, fine clothing and an elephant, while in return allocating favours, positions and contracts.[6] His merging of the private and public parts of his role is characteristic of what is often described as 'old corruption'. Across the Indian Ocean in southern Africa, Cecil Rhodes had no scruples about using bribes to get what he wanted in building his vast De Beers mining empire, with missionaries and governors on his payroll. He believed 'every man had his price'.[7] One grim example of bribery in the Kimberley mines occurred during a smallpox epidemic in 1883, when the mine bosses (though possibly not Rhodes) bribed the local doctors to declare that the disease was chickenpox; the mines were allowed to stay open, and 700 people died (of whom 51 were recorded as being white).[8]

Colebrook and Rhodes were big beasts in the colonial world; the real damage was perhaps done by the mid-level officials who day in, day out, used their power to extract money, land and commercial advantages for personal gain. The twentieth century may have seen less abuse than the nineteenth, but only barely so; and it is no surprise that many leaders of anti-colonial independence movements cited the corruption of British rule as a motivating factor. Gandhi, for instance, wrote: 'Civil disobedience becomes a sacred duty when a state becomes lawless or corrupt.'[9]

One of the unintended consequences of decolonisation is that some parts of the former British Empire have rampant corruption today. This is not universally true: Singapore, Hong Kong and New Zealand stand out as having lower levels of corruption. By contrast, Pakistan, Sudan and Zimbabwe are examples of former British colonies with a high prevalence of corruption. How power was handed over, to whom and in what circumstances seem to be some key determinants of success – as well as the underlying stability and governance of the colony at the time of independence. Put plainly, if you pass on a corrupt style of government to a group of people who have not before been in government, against a background of civil unrest, it may not be surprising if corruption takes hold. In those former colonies where corruption thrives, we cannot escape the probability that today's corruption is, in part, the legacy of British colonial rule.[10]

Our focus here, however, is not the Empire itself, but rather how corruption within the former colonies may affect the United Kingdom of today. The movement to 'decolonise' thinking in corruption studies, as in many academic fields, can be seen in part as an attempt to correct past assumptions that have neglected or ignored corruption in the Empire; although some argue that there is a danger of over-correcting by over-emphasising the corruption of the past, which may give an unbalanced picture. In my view, those who warn that we must learn the lessons of colonialism are not necessarily using the sins of the past as a stick to beat the modern-day United Kingdom. It is reasonable to argue that it is precisely to prevent the UK ending up like some of its former colonies that we need to do better in terms of basic governance. The lessons of the Empire are the lessons not of foreigners, but of how British people have behaved and governed in the recent past. It brings to mind the comment of a London-based Nigerian investment banker during a conversation we had in a London club: 'I used to think that Nigeria and the UK would gradually come closer regarding levels of corruption; I was right, but not in the way I thought. In fact, it's the UK coming closer to Nigeria, not the other way round.'

So what is the Empire's residual impact on corruption in the UK today? I think we can discern five aspects.

Racism-linked Corruption

The UK has periodically welcomed immigrants from the Empire, which in many circumstances has led to an imbalance of power. In simple terms, incomers to a country often lack social power and access to formal positions of power. Their low status can lead them to be regularly in a position of dependency on those who do hold power. Such an imbalance can be extended and exacerbated when the immigrants are persons of colour and a racist component comes into play. A well-known example is the Stephen Lawrence case, which was investigated by the Metropolitan Police after a group of white youths murdered a Black teenager at a bus stop in a racist attack. The serial failures of the Met first to conduct a proper investigation and then to bring the killers to justice led to a number of inquiries, including the Macpherson Report of 1999, which found the Met to be 'institutionally racist'.[11] I use that tragic case to illustrate this point because Lawrence's parents were immigrants from Jamaica, faced on the one hand with the social power of a gang of white youths linked to local crime bosses, and on the other with the official power of the police who did nothing to help them – and may even have colluded with the crime bosses to protect the gang. It seems plausible that the dismissive attitude of the police towards a Black victim and his family could have encouraged police officers to act corruptly through collusion or cover-up.

Across the Atlantic, the death of George Floyd in Atlanta, which sparked the Black Lives Matter movement, showed a more extreme manifestation of the link between corruption and racism. When Floyd was held down by a police officer such that he could no longer breathe, the entrusted power of the police was being abused; the officer allegedly gained personal gratification from this exercise of power, and the public interest was harmed by what was later judged in court to be murder. We can see in this example how personal and institutional racism can be intertwined with corruption.

This also introduces a more complex question: does the imbalance of power for disadvantaged or under-represented groups mean that they are disproportionately subjected to abuses of power? If so, we might conclude that they are more likely to be the victims of corruption. And if there is institutional racism, as was found in the Macpherson Report on the

Met's handling of the Lawrence case, does that raise the probability of structural corruption?

Bringing this back to the subject of Empire, we can see from these examples that post-colonial immigration comes along with imbalances of power, particularly for certain groups; while the lingering assumptions of the Empire that some people were inferior might make it more likely that they will suffer from abuses of power.

Moral Superiority

Britain's perception of itself as a moral centrepoint within the Empire – home to the king and the Church of England – was reinforced by victory in the Second World War. No wonder we think we are special and superior to corrupt foreigners: we had an empire to prove it.

Moral Inferiority

In contrast to that moral superiority, the shameful corruption within the Empire revealed that, in the right circumstances, British officials could both be corrupt themselves and preside over a corrupt system. It is an important reminder that there is nothing innately un-corrupt about being British – we can be just as corrupt as anyone else.

Overseas Territories

The UK has fourteen territories spread across the world – the remnants of the Empire. Some of these, most notably the British Virgin Islands and the Cayman Islands, have become major international financial centres associated with corrupt capital flows.

Investigative journalists and leaked documents have in recent years helped to lift the lid on what is going on. Most notably, the Panama Papers, a leak of 11.5 million documents that revealed who was keeping their money in offshore accounts around the world, demonstrated the central role of the UK's territories in allowing corrupt individuals to hide and launder their stolen wealth. These Overseas Territories are able to market themselves as financial centres in part due to the rule of law and security of property rights, which are implicitly guaranteed by the UK connection, as well as the historically close connections to the City of London, which plug them into the global financial system. Like much of its historical attitude to the Empire, the UK's attitude has tended to be that its Overseas Territories are out of sight and out of mind, and so the issue of corruption has never been a priority. However, these so-called secrecy jurisdictions play a central role in a damaging global system of illicit financial flows by permitting the proceeds of corruption to be stashed offshore. An interesting recent development has been that, as the global spotlight has started to shine on these territories, corrupt capital has been diverted elsewhere. Dr Daniel Haberly has painstakingly traced the flows; he finds that the residual plumbing of the British Empire – historical connections of common law, structures like trusts, and professional qualifications – helps corrupt money to flow more easily, most notably in what he describes as the 'Dubai–Kong' axis between the former British territories of the United Arab Emirates and Hong Kong.

Immigrant Corruption

One of the long-term consequences of Empire is that many immigrants from former colonies come to the UK. If they come from areas of the world where corruption is prevalent, do they bring those norms with them? A comparable question was addressed by Baroness Casey in her audit of child grooming gangs published in June 2025. She was grappling with the delicate issue of the ethnicity of the perpetrators,[12] aware that pointing the finger at specific ethnic groups could contribute to community tensions or lead to hate crimes. When we look at the ethnic origin of those who perpetrate corruption in the UK, a similar issue is present. We must be wary of claims that corruption is an overseas disease that is spread by immigrants to the UK: our history tells us otherwise. But some legitimate questions have not been examined. For example, are immigrants from countries that have a high prevalence of corruption likely to act corruptly within the UK? Might any corrupt behaviour be further reinforced by patrimonial networks, which expect clan or ethnic loyalty to be placed above loyalty to the state? Or could it be that those who have come to this country to escape corruption act with higher levels of integrity than is the norm in the UK? We do not have the data either way, although the instances of bribery we encountered in the Introduction – the first three prosecutions under the Bribery Act – did suggest that some UK corruption might have an ethnic dimension.

It is possible that there may be a link between immigrant communities and corruption, but careful research needs to be done. On an optimistic note, the most relevant and widely cited piece of research looked at how students from countries where corruption is prevalent change their views over time.[13] Abigail Barr and Danila Serra's study at Oxford University found that 'time spent in the UK was associated with a decline in the propensity to bribe ... We conclude that, while corruption may, in part, be a cultural phenomenon, individuals should not be pre-judged with reference to their country of origin.'

Where does this leave us? At the very least, we can see that the imperial legacy is unresolved. The impression is reinforced that we have a national capacity for complacency about corruption, not because the story of British corruption in the colonies is serially denied, but because there is a profound indifference towards and ignorance of it. The standout message is that, in the right circumstances, the British are more than capable of corruption.

In this chapter we have looked at two key areas of the United Kingdom's long-standing self-image, as a stable constitutional monarchy and ruler of the largest empire in history, which are both underpinned by a sense of moral superiority. In reality, the monarchy, which we might expect to be a bastion of integrity, has been on the borderline of corruption because of the actions of senior members of the royal family. The legacy of the British Empire in relation to corruption is complex, not least due to structural racism and present-day immigration, and illustrates the unresolved impact of our history on the present day. This suggests that the residual attitudes of the Empire have yet to work themselves out of the UK's body politic.

6

THE PRIVATE SECTOR PARADOX: IS IT, OR ISN'T IT?

The paradox of the private sector is that lots of its activities seem to result in the same outcomes as corruption (inequality and injustice, to name two), yet individual companies often do not seem to be corrupt – at least according to standard definitions. In this chapter I will try to unpick that paradox, while examining the grey areas about what constitutes private sector corruption. We will also cover some aspects of private sector business that are broadly accepted to be corrupt in order to illustrate the core argument: that there is plenty of private sector corruption on show, even without engaging in a debate on whether neoliberalism and capitalism are corrupt.

Let's start with a brief anecdote from fifty years ago, when the idea of corporate corruption usually brought to mind straightforward bribery by a company to obtain government permits or contracts. My first experience of this came in the late 1970s, when I was about ten years old. For several days, the headline news was a story about a close family friend who had been sent to jail in Iraq; the charge was that he had paid a bribe to secure a contract selling commercial vehicles to Saddam Hussein's government.

I had no idea what corporate bribery was – all I understood was that the adults in my family were outraged. Our friend was known as a man of the highest integrity – a committed Christian who, as various members of his family explained to the Foreign Office, would never contemplate committing such a crime. Nine years later he emerged from the Iraqi jail, having learned Arabic along the way, and told his side of the story. It transpired that a bribe had indeed been offered – but by his German competitor. And when our friend had tried to cry foul, he was in short order accused, convicted and locked up, following a summary judicial proceeding that was common in Iraq at that time. The witnesses who could attest to his innocence were also accused, and then executed. Of course, the officials who had been bribed by his competitor were keen for the truth not to come out, and locking him away must have seemed a good way of protecting the gains from their corrupt contract. As a postscript, I should say that he went on to live a full life, but his family always bore the memories of those terrible years.

Those were the days before the OECD's Anti-Bribery Convention, which was agreed between the countries with the largest economies and designed to put a stop to big companies paying bribes overseas. My family friend's experience tells us two important things. First, that bribery is a form of corruption closely associated with companies. But also that corruption by companies often takes place overseas – and this story seemed to support the perception in this country that foreign companies are more likely to pay bribes than British ones.

Corporate bribery is unambiguously a form of corruption. One of the recent advances in the UK's anti-corruption armoury was the introduction of the Bribery Act in 2010, which enshrined that OECD Convention in law. As a result, British companies should be in no doubt that they must not pay bribes overseas (though some still do – the Serious Fraud Office investigates a number of cases each year), but the debate around what else should be categorised as private sector corruption rapidly gets into grey areas. If our picture of corruption in the UK is to be accurate, we need to tease out what is genuinely corrupt from other forms of harmful, unethical or illegal behaviour – which also means once again addressing the complex task of working out the difference between corrupt behaviour and a corrupt system.

If we trace the root of corruption to the question of who holds power, companies – and multinational corporations in particular – seem to be firmly in the frame. We have recently seen in the US that the so-called 'broligarchs' – the small group of mega-rich tech company bosses – can help to influence an election through political donations and then use that access and influence to rig the rules in areas like the regulation of content moderation, so that they and their companies gain ever more wealth and power. Tech bosses, especially those who own social media platforms, have both enormous wealth and enormous influence – just like the media magnates of yesteryear. Other global companies in a variety of sectors, including oil and food, also wield huge power, not only within their own business empires but also over the lives of everyone else. Financial markets and those who work within them seem to be able to dictate what governments can and cannot do in terms of tax policy and spending on public services – as we saw with the infamous Liz Truss mini-budget in 2022, when the reaction of the markets caused a complete reversal of government policy in just a few days.

Of course, corporations of such size and power have long existed. We need only think of the trading and industrial champions of the British Empire like the East India Company and the Tate & Lyle sugar company – or the manufacturing giants of the twentieth century such as car and defence companies, to name but a few. Has something changed? Most corruption analysts would say it has.

There has been a profound shift, from a time when most infrastructure and public services were owned and run by the state to an economic model of privatisation and outsourcing. This went hand in hand with the collapse of communism, which for many companies opened up new markets, as well as introducing competition from low-cost manufacturing, and apparently validating capitalism as the best way to run an economy. Giant state-owned enterprises were privatised across the world, while in the UK industries such as coal mining effectively closed down. Regulation and state control were rolled back in the name of the free market. Manufacturing was moved offshore to places where labour was cheaper. In the UK, a great deal has changed in the space of a couple of decades; almost every aspect of the individual's interactions with the state and public services now involves the private sector in some way, from school meals and rail travel to energy provision and sending a letter through the post.

Some scholars argue that capitalism is inherently corrupt. Its triumph has been in changing the balance of power between the state and the private sector, which is sometimes described by the term 'neoliberalism', a description of how the tentacles of the private sector increasingly extend into all our lives. One strand of scholarship equates neoliberalism with corruption, for the reason that the outcomes are similar: the accumulation of power and wealth by companies, financiers and business leaders; unequal wealth distribution; impunity and a lack of accountability before the law; and the ability to move funds and activities nimbly between jurisdictions to take advantage of gaps and loopholes in laws, regulation and enforcement.

Those are all bad things, of course; but it seems to me that simply equating neoliberalism or capitalism with corruption without further evidence risks stretching the boundaries of what may plausibly be described as corruption. Even if capitalism and corruption can sometimes lead to similar outcomes, what about the occasions when capitalism generates wealth and innovation? Of course, most people find it highly objectionable when corporate power is used in a way that seems to champion private interests over the public interest, but economists such as Professor John Kay argue that this is a distortion of capitalism rather than its essence – and particularly risky in contexts like the privatisation of essential services. He says of the privatisations in the Thatcher years: 'The idea that such arrangements will work if institutions whose purpose is to maximise the value of their shares are constrained by a sufficiently extensive rule book is implausible and has failed. This invites smart and greedy people to find ways to extract revenue from the business while pushing the limits of the rules.'[1]

It is fairly clear how that is undesirable for society, but is it corrupt for a company to find loopholes and maximise its profitability? As Kay points out, companies can still be regulated by the state. Of course, that itself represents a vulnerability when those same companies can be involved in regulatory capture through the dark quartet of lobbying, political donations, conflicts of interest or the revolving door. Although if, as Kay suggests, regulators are being outsmarted rather than captured, this does not automatically suggest corruption.

It may be that at a certain point capitalism becomes so detrimental to the public interest that we enter a post-capitalist age of monopolies whose power exceeds the power of the state to control them – and that's the concern around tech companies today. This question of whether capitalism and neoliberalism are examples of structural corruption remains contested. For the purposes of this book, I leave readers to make up their own minds based on the evidence presented.

There is, however, no doubt that privatisation and outsourcing have blurred the lines between the private and the public sectors. In particular, should private companies necessarily be expected to act in the public interest while delivering public services? Put another way, if a private company empties your bins, is it primarily responsible for making a profit or for keeping the streets clean? And what should happen when those two ideas come into conflict – for instance, when the company's contract with the council requires it to empty 100 bins in a street, but the division of some houses into flats doubles the number of bins? The private interest may prevail either if the company sticks to emptying 100 bins or charges a premium for emptying any more than 100.

In my view, the danger here is represented by 'the duck problem'. We might imagine something is corrupt if it looks, walks and quacks in the right way – and that's the reasoning often applied to things that people do not like about the private sector. The phrase was first used in the eighteenth century, when the French inventor Jacques de Vaucanson designed a mechanical duck.[2] It did indeed look, walk and quack like a duck, and reason appeared to suggest to French philosophers that it therefore *was* a duck – which, of course, it wasn't. In the same way, we need to be cautious in saying that because something seems to have the same effect as corruption, it is therefore corruption. It may well be, but we need other tests to find out.

The application of our four-step test seems to represent one way out of this maze: can we see entrusted power, abuse, private gain and harm to the public interest? As we have already seen, it builds on definitions of corruption that placed the idea of abusing public office at their heart. And moving from the concept of 'public office' to 'entrusted power' allows us to evaluate whether privatised or outsourced public services providers are holders of entrusted power.

We might consider a few examples to help illustrate these complexities. First, the hotels at Heathrow Airport – an example of power perhaps having been abused that most analysts would not regard as corrupt. In March 2025, a fire at an electricity substation near Heathrow closed the airport for a day. Desperate travellers needed places to stay, and all the hotels in the area responded in the same way, with immediate and large price rises: the nightly price of a hotel room that would normally cost £87 rose to £379. There are good explanations for this: the surge pricing that was enabled by booking algorithms, and the standard economic analysis of supply and demand in a free market. But was it corrupt?

Shocked tabloid newspapers accused the hotels of abusing their monopoly to profit at the expense of travellers who were already suffering. Those academics who regard capitalism as analogous with corruption might argue that such a monopoly is inherently corrupt because it concentrates power in the hands of those who do not operate in the public interest. If the government had introduced a price cap, or had the hotels been state-owned, this would not have happened. A more conventional definition of corruption would see this sort of behaviour as unethical price-gouging, but not as corrupt. Perhaps the main difference concerns the question of what kind of 'power' the hotel companies have. In this case they are exploiting, perhaps even abusing, an unexpected and unusual market power, but they are not abusing 'entrusted power' – after all, they are not in any official position or authority. This is essentially a standard commercial transaction, with prices and profits in plain sight.

In this case, the private sector seems to be operating against the interests of society – which might be potentially described as corruption if our definition were to be very broad. But our four-step test suggests otherwise.

To complicate this further, we will now examine three cases that are less clear-cut because they involve the private provision of public services. There are dozens of examples of companies failing in the delivery of public services, and it often seems astonishing how seldom anybody is held to be directly or personally responsible. How was it possible, for example, in December 2024 that the boss of outsourcing giant Serco could receive a huge bonus while a seventy-seven-year-old climate protestor had to spend Christmas in jail because his company could not provide an electronic tag small enough to fit her frail wrist?

And what about the part-privatisation of the NHS known as the Lansley health reforms of 2012?[3] These allowed GPs to form 'clinical commissioning groups', which permitted them to benefit personally from running their practices as a business. Some GP clinics have had private equity investments, further exposing the NHS to market forces. While most GPs still earn modest salaries, a small number earn more than £200,00 each year, and in 2023 it was widely reported that one individual had earned more than £600,000. There are a number of ways in which this can be done, including incorporating lucrative private cosmetic procedures into the GP practice or taking over other local clinics and running them as a group. This is all legitimate and might be considered to be purely down to hard work or clever management of the system; as long as the patients are well served, it is hard to view it as an abuse of entrusted power.

There is no shortage of such examples, but there are no clear answers. We might try to find a way through by looking in depth at three contentious areas, involving privatised and outsourced public services and a botched public procurement.

We will start with the provision of children's care homes. Local authorities in the UK are obliged to provide residential places for children who are taken into care. Traditionally, these youngsters would live in children's homes that were run by the council or by religious institutions. Over the past two decades, private children's homes have started to provide large numbers of places, and increasingly these have been consolidated into bigger businesses and taken over by private equity firms.[4] Today some 83 per cent of children's homes are in private ownership, and the average annual cost to the state per child in care is £281,000 – five times as much as keeping an adult in prison. Some councils pay £63,000 a week for keeping a single child in care when there are complex care needs, specialised staff and a high ratio of staff to children.

The profits from private children's homes are vast, and the cost to the taxpayer is huge. Yet the standard of care they provide is often very poor; researchers from Oxford University concluded that private sector providers were much more likely to be rated of lower quality than those in the public sector.[5] But is this corrupt? Let's run the test. Running a children's home to a poor standard is, of course, harmful to the public interest. There is private gain from doing so – the private equity owners make plenty of money. There is entrusted power, too: the state is delegating its power over the well-being and upbringing of children in care to the private sector.

And is this power being abused? It's hard to argue that profit-making – even profiteering – has any intrinsic relation to the quality of children's upbringing. A profit-making enterprise could still provide high-quality care. And profit-making is, after all, what companies are set up to do, and is simply the natural consequence of involving the private sector. The poor stand-ard of care they offer could simply be considered poor service provision rather than an abuse of power. Even in an extreme case, such as when care is negligent and allows local gangs to groom young girls for sexual exploitation, it is not clear that the entrusted power was being abused; the care home managers were not involved themselves – they were just running a shoddy operation.

So, at face value, while this is clearly a situation where lots of things are going wrong, the corruption label is hard to apply to children's care homes. However, it is a grey area. There is a legitimate argument that the power of the care home industry over young lives is so important that any failure to deliver what society expects from a provider is an abuse of that power. But if we conclude that the care home industry, or even an individual children's care home, is corrupt, where does the responsibility lie? Is it with the individuals managing the care home, or the executives of the company that owns and operates it on behalf of private equity investors? Or even with the private equity firm's board of directors, or the local authority that contracted the private firm?

We can see that, when a private company is negligent in its running of care homes while making a huge profit, it is possible to make an argument that corruption is present; but the case is not clear-cut.

For our next grey area, let us turn to Thames Water. You can only obtain your water through one water company in the area you live in, meaning that it has a monopoly. Although it was for a long time state-owned, it is now a private company – though it continues to provide a public service. Its service is twofold: the provision of clean water and the safe disposal of sewage. It usually does one of those things well – providing clean water – but the other one very badly. Let us try applying the four-step test.

Flooding rivers and the English coastline with raw sewage is not in the public interest. Anyone who has recently tried to swim in the seas around many of England's most famous beaches will have risked finding themselves sharing the waters with all sorts of undesirable human waste, dumped there by the local water company. There is private gain, both for the company that makes a profit and for its executives who receive performance-related bonuses. This became a particular bone of contention at Thames Water when, even after years of poor performance, bonuses of £18.5 million were awarded in 2025 to twenty-one of the company's executives – apparently linked to the performance of the company's financial engineering rather than the prevention and clean-up of the pollution. There was also enormous gain over the years for the private equity owners, particularly in the case of the Australian bank Macquarie, which was reported as loading Thames Water with debt while at the same time taking out big dividends. The BBC reported that Macquarie had made annual returns of between 15 and 19 per cent, all while adding an extra £2 billion of debt to the balance sheet before exiting in 2017. Meanwhile, a judge imposed one of several fines while noting that there had been 'inadequate investment, diabolical maintenance and poor management' – all denied by Macquarie, which issued its own 'factsheet' in 2023 about its ownership in the period 2006–17 that explained that there was a 'misrepresentation of the data'.[6]

We can see harm to the public interest and private gain, so now we come to the question of whether a privatised utility has entrusted power, and if so whether it has been abused. The entrusted power seems unarguable – access to clean water is a fundamental human right, delegated in this case by the state to the privatised company, along with the responsibility to keep the rivers and seas free of sewage. Yet the levels of pollution caused by the company not fulfilling its duties have been extreme, and this might be considered an abuse of entrusted power. During 2021 and 2022, 72 billion litres of raw sewage were released into the River Thames alone. A couple of years before this the company was fined for 'reckless failure' in a similar incident – just one of many occasions over the years in which courts, campaigners and regulators have pointed to a company that has failed to fulfil its duties and obligations. By 2025, the company was being fined £122.7 million by the regulator Ofwat, which said Thames Water had 'let down its customers and failed to protect the environment'.[7]

The extraction of dividends from the company by Macquarie and other owners had meant there were fewer funds to invest. The water companies themselves argue that they have been hampered by a Victorian sewage infrastructure, a rapidly increasing population and deluges of rain in part due to climate change. Moreover, everything they did was agreed with Ofwat. It is unlikely that private equity companies think of themselves as corrupt: they would argue that they were simply leveraging loans, as is normal in their line of work, paying dividends to themselves and paying fines when the regulator required. So this remains a grey area, in which everyone can make their own judgement based on their preferred definition of corruption. In my view, this complex example of privatisation gone wrong does exemplify how the four-step test can be a useful pointer to structural corruption: the triumph of private interest over public interest is simply baked into the system here.

For the third of these grey areas we will look at the 'VIP lane' for the procurement of personal protective equipment during the Covid-19 pandemic. In the heat of the crisis, when the UK was suffering from an extreme shortage of medical equipment, ministers suspended government procurement rules and created a special way in which a small group of politicians and civil servants could refer companies to a fast-track procedure known as the VIP lane. This was later found to be unlawful in a High Court ruling, although the same ruling found that some of the companies that had been fast-tracked due to their political connections would probably have won contracts anyway.[8]

The VIP lane has subsequently been analysed in detail by Transparency International, and the results are not pretty.[9] Researchers who study procurement have recently developed a 'red flag' methodology to identify where there might be corruption risks in government spending.[10] Applying this approach to 5,000 Covid-related contracts, TI found 135 contracts worth £15.3 billion that had three or more red flags for corruption, indicating that they should be thoroughly investigated – and, most worryingly, many of those were very large contracts. In total, around a third of spending on Covid-related contracts had that number of corruption red flags. Of these 135 red-flagged contracts, 51 – worth £4 billion – went through the VIP lane. Further work by Spotlight on Corruption has found that £1 billion of PPE bought from twenty-five suppliers who went through the VIP lane was later deemed not fit for purpose.

Companies referred through the VIP lane included those owned by party donors and friends and acquaintances of ministers, political involvement in public procurement that was highly irregular. As the experts in this field, the Open Contracting Partnership, later wrote: 'we work in over 50 countries: we don't know of any other country that put a formal process in place to prioritise emergency contracts based on political referrals and on politicians deciding who had stocks of PPE or not.'[11] An example of a political referral through the VIP lane is Meller Designs, whose chair was a Conservative Party donor. David Meller was referred by Michael Gove, whose leadership bid Meller had previously supported. His company had no prior experience providing such equipment, yet secured contracts worth £163 million; their annual profits in that period rose from £144,000 to £13 million.[12] The Good Law Project, an NGO that has looked in detail at Covid-related government spending, found that 'More than £8.4m worth of PPE delivered by Meller Designs was unsuitable for use in an NHS setting. Three of their six PPE contracts were signed at above-average prices, with markups of between 1.2 and 2.2 times.'[13]

In several cases, the companies that sold the kit had been created solely for this purpose, and the individuals involved had no track record of providing healthcare equipment. PPE Medpro, the company linked to Baroness Mone and Doug Barrowman, was one of those. Often the equipment that came via the VIP lane seems to have been procured at prices that far exceeded market rates – according to the Good Law Project, PPE worth £925 million that came via the VIP lane was bought at prices on average 80 per cent higher than the prices offered by suppliers who came through other routes.

Large quantities of the equipment were unusable – an estimated one in five items of PPE was not fit for purpose.[14] This was a significant cost to the public purse, as the government spent a total of £12.3 billion on PPE;[15] and as the PPE Medpro and Meller Designs examples illustrate, the suppliers who came via the VIP lane could make enormous profits. For months, the government tried to keep the details of who had benefitted from VIP lane contracts secret, fighting court battles to prevent campaigners from finding out. Some of the names of the people involved remain confidential to this day. In sum, the VIP lane was unlawful and secretive and favoured companies with close links to politicians, which often supplied unusable equipment at high prices.

Why are we even considering this to be a grey area when it sounds straightforwardly corrupt?

Let's try looking at it from another perspective. Yes, these people had contacts within the Conservative Party or government that gave them access to the VIP lane, but they also had sufficient entrepreneurial spirit, along with important access to Chinese manufacturers, that meant they could promise supplies at short notice at a time of high demand. There is no doubt that it looks bad – government cronies being awarded special contracts at high prices is something we might expect to see in countries well known for high levels of corruption. But this was a national emergency, it was all hands to the pump, and the market rate for PPE kit was hard to establish given the worldwide demand. Of course, all that could be true – and there could be corruption as well.

In this case of the Covid VIP lane we can see entrusted power held by ministers and officials, and private gain by the newly established companies selling high-priced equipment to the NHS. But do we see that power being abused – and if so, are the people who are abusing the power also making the private gain? There are so many different players that it is hard to make a judgement. Was it abuse by the minister who set up the VIP lane or the officials who allowed in companies with no track record? Was it the member of the House of Lords who aggressively lobbied for her own company but denied she was involved with it, or the ministers and MPs who referred their party donors to the VIP lane? Or the companies that provided substandard kit and made excess profits just because they could?

On the available evidence, I would classify the existence

of the Covid VIP lane as a result of panic and incompetence at a time of crisis rather than corruption. The companies who provided substandard kit were arguably engaging in fraud. Profiteering was unethical, but it was enabled by the NHS being willing to overpay when the Treasury temporarily removed the usual limits on spending.

We can, however, also see that the VIP lane was top of the class for corruption risk: the multiple red flags both about individual contracts and the system as a whole suggest that, if more information were to come to light, it is likely that at least some corruption would be identified, and the entire VIP lane itself might be branded corrupt. For example, if it were to transpire that it was intentionally set up to allow funds to be channelled to cronies and party donors, that certainly would make it corrupt. Likewise, if any minister or official colluded in the awarding of contracts to cronies, that would also have been corrupt. And if a member of the House of Lords was abusing their power as a parliamentarian to gain privileged access for their own company, that also looks like an abuse of entrusted power for private gain – and harmful to the public interest if the goods supplied were overpriced or unusable. We may currently give the benefit of the doubt to the Johnson government for being incompetent rather than corrupt, but the judgement could easily go the other way. We might have hoped that the Covid Inquiry would settle this question – but as a later chapter on public inquiries will show, we should not be too hopeful.

While the VIP lane scheme may have been unlawful without being intrinsically corrupt, we can also see that the panicked decisions and an indifference to whether corruption might result undoubtedly opened the door to it. Many corruption experts at the time advised against such a course of action for precisely this reason, only to be ignored. The result was a corruption-prone system that almost certainly resulted in some corrupt deals. If there is ever a proper investigation into Covid corruption, we may find out which deals were corrupt and which were simply ill-advised.

Children's homes and water companies operate in a grey area where society pays a lot to private companies but comes out badly. The same is sometimes true of public procurement from the private sector. Through one lens it may look corrupt, but it might only be that way as a result of incompetence and negligence.

All these grey areas make it hard to ascribe a definitive label, and they also demonstrate how applying the four-step test does not always give a conclusive answer: it can be a helpful guide to many types of corruption but it does not determine whether the 'neoliberalist' approach of passing as much as possible over to the private sector is fundamentally corrupt. So with cases such as the Covid procurement scheme, the best we can do is weigh up the evidence and make a judgement: and since a judgement is inevitably subjective, one person may reasonably think some of these private sector activities are corrupt, and someone else might equally reasonably think they are not.

However, even in the grey areas there are some things we can usefully observe. I think the children's homes and Thames Water are cases where we might reasonably argue that the failures are not just poor customer service but fundamental failures in duty. It is unfashionable to talk about private sector companies having a duty to society, but when they are delivering vital public services that's clearly the case. They are not just filling in potholes; they are providing public services that touch on people's fundamental rights. We might even say that the unregulated private provision of public services contains such an inherent conflict of interest that corruption is 'baked in'. In other words, if the system has been set up with such an inherent tension between private and public interest, it might inevitably default to a form of structural corruption, even if that was not the intention of those who created it, nor the motivation of those who are participating in it.

The government recognised this tension with its decision in 2013 to apply the Nolan Principles of standards in public life to private companies that are delivering public services.[16] However, little has actually changed: a report in 2018 found that 'many service providers continue to expect that setting and enforcing ethical standards remains a matter for government alone'.[17] There seems to be a double standard – an ambiguity – in applying such principles to the private sector.

For instance, imagine if, in the case of children's homes, sewage discharges or unusable PPE, it were public officials who were being this negligent. What would we think then? Essentially, the negligence seems to result from the services being run simply to enrich those in charge rather than to provide the best possible public service. Sewage releases can be prevented with investment; children's homes can provide excellent care if they are staffed by those with experience, training and a sense of mission; usable Covid equipment can be procured at a fair market price, even during a time of crisis, as some UK companies and other countries like Canada and Germany showed.[18] If these services were being provided by public officials who were prioritising their own private gains – whether higher salaries, bonuses, or promotion as a result of gaining a reputation for cost-cutting – by paring back services, those public officials might plausibly be described as corrupt. So why would we not say the same about the private sector?

Perhaps the problem is that the way these things are set up

means that, when the state delegates entrusted power to the private sector, no one is accountable for its abuse. A company's duty to its shareholders is considered to be the prime driver of the corporate mission, with its responsibilities to public service delivery reduced to measurable key performance indicators and not an overall sense of duty to the public.

Somewhere in the transfer of power from the state to private companies, we seem to have lost the concept that failing to act in the public interest is an abuse of entrusted power. We might consider corruption as baked in to such scenarios if the private sector companies were unregulated but, with the exception of procurement during the pandemic when regulations were suspended, all these services are theoretically regulated. One of the issues is that the regulators have failed. For example, it seems extraordinary that year after year Ofwat, the water regulator, allowed financial engineering to drain money from the water companies and pollution to mount with little sanction. That is partly a failure of government: pruning the remit and resources of regulators in order to save money or 'attract investment'.

I do not think that privatisation and outsourcing in the UK represents a deliberate attempt to create opportunities for corruption by the politicians and civil servants who have set up a system through which public funds flow to their friends and acquaintances. As earlier chapters have illustrated, our national tendency is to ignore corruption; it may be that we need an approach to privatisation and outsourcing that acknowledges the inherent risk. There could be greater recognition of the responsibilities that come when the state delegates entrusted power to the private sector. Perhaps we need contracts stipulating that if there is an abuse of entrusted power, someone, whether the board of directors or the company's senior executives, must be held individually accountable. We certainly need regulators that are up to the job, and they must be immune to the possibility of what is known as 'regulatory capture' by those they are in charge of regulating.

Regulatory capture describes the situation in which lobbying, political donations, the revolving door, senior appointments and even intellectual capture can be used by companies to rig the regulatory rules in their favour. It is often done via industry bodies so no individual company is implicated, and it happens in all sectors – from food, agriculture and energy to tech, water, financial services and pharmaceuticals. The banking sector as it existed prior to the global financial crisis is often held up as the classic example of successful regulatory capture:[19] the rules were manipulated at both a national and an international level to allow excessive risk-taking, with the public finances acting as a back-stop if such risk-taking ever led to the banks making substantial financial losses. Like so much in this field, regulatory capture may sometimes be corrupt, but it generally exists in a grey area in which private interests prevail over the public interest.

Further exploring the conflict between public and private interest could draw us back into a discussion about the innate tendency to corruption of neoliberalism and capitalism – a worthwhile question, but one for another book.

We can establish that there are both corruption and corruption risk in the private sector without such a debate. To do that, we will now focus on some cases where everyone agrees there is corruption – they give us more than enough fuel for a discussion on whether something needs to be done about the private sector.

As with so many other areas of the UK, an underlying question is whether there are a few rotten apples or a rotting barrel. My answer for the private sector – as for the public sector – is that we have enough evidence to show that a large number of individuals will become rotten if the incentives are right; to prevent the barrel becoming rotten we need to make sure that such incentives are not in place, and that our defences are strong enough. Let's look at some cases of out-and-out corruption: a nuclear power plant, a company supplying supermarkets with potatoes, a concert at the Brixton Academy in London and the construction and property development sector.

If there's one place where we might hope that decisions on engineering and repairs are taken with safety and proper procedure as the prime consideration it is in a nuclear power station. This is an area where standards should never compromised by bribery. People might assume that such things could happen elsewhere – in the former Soviet Union or India, perhaps – but surely not the United Kingdom.

Yet at Hinkley Point C power station in Somerset, currently under construction at a cost of £46 billion, the man with the unusual job title of 'Head of lifting and temporary works' was demanding bribes from contractors and awarding contracts on that basis. At an employment tribunal it was said of Ashley Daniels: 'He was known as asking for favours, was self-entitled and greedy, was cheeky and a greedy little toad.' In other words, a serial bribe-taker. In the case that came to light, he was found to have been taking bribes from a crane-hire company over a two-year period, including boxing match tickets worth £2,000 and a quad bike worth £11,000. The setting in which the bribery came to light, at an employment tribunal, was unusual; it arose because the project director at the crane-hire company who was paying the bribes was dismissed for gross misconduct when his employer discovered them. He took the case to a tribunal, as though his bribe-paying was standard behaviour and not grounds for dismissal.

This case tells us a few things. Most obviously, that bribery takes place within the UK's private sector, and need not involve public officials. On a £46 billion project, there are substantial temptations and opportunities for individuals to make personal gain through abusing their positions of power. There was serial bribery, involving a number of people, which stayed hidden for a long period. And this came to light not because of a police investigation, whistleblowing or investigative journalism, but because the bribe-payer was fired and took his grievance to an employment tribunal. Although the company was slow to catch on, it did dismiss the bribe-payer when it found out about the bribes rather than carry on getting contracts through paying them.

As to how typical this is of private sector corruption within the UK, we can only speculate. Some sectors are particularly high-risk, due to the size of the contracts involved – such as defence, healthcare and the extractive sectors (oil, gas, mining and forestry). In other sectors, the remuneration schemes might incentivise kickbacks – when the personal rewards for landing a deal or securing a contract are so high that offering a bribe might seem worthwhile. The government's Economic Crime Survey from 2024 gives some insight: it estimated that 117,000 bribes had been offered over the preceding twelve months by one UK business to another; and that a much smaller proportion of businesses (less than 0.5 per cent) had to give or were asked to give a bribe to a UK public official in the past twelve months.[20] The researchers estimated that £309 million of bribes was offered, with a mean value of £2,640.

Next time you are doing a price comparison in a supermarket and can't understand why the same item costs more in one shop than another, consider the following story. In the Sainsbury's potato bribery case, two directors from a company supplying potatoes paid bribes to the buyer at the supermarket chain who was in charge of ordering them. This was a contract for 45 per cent of all the potatoes supplied to Sainsbury's, worth a staggering £40 million a year. The bribes to the supermarket's buyer were worth £4.8 million over three years, allowing him to treat himself to an Aston Martin and extravagant holidays. In return, the potato supplier retained the contracts.

We might ask where the harm is in that relationship. It is simple. Because their potato buyer was more interested in personal gain than buying potatoes based on the usual criteria of quality and price, Sainsbury's was no longer getting the best available prices. As a result, the supermarket overpaid for its potatoes by £8.7 million, a cost that was passed on to customers. This is not to say that corruption in supermarket supply chains is widespread, but we can see both the risks and the incentives. It would be naïve to think that it doesn't exist.

Bribery in the private sector can also have tragic consequences. At the Brixton Academy music venue in London in 2023, overcrowding at a sell-out concert caused a crush in which two people were killed. How did the accident come about? A whistleblower later told the BBC that private security guards were regularly allowing 'a couple of hundred' extra people into venues, including the Brixton Academy, in exchange for money. On this occasion 'There were people taking money ... some staff made £1,000 cash.'[21] In corruption terms, the guards solicited bribes to allow in extra customers – to a level that proved not only unsafe, but fatal.

One sector that is generally agreed to have a high corruption risk is construction. A combination of large budgets, lack of standardisation between projects, complex supply chains involving lots of suppliers and the way in which bids are structured has made corruption prevalent.

We know this conclusively because it is one of the few areas in which there has been detailed research. For example, a survey by the Chartered Institute of Building in 2013 found that 48 per cent of construction professionals felt corruption was commonplace within the industry, while 35 per cent admitted to having been offered a bribe or incentive on at least one occasion.[22] Research by the University of Portsmouth in 2021 reinforces this picture:[23] their mid-range estimate is that £35.7 billion would be lost in the five-year period from 2021 through fraud and corruption on UK government infrastructure projects. Although this lumps fraud and corruption together, and we might expect fraud to be the major part, that still leaves a substantial sum lost through corruption.

From the cases involving corruption that have come to court, we can glimpse how it operates in the UK construction sector. Two instances in rail construction illustrate the scale of the problem. The upgrade of Farringdon station as part of the Thameslink project saw four people jailed after one of those involved became a whistleblower and reported the bribery to the Mayor of London's office in 2011. In this complex scheme, a company called Alandale Rail obtained the contract to supply safety critical staff to the contractors running the project, a joint venture between Costain and Laing O'Rourke. The directors of Alandale Rail were able to undercut rival bids after being fed inside information by a senior health and safety manager inside the joint venture, whom they called 'our man in Havana'. They rewarded him with bribes of £140,000. Having won the contract, they compounded the corruption with fraud, also signed off by their man on the inside, pushing up the value of the contract (and therefore the cost to the public) from £2.1 million to

£5.2 million. They did this by employing 'ghost workers' who did not exist except on paper.

A second rail-related bribery case concerned the extension of the Jubilee Line in London. As seems to happen fairly often in complex cases of financial crime, the trial of the six defendants collapsed in 2005, having lasted for twenty-one months. In this instance, the collapse was caused by problems with the jury – in such a lengthy trial, there had already been a pregnancy and illness among the members, before one juror went on strike, saying he could no longer continue as the case had led to a financial dispute with his employer that needed to be resolved before he would carry on. But a seventh defendant had previously pleaded guilty to related charges, which means we know there was certainly some proven wrongdoing in the contracting, even though the substantive bribery charges remain as allegations as there was no appetite for a retrial. These allegations were spectacular. The prosecution claimed that bribes worth tens of millions of pounds had been paid by contractors to secure lucrative contracts. The alleged bribery in this scheme followed a very similar pattern to that in the Farringdon case. In this incident, senior managers from a surveying company called RWS were accused of bribing London Underground officials to gain inside information that allowed them to win contracts, and once they had the contracts the costs were allowed to increase. The police estimated the contractors had overcharged London Transport by £200 million.

These snapshots indicate that bribery in the construction sector can involve big money. And looking at such stories alongside the survey finding by the Chartered Institute of Building that a third of managers in the sector have been offered a bribe,[24] we can see it is not uncommon. If we are to look at corruption in the private sector more generally, we would need to know how far bribery and corruption in the construction sector reflect practices in other sectors. The recent government Economic Crime Survey, referred to above, has given a glimpse of this, incorporating a table of prevalence rates of bribery per sector, based on an opinion poll carried out among 3,477 companies in 2024. This tells us that five sectors have levels of bribery that are above average for the UK private sector: construction, real estate, utilities and production, information and communications, administration, and service and membership organisations.

This, of course, raises an important question: why are some sectors apparently more prone to bribery and corruption than others? We can certainly identify some characteristics that make a sector more high-risk: for example, where there are high-value contracts, and where certain individuals have discretion over the awarding of contracts or subsequent amendments. Rational choice theory tells us that some people will take advantage of the opportunities that are presented. But we can also see that, when such behaviour becomes the norm, bribe-paying seems to be legitimised – or normalised. This theme – of corruption becoming a norm – arose in the earlier chapter on politics, and we will see it again in other institutions such as the police.

Unlike the grey areas explored earlier in this chapter, the case studies above can be labelled more definitively as corrupt because we have enough evidence to make a clear judgement. In other cases, due to the strict libel laws we have in the UK, while the facts can be presented it must be left up to the reader to decide whether the label of corruption should apply. Consider, for instance, the events at the Weavers Quarter, along with other developments in the London borough of Barking.[25] This information came to light through the excellent investigative journalism of *The Londoner*, an online newsletter. Barking

Council had awarded building contracts worth hundreds of millions of pounds, with councillors receiving perks from the companies that won the contracts; in one case, the daughter of the council leader worked for one of the firms. In total, seven Barking councillors took jobs or hospitality from the construction industry or firms linked to it, and the gifts alone were reportedly worth £27,895. Perhaps most revealing is the response from one of the construction companies that such payments were 'legitimate and in line with standard industry practice'. This seems accurate: no laws appear to have been broken, and it happens all the time.

In all the cases we have looked at so far, whether in a grey area or definitively corrupt, the private sector looks deeply unimpressive. That might seem to reinforce the view that there is something inherently corrupt or corrupting within capitalism or neoliberalism, but the picture is not entirely negative. Many companies have honest staff who want to do a good job and have no intention of acting corruptly or perpetuating a corrupt system. In light of anti-bribery laws enacted across the world as a result of the OECD Anti-Bribery Convention, most large companies put in place anti-bribery and corruption (ABC) systems. We have discovered over the past three decades that, if the laws and penalties are operational, companies can usually be persuaded to do the right thing. These ABC systems often incorporate whistleblowing procedures, and periodically companies self-report to the authorities – a big change since my family friend was jailed in Iraq in the 1970s.

Returning to the theme of this chapter, at the heart of the private sector is a paradox. Lots of private sector behaviours – not to mention the free-market economy itself – produce outcomes that appear corrupt. They certainly prioritise private interests over the public interest. This points to an ambiguity that we find time and again in liberal democracies, in which powerful interests seem to dominate the political economy and end up with the spoils – and all within the law. Business can be seen as prone to operating corruptly, a risk magnified by what is described as neoliberalism because this prioritises private interests over public interests. Effective government and regulation are required to keep in check the self-serving instincts of the private sector; but this risks attempts by companies to seek what is known as 'regulatory capture' via the dark quartet of lobbying, political funding, the revolving door and conflicts of interest. However, describing capitalism and neoliberalism as inherently corrupt seems to me a little too glib. They may be considered undesirable for a whole host of reasons, but that does not make them automatically corrupt. It is at best a contested space: some scholars will plausibly apply that label.

By contrast, we have seen in this chapter that there is out-and-out corruption in the UK's private sector, with perverse incentives to encourage it. Many companies occupy a grey area in which what they do could either be interpreted as corrupt or tip over into corruption. Better regulators and more nuanced legislation about privatisation, outsourcing and procurement could move those approaches further from corruption. The key message is that, in too many areas of the private sector, there is an undesirably high risk of corruption – and that must be addressed.

7

MEN IN SUITS: THE OLD AND NEW ESTABLISHMENT

David Lammy, appointed as Deputy Prime Minister to Keir Starmer in 2025 following a stint as Foreign Secretary, does not think much of men in suits. In a speech on corruption a few weeks before the 2024 general election, he said: 'It is important to understand a simple fact. There are men in suits behind every crime [of grand corruption]. Every time a kleptocrat launders money or evades sanctions through British territory, they are enabled by hired help ... An incorporation agent, a banker, a lawyer, an accountant ...'[1]

The phrase 'men in suits' has traditionally been applied to people in a position of authority who work behind the scenes to fix things. It brings to mind a network of civil servants, bankers and other senior figures who comprise that vague but recognisable concept, the British establishment. However, Lammy is using the phrase slightly differently, to describe a new kind of establishment that has played an important role in recent years in relation to corruption.

This chapter will focus on this new establishment; my working hypothesis is that there has been a subtle shift in power – or at least in influence – from groups like civil servants to other influential groups such as lobbyists, fixers and advisers. We will find out who these new men in suits are, and whether what they do is corrupt.

Meanwhile, the old establishment carries on, though at times it seems almost like a parody of itself. Think, for instance, of a character like Jacob Rees-Mogg, educated at Eton and Oxford, who was director of an investment management firm in the City before becoming an MP and cabinet minister. With his silver-spoon background and old-fashioned upper-class drawl, it seems inevitable that he would end up where he did, and he seems to epitomise the old establishment. But he was hardly a friend of the civil service's men in suits who are traditionally seen as the heart of the British establishment. As Minister for Government Efficiency he described the civil service as the 'Whitehall blob'[2] and characterised himself as a reformer rather than a conservative, attempting a slightly unconvincing populist rhetoric as a presenter on the anti-establishment TV channel GB News before losing his seat in the 2024 election. His erratic career demonstrates that the old certainties and alliances among the traditional men in suits have broken down.

In fact, even people who might most obviously seem to be part of the old establishment seem keen to claim it is something other than themselves. Oxford-educated former prime minister Liz Truss claims that what she calls the 'Deep State' was actively working against her: 'the Bank of England, the Office for Budget Responsibility and even MPs within the Conservative Party fought back against my government's efforts to generate growth'.[3] She concludes that 'Patriotic Brits have had enough. They've had enough ... We want Elon and his nerd army of "Muskrats" examining the British Deep State.'[4] She seems to be arguing that a subset of the establishment has deliberately conspired against her. It is not a view widely shared among those of sound mind but this does illustrate that, although it is easy to set up the notion of an elite establishment as the source of the nation's problems, it is no longer clear who is in the establishment – and what its shared interest might be.

So how exactly should we define the British establishment? One school of thought is that this old establishment embodies an underlying corruption that standard definitions and indices of corruption have failed to capture. We can see this line of thinking, often associated with a left-wing ideology, in the work of popular polemical writers such as Owen Jones. He contends that a powerful elite 'manage democracy, to make sure that it does not threaten their own interests'.[5] An academic essay collection with the compelling title *How Corrupt Is Britain?* concluded that there is a 'quintessentially British brand of corruption' that seems inseparable from the establishment, with 'a routine practice that is used for maintaining and extending the power of corporations, governments and public institutions' linked to 'the slow and pernicious onward march of a neoliberal political economy'. In fact, a large number of books have over the years regarded the British establishment as unhealthy, rotten or even corrupt.

How accurate is this picture today? One of the privileges of running a charity like Transparency International is that you get to view what is usually described as the establishment from the inside – and I found the opportunities to be part of the establishment's gang came thick and fast. A few occasions among many stick in the mind, from private meetings with the Lord Mayor of London to talk about money laundering to conversations with judges at the Old Bailey about the human rights implications of an anti-corruption law on unexplained wealth orders (UWOs). A typical instance was in the queue for the cloakroom of the annual Ambassadors' Ball at Buckingham Palace, where I found myself standing between the Attorney

General and the Defence Secretary – and later, in the line-up to meet the Queen, having already met the chairman of a FTSE100 mining company, I was exchanging pleasantries with the director of the Science Museum. I recall talking to the Archbishop of Canterbury at the Commonwealth Summit, amid world leaders and their ambassadors. I discussed national security threats with the former head of MI5, and had lunch at the Athenaeum with a former private secretary to William Hague. And I went for meetings at 10 Downing Street – saying hello to our ambassador to China on the way in – to persuade special advisers that the UK needed an anti-corruption strategy.

With Oxford University and the City on my CV, I could mingle unobtrusively in such circles, even though the bulk of my working life was spent in the very different spheres of charities and academia. As time went on, I increasingly encountered contemporaries from Oxford – including David Cameron and Boris Johnson – who had taken a different career path and were now running the country and some of its major institutions. This is the classic view of the British establishment: people of a certain educational background congregating in exclusive places, and doing each other favours according to an unwritten set of rules. It is sometimes described as the 'chumocracy' – rule by chums, some of whom are in public office while others hold positions of influence in business and elsewhere. To the majority of people, who only get an occasional glimpse of this privilege and entitlement, it may feel as though the country is being run by these men in suits, with the implication that a narrow elite has tilted the playing field in their own favour so that they can retain money and power.

This cynicism about the establishment echoes the academic literature on institutional and structural corruption in the US by writers such as Lessig, Thompson and Johnston, whose work is described in the first chapter of this book. They view the links between business, a rich elite and politics as having undermined democracy. In their framing, corruption should be viewed not just as involving corrupt individuals; rather, a whole political economy may be corrupt when it is no longer operating on behalf of the ordinary citizen. American philosophy professor Mark E. Warren describes this as 'duplicitous exclusion' – ordinary people are duplicitously excluded from real decision-making, which is captured by vested interests that operate in their own favour.[6]

So, does anyone represent the real people? This is typically the claim of populist politicians.[7] Paradoxically, when a populist gets into a position of power they find themselves at the heart of the machine, and so might then be considered part of the establishment. A common response from the populists is that they are fighting a valiant fight against dark forces trying to prevent them acting on behalf of the real people – just as Liz Truss feels she was taking on the 'Deep State'. In the UK, this kind of rhetoric has been increasingly adopted by the right wing of the Conservative Party, as well as Reform UK and – at the other end of the political spectrum – the followers of hard-left politician Jeremy Corbyn. In 2022, the then Home Secretary Suella Braverman claimed that an unelected 'Guardian-reading, tofu-eating wokerati' was undermining the effectiveness of the Conservative government. It is not clear, however, why the public-school-educated former City commodity broker Nigel Farage MP or Cambridge-educated barrister Suella Braverman herself are entitled to describe others as part of the establishment without applying the label to themselves.

As my own experiences show, there is undoubtedly a ruling elite in Britain – as there is in most other democracies. Gaining an excellent education, having good connections or the acquisition of wealth opens the door to political power or influence. But is this corrupt?

We can see that business does lobby government and civil servants to get what it wants, and senior figures from Westminster and Whitehall frequently move with ease through the 'revolving door' into senior corporate roles, including company boards, but there is no clear evidence of systematic collusion that operates against the public interest. Long periods of ineptitude, regular scandals, groupthink and an inbuilt aversion to risk are signs of an unhealthy system – as are rising inequality and large corporate profits resulting from a weak regulatory or legislative regime. But whether or not this indicates corruption depends to a great extent on how those in charge are exercising their power. Is it in their own self-interest, or do they believe that they are acting in the public interest?

At the risk of underplaying the perniciousness of the old establishment, I would not tend to characterise it as innately corrupt, even though it carries a high level of corruption risk. It is a network of senior people who have a great deal in common, in terms of both background and interests. They quite often use their power and influence to promote those common interests, but they do so by bringing to bear their influence rather than through capture, in the sense that their success in bending events and circumstances to their own interests is by no means guaranteed. This does not mean I think the old establishment is a force for good, but too much of the rhetoric on establishment corruption seems to err towards unsubstantiated conspiracy theory. It is clearly hard to distinguish between an establishment that is self-interested and an establishment that is corrupt, but simple recourse to the label 'structural corruption' to describe the shifting networks and connections of the old establishment does not do justice to the complexity of the situation.

Peter Mandelson presents a very interesting example of the transition from the old establishment to the new. After a career marked both by moments of political brilliance and serial scandals, usually involving rich people from whom he wanted money or favours, he was finally undone through his relationship with the American financier and sex offender Jeffrey Epstein. Documents that came to light in early 2026 seemed to suggest that Mandelson had from time to time leaked confidential government information to Epstein, and that he and his husband would periodically receive funds into their bank accounts. If these allegations were to prove true, this would be an open-and-shut example of corruption.

At first sight, it might also look like a classic example of the establishment at work, with the nexus of business and politics and behind-the-scenes market manipulation. But viewed in another light, it seems to tell a different story. What we can see here is no longer some mutual back-scratching among the old establishment, but a senior political figure enjoying the high life and blithely passing on state secrets to a foreign businessman while ignoring the national interest. The charge of corruption seems unanswerable given this set of facts. We might feel that Mandelson was not a typical figure – his serial scandals perhaps indicate he was unusually attracted to the global high life, and particularly open to seduction by wealthy foreigners and all they had to offer. Yet we can identify similar characteristics in the cases of Johnson at Lebedev's Umbrian villa and the donations of overseas oligarchs to political parties. In all these examples, significant overseas wealth, via the medium of unscrupulous individuals looking to advance their personal interests, has been dangled or deployed to influence British politics and politicians.

The Mandelson–Epstein affair gives us an important insight into how the new establishment differs from the old: the relationships are still personal but the networks are now global, and it thus becomes harder for the protagonists to sustain the argument that their personal and the national interest are somehow aligned.

Epstein's networks extended into elite circles around the world, and that brings us to the question of whether the idea of an establishment is in any way particularly British. Many countries have a well-networked elite of politicians, civil servants, lawyers and businesspeople who were educated in a small number of schools and universities and mix in the same places. They often count in their number senior figures in the media and the arts.

In the US, this is eloquently described by Donald Trump as 'the swamp' – and there is a grain of truth in his analysis. Just look at the relationship between the tech bros and senior politicians in the US – Elon Musk and Trump himself being obvious examples – many of whom were educated in the same small group of Ivy League universities. And you might also remember that Trump's first Secretary of State was the former CEO of oil giant Exxon-Mobil Rex Tillerson – just as George W. Bush's Vice-President, Dick Cheney, was once the CEO of government contractor Halliburton. The Australian website gameofmates.com has a colourful description of this phenomenon: 'Mates in big corporations, industry groups, government departments, the halls of parliament and the media skew the system to suit each other.'

In France, three of the country's four presidents since 2000, as well as four prime ministers and a host of business leaders, were all educated at a single specialist educational institution, the École Nationale d'Administration. In all the leading global financial centres, from London to New York to Geneva to Dubai, business leaders are close to policymakers. In other words, elites all over the world tend to look very similar.

There is a definite downside for the health of society, politics and the economy in drawing on a small talent pool. This contributes to what is described as the 'opportunity gap', which on the one hand leads to a stultifying complacency among the incumbent elite, and on the other hand locks out talent, energy, new ideas and innovation from newcomers. But the existence of such an elite and the societal problems associated with it may or may not be described as innately corrupt. I think we must accept that describing the old establishment and chumocracy in this way is ultimately a matter of personal opinion. As in other chapters, we are on much firmer territory if we apply the four-step test and try to find some common ground among those who are seeking to identify corruption in this area of our national life. Like before, we would ask: do these members of the old establishment abuse entrusted power, and is there private gain that is harmful to the public interest? We will have a look at some case studies to which we can apply the test; that will help us to discern where there has been corruption, but will also reinforce the picture of complicity and complacency. And we will also see that the rise of a new establishment of professional enablers and fixers, who have in some ways supplanted the old establishment in influence, has been closely linked to corruption.

In the UK, as in France, membership of the elite is often particularly linked to educational background – of thirty UK prime ministers since 1900, nineteen were educated at Oxford; 63 per cent of Rishi Sunak's cabinet ministers were privately educated. Embedded – and rising – levels of inequality seem to indicate that the economy does operate in favour of those who are already in the elite.

While this may not be inherently corrupt, the relationship with corruption can be close. Among a group all thinking in the same way, norms can shift so that things become acceptable that should not be so: a good example is the MPs expenses scandal, in which many MPs who considered themselves to be people of integrity and serving the public interest nevertheless acted in ways that ranged from unwise lapses of integrity to the blatantly corrupt. There can be a failure to spot corruption because there is a greater tolerance of what others in the chumocracy are up to; and a failure to deal with it appropriately, as the chums are ultimately supportive of each other.

What I think we see with the UK's chumocracy is the result of a kind of inbreeding – precisely the reasoning that Emmanuel Macron gave when he took the decision to close down the École Nationale d'Administration in 2021. Over time, those who are part of the elite can view themselves as key upholders of the public interest simply by virtue of being members of the elite, even if they are profiting along the way. On the other hand, the UK still has plenty of genuine public servants who do try to operate in the public interest; they can be found in many places including the civil service, judiciary, local government, the police, and even politics. Not everyone is exclusively self-interested, and many have come to their positions through talent and not simply by going to the right public school.

So, is the UK's inbred self-interested elite merely undesirable, or is it also corrupt? To work out which sort of system exists in the UK, let's look at both the old and the new establishment, and see how they measure up against charges of corruption.

Our starting point is the UK's financial services industry, colloquially known as the City. Whether we are talking about the old or the new establishment, the City is seen as a prime location for the men in suits, who are thought both to gain great wealth and exert a heavy influence on government and politics to allow these favourable conditions to continue.

For those who argue that the City is fundamentally corrupt, the prime exhibit seems to be its role in the 2008 global financial crisis. Huge national and international banks, having previously made large profits and paid their employees vast bonuses, were on the point of financial collapse and so were subsidised, at great cost to the taxpayer. The wider world became aware of complex financial instruments that had played a role in both enriching individuals who worked in the City and increasing market-level risk to breaking point. Regulation had been scaled back by a government receptive to the argument that a thriving financial services sector was good for economic growth. A few years later, ordinary people were still paying the costs in the form of austerity and economic stagnation – yet banks were back to making profits and awarding bonuses. Surely that was corrupt?

I had stopped working in the City a few months before the crisis; when I visited a trading floor shortly after it peaked with the collapse of Lehman Brothers in late 2008, all the talk was of what bonuses people felt they deserved. There seemed to be no recognition that ordinary people's pensions had lost hundreds of billions of pounds in value, and that the managers of those funds might therefore not deserve a bonus at all.

I struggle to define the role that the City plays in the capital markets, or the political economy as a whole, as being corrupt, though I accept that it is an argument that some scholars will make. Let's apply our four-step test. We can see there was private gain in the overheated markets before the financial crisis, and the bailout from the public purse suggests that this was against the public interest. But do banks have 'entrusted power'? And was there 'abuse' of this power?

At a stretch, it is possible to argue that the role banks play in society means they have entrusted power. The difficulty with such an argument is that it could equally be applied to any sector that provides a service – the energy companies that provide fuel for our homes and cars, the shops that sell us food and clothes, the farming that grows our food and the tech companies that provide us with screens and connectivity. In my view, they do not really have entrusted power, which would imply some kind of official status.

Of course, some people firmly believe that the City, as the engine of capitalism, corrodes society from within. If you do believe that capitalism and the City are rotting our political economy, that would make them corrupt in quite an old-fashioned sense. It is certainly possible to create a definition that supports that case – but we might be able to describe anything as corrupt by designing a definition to fit. We must be wary of labelling all sorts of ills as being corrupt. But be in no doubt: I viewed the City from the inside, and some of the behaviour I witnessed was morally repugnant.

One of the arguments that the City is corrupt rests on the premise that it unfairly rigs the political economy, through exercising a secretive influence on politicians and the Treasury, facilitated by the chumocracy of mutual connections and acquaintances. For example, the reluctance of successive governments to apply wealth taxes, their apparent keenness to privatise public services and the lifting of caps on bankers' bonuses have all been taken to illustrate that politicians bend before the City's wealth and power – the old establishment at work. However, there are sensible alternative explanations about why those policies have prevailed. For instance, there is a plausible argument that wealth taxes drive mobile high-income earners to relocate overseas, which results in a reduced tax take overall.

Furthermore, there are strong counter-examples of how the City's influence with politicians can be overestimated. If we consider the departure of the UK from the European Union, it is clear that the hard Brexit pursued by the government of the day harmed the City. One key red line for the City of London Corporation was 'equivalence', the system by which UK financial services firms could continue to access the EU because the regulatory and supervisory regimes were considered 'equivalent'. It was deemed fundamental if the City was to flourish post-Brexit – only to be rapidly sacrificed by the UK negotiating team. I was at a meeting in the Guildhall when that news came in; senior officials were white-faced with shock.

A second, and entirely anecdotal, example relates to the City Remembrancer, a position dating back to the late sixteenth century whose role is to provide a backchannel between the City and parliament, reminding MPs of the City's interests. Many campaigners view the role with suspicion. As it happens, I had met with the Remembrancer while the Bribery Bill was going through parliament in 2009–10. A barrister by training, he was supported by a team of civil servants. What struck me during the bill's negotiations was that, though he and his team were close to parliament, at TI we seemed to have much better intelligence about what was going on – and, on that occasion, perhaps greater influence. This is not to say my experience at that time was typical, but it does demonstrate that, while close links undoubtedly exist between the City and other arms of the British elite, that does not mean decisions are always taken in the City's favour.

But there is still a problem. I said earlier that the risk with chumocracy is that an inbred bloodline both fails to spot corruption and is ill-equipped to deal with it – and that is the case with the City's facilitation of global corruption. In this, the City is both complacent and ultimately complicit.

How does this work? It is simple. Think of someone who has accumulated vast wealth under suspicious circumstances

– perhaps an African president, the head of a privatised state-owned enterprise in central Europe or the uncle of a Middle Eastern dictator. What do they want to do with their millions of pounds of assets? They want to keep them somewhere safe, to enjoy spending the money without the scrutiny that might come at home. To live a luxury lifestyle and move freely among the global elite while appearing utterly respectable, and passing on their wealth to the next generation. There are a few places in the world that can help you with this, like Switzerland and Dubai. London is another such place, and has been highly successful at attracting that kind of money.

I have discussed this problem many times with leading politicians and figures in the City. When I sat on an advisory panel for the Lord Mayor, I found I could interest almost no one in the fact that the City's reputation overseas was increasingly as a haven of dirty money. There were two stock responses: that it was a low priority compared to other challenges, and that the UK has a world-class anti-money laundering (AML) system, so we need not be unduly concerned. It is true that this was at the time of Brexit, when the City was reeling from the bad hand it was dealt by politicians at Westminster – but the complicity and complacency long predated the Brexit crisis.

How true are the claims that we have a world-class AML system – and surely that should be an adequate defence against dirty money? Sadly not. The global AML regime was put in place in the late 1980s, by the Paris-based Financial Action Task Force (FATF). It was initially designed to tackle organised crime, then terrorism and eventually the proceeds of corruption, which always came a poor third to those other priorities. Although the UK does well on FATF's periodic reviews because we can tick all the boxes to show that many policies and procedures are in place to deal with the proceeds of crime, we know that lots of dirty money still flows into the UK – estimated by the National Crime Agency to be at least £100 billion per year.*

But the problem is not just the relentless flows of dirty money. The AML system only kicks into action when there is a provable crime generating the dirty money – but kleptocrats and corrupt oligarchs will generally not have committed a 'crime' in accumulating their wealth. Instead, they have typically captured the judiciary, parliament and law enforcement, while neutralising the press and civil society, along with any opposition. There is no provable criminality at the heart of their wealth, and so their funds that flow to the UK are not even included in the NCA's annual figure of £100 billion.

We know this to be the case because leaks such as the Panama Papers and Paradise Papers have given a firm evidential basis to what previously was based on anecdotal evidence, one-off cases or theory-based assumptions. The treasure trove of documents that have been leaked over the past decade – forensically examined by excellent investigative journalists at organisations like OCCRP and ICIJ – has given documented proof that the world's kleptocrats and corrupt oligarchs have been transferring billions of pounds of wealth from their own countries, via secrecy jurisdictions like the British Virgin Islands, to destination countries like the UK. For example, Igor Shuvalov was Russia's first Deputy Prime Minister from 2008 to 2018, as well as chair of the Russian bank VEB, which financed the Sochi Winter Olympics. His closeness to Putin caused him to be added to the UK's sanctions list in 2022,[8] although the relationship had been well known for almost two decades prior to that.

---

* To give some context, the UK's GDP is around £2 trillion per annum – so the NCA figure of £100 billion represents about 5 per cent of that.

Shuvalov's official income and declared assets are both known because – before the law was repealed – such declarations were a legal requirement for Russian politicians. In 2014, his asset declaration listed his official salary as £112,000, and the joint wealth of Shuvalov and his wife was listed as £634,000. And yet the leaked Paradise Papers revealed that, via his wife and daughter and a series of shell companies, he owned assets around the world, including London properties valued at £15 million, and his net worth has been estimated at around £200 million.[9] Shuvalov is just one of many examples that have emerged over the years showing how easily corrupt capital can evade the global AML regime.

To many, this ability of those who are most corrupt to bypass the AML system seems deeply ironic. The reason you need to produce utilities bills and proof of address and identity when undertaking standard financial transactions such as opening a bank account or taking out a mortgage is a defence against money laundering, yet the very people the AML system is designed to catch seem to sail through it. This is why we can fairly describe the City as complicit and complacent with regard to corruption. Complicit because the efforts to exclude the proceeds of corruption have been half-hearted at best, and complacent because the attitude is generally that there is not a serious problem to be addressed.

To illustrate the point, we can do no better than to look at the role of lawyers, a key part of the network of businesses that make up the City – and one of a number of professions who are complicit and complacent when it comes to kleptocracy, state capture and grand corruption. Much of my own recent research has been into lawyers, and so I have seen for myself that we have the evidence to confirm the hypothesis that they play a key role in what is known as 'professional enabling'.

Lawyers also provide a bridge between the old and the new establishment. They once exemplified the old establishment – staid, cerebral and impartial advisers – but the legal profession has changed beyond recognition in recent years. Deregulation and the emergence of the global role of the City have led to the financialisation and Americanisation of the legal profession in this country. The world of the staid professional firms that were a byword for discretion and integrity has been left behind, and replaced by the emergence of much larger firms whose style, culture and appetite for revenue is much more nakedly commercial. Symptomatic of this, the starting salary of a junior lawyer in a large City firm is currently £180,000. It should be no surprise if firms, in search of wealthy clients to recoup such costs, are prepared to act on behalf of anyone who knocks on the door.

Like banks and accountants, lawyers are often described by campaigners as 'professional enablers' of corruption. Such professionals are necessary to move money around the world using complex financial structures; they help to keep it safe, and to legitimise and increase the wealth of their kleptocrat clients, using legal means such as raising capital in Western markets. It is often said that lawyers are the keystone in the architecture of professional enabling, because so many activities and transactions require them.

Through dozens of interviews with lawyers and some innovative research techniques, such as the analysis and categorisation of comments posted to press articles, my research team have examined the decline in professional ethics over the past two decades, during which time a lawyer's duty to the public interest has been superseded by a minimalist view of a lawyer's role as simply being to help clients use the law to their advantage. During my research I have met many lawyers who are themselves bemused, and sometimes rather aghast, at how their profession is changing. But it is also clear that major City law firms, as well as a host of smaller boutique ones, have been seduced by lucrative business, such as capital raising and wealth management, to act for those whose funds are the proceeds of corruption. The Syrian case study below is an excellent illustration of this.

These law firms, backed by their professional bodies like the Law Society and Bar Council, have become adept at justifying this. They claim it is an issue of access to justice, that everyone has a right to representation, and that as lawyers they are obliged to put their clients' interests first. In fact, this is based on an interpretation of a US-based approach to lawyering that equates the ethics of practising criminal law (where everyone, even murderers, can expect a lawyer to defend them) with those of commercial law. Modern legal ethicists tend not to support such a point of view – at best, the law firms' self-serving justifications can be described as contested, and certainly not some kind of absolute truth.

The law firms are usually well aware that they are acting for those who are implicated in grand corruption, state capture and kleptocracy. However, they feel justified in doing so because there is no provable criminality at the heart of their clients' wealth, and therefore acting for them is within the current AML rules. If parliament wants to change the rules, they will act within the new rules; but for now, the law firms are acting like you might expect any business to act. The traditional notions of professional ethics and upholding the rule of law in the public interest have been set aside, perhaps exacerbated by the significant increase in aggressive US law firms in London. A retired senior partner of one of the City's most prestigious firms told the *Financial Times* that 'their business model is much closer to investment banking than it is to many other law firms'.[10] The pursuit of profit over principle might be expected of investment banks, but it comes as a surprise to find this in the blue-chip City law firms that have for centuries been afforded a special status through a compact with society that the law and its lawyers operate in the public interest. The old establishment is now serving new masters.

One case that illustrates this very well is that of Rifaat Al-Assad, uncle of Syria's brutal dictator Bashar Al-Assad.[11] Rifaat was widely accused of war crimes – indeed, he was known as 'the Butcher of Hama' – and his vast wealth was in 2020 found by a court in France to have been the proceeds of crime and corruption. His London property portfolio included the Highgate mansion Witanhurst, second only to Buckingham Palace in the list of the capital's largest residences. Rifaat's legal representative from 1999 to 2015 was the Old Etonian Mark Bridges, head of private international wealth at Farrer & Co, a City firm founded in 1789. And just to consolidate the sense of chumocracy, Bridges also acted as the queen's solicitor and was knighted in 2019.

When the relationship between the blue-chip firm and Assad's uncle was exposed by The Bureau of Investigative Journalism (TBIJ), Farrer & Co explained that they had been 'provided with credible information … which fundamentally contradicted the claims being made in the media about Mr Al-Assad.' In other words, though the allegations about Al-Assad were well known, there was plausible deniability. This was active involvement with a war criminal who had acquired his wealth by corrupt means, but the City firm was able to claim that the involvement of one of its partners was unwitting complicity. Since the allegations were denied by the client and unproven by other means, they felt it was legitimate to represent the Butcher of Hama. From the perspective of campaigners, such justifications epitomise the complacency that accompanies the complicity: law firms feel comfortable in setting aside ethical considerations and taking on such a client, as long as it is legal to do.

An equally disturbing case is that of Yevgeny Prigozhin, then head of the Russian mercenary Wagner Group, which played a prominent role in the invasion of Ukraine, and prior to that in ruthless operations in Africa and Syria. When Eliot Higgins, an award-winning journalist with the independent research collective Bellingcat, posted five tweets highlighting the role of Prigozhin and the Wagner Group, he was sued for libel. Such frivolous cases, designed to suppress critics by loading them with costs and legal procedure, are known as SLAPP suits. Despite being under sanctions, Prigozhin found a boutique law firm in London, Discreet Law, to represent him. The case was eventually dropped, leaving the journalist with a £70,000 legal bill. Discreet Law was referred to the Solicitors Regulation Authority, which declined to take action.

Such SLAPP suits have become common in the UK, with law firms being willing to act for unsavoury clients who have baseless claims but bottomless pockets. They have been documented by the Anti-SLAPP Coalition,[12] which highlights several well-known cases, such as the action by former Chelsea FC owner Roman Abramovich against the author Catherine Belton for her book *Putin's People*, and a group of Kazakh oligarchs against the *Financial Times* journalist Tom Burgis for his book *Kleptopia*. In 2022, the Isle of Wight MP Bob Seely became so incensed at such cases that he took the unusual step of naming specific lawyers in parliament, mentioning the 'amorality' of Harbottle & Lewis, CMS and Carter-Ruck. He asked, 'How on earth have we allowed this to happen? I would love an answer from a lawyer in government. A free press should be intimidating kleptocrats and criminals. Why have we got to this position in our society – a free society, the mother of parliaments – where we have kleptocrats, criminals and oligarchs intimidating a free media?'

The larger blue-chip law firms that are involved with kleptocrats do not usually deal with SLAPPs, as they generally specialise in other types of legal work. But the profession as a whole has been willing to let this sordid practice continue, with regulators and professional bodies defending it as though they were defending human rights. As with the case of Assad's uncle, in the Prigozhin case we could debate the precise legal rights and wrongs – but that would miss the point. In both cases, a London law firm felt able to act for an alleged war criminal with extensive unexplained wealth. And it was all within the rules.

In these cases, we see the UK playing a role in supporting global corruption. The corruption itself may have happened elsewhere, but the funds were welcomed here, assisted by law firms, banks, accountants and other men in suits. Some scholars make the argument that these lawyers are themselves corrupt; they have a form of entrusted power, having been granted a privileged position by society – and that in acting as professional enablers of kleptocrats they are abusing it. In my view, this stretches the definition of corruption, but it does highlight how far a respectable profession has lowered its ethical standards, that it can be plausibly seen not only as enabling corruption but as acting corruptly itself.

It is this type of behaviour that the writer Oliver Bullough has described as making Britain the 'butler to the world'. One of the things I most like about this phrase is that butlers are the classic men in suits. They look impeccably smart. What is the difference between a suit worn by a butler and one worn by the master? The discerning eye may detect a difference in cloth and cut, but that can be hard to spot. In *The Remains of the Day* by Kazuo Ishiguro, the butler encounters precisely this ambivalence when removed from the grand house over which he presides: outsiders are not quite clear whether he is servant or master. In essence, the difference is not the suit but the function. Bullough's argument is that Britain's men in suits have gone from being masters of the world, when the City and the civil service presided over the Empire, to being servants to the world.

These men in suits, professional enablers who service the ultra-wealthy, are the new British establishment – and they are not picky about who their clients are, as long as they have sufficient wealth. They are fixers who often mix business with the world of politics. The dark quartet of lobbying, the revolving door, political party funding and conflicts of interest have long been a problem at Westminster, giving those with wealth privileged access and influence. As we saw in Chapter Four, the thin line of defence to prevent this turning from legitimate activity into corruption rests on the integrity of those who are in power. Onto this fragile existing system has been grafted a new phenomenon: fixers for hire.

We may think of fixers as people who can help get things to work in countries that are dysfunctional. When I visited Ethiopia just after the end of the civil war, my hotel in Addis Ababa provided me with a fixer who could get me to the places I needed to go to, help me get into places with local knowledge and contacts, and organise a few excursions. Used the world over by journalists and businesspeople, they were traditionally associated with the concierge services of the grand hotels.

However, the rise of the global super-rich has seen a rise in concierge services that are no longer attached to hotels but operate as businesses in their own right. They are among a group of service providers that act as the 'butlers to the world'. These butlers also include lawyers, accountants, wealth managers, private medical providers, elite schools, private security and the lobbying and PR firms who can offer so much help to their clients.[13]

Some of this butlering may be amoral without being directly damaging to the UK. For example, when a corrupt Nigerian politician comes to a private hospital in London to have an operation, they are not doing this country any harm. But some of the butlers are trying to make the UK, its policies and economy more amenable to their clients, which can harm our own political economy and society. Moreover, it is unlikely that an individual who has come to wealth and power through corrupt means in one country will suddenly change their spots when they come to the UK – but they will understand how the game is played here: they need the butlers to help them out.

Much of this takes place in secret, so it is hard to find out what is happening – but we do get occasional glimpses from court cases, investigative journalists and document leaks. One recent example is the role that London-based PR firm Bell Pottinger played in trying to clean up the reputation of the corrupt Gupta family during the state capture scandal of President Jacob Zuma in South Africa. The firm's founder had previously observed that 'morality is a job for priests, not PR men' – and this attitude was fully on show when Bell Pottinger broke the Wikipedia rules to manipulate the entry on the Gupta family, launched an anonymous social media campaign to support them and used a range of lobbying techniques in London and South Africa to paint their corrupt clients as victims rather than criminals.[14]

Lobbying has existed for a long time, so if we are to describe it as part of the new establishment we need to work out whether anything has changed. There is still continuity with the old-style lobbying, and particularly the secrecy with which the system operates, but I think we can discern that there have been clear changes around the new breed of fixers.

First, access to the establishment has been opened up to foreign money. This has been a gradual process since the 1970s, when Arab states started investing in UK assets and property, and it has accelerated since the 1990s with the advent of money from Russia and the former Soviet Union and more recently from China. Each new wave has been in search of a safe haven where wealth can be stored and grown, access to a luxury lifestyle in a peaceful and stable country, and related reputational benefits. The men in suits – the professional enablers – are now regularly operating on behalf of wealthy individuals, companies and governments from overseas. The intermingling of rich foreigners with the establishment has been enabled by political donations, cultivation of the right contacts, spending money in the right places and educating offspring within the educational networks that give access to those with power and influence. This system is often on full display in the pages of glossy magazines.

Second, there is now a more blatant merging of politics and financial interests on behalf of wealthy foreign clients, with no apparent consideration of the national interest by those who are fixing and enabling; indeed, one of the 'concierges' in recent years became a chairman of the Conservative Party with a remit to raise for them as much money as possible, and another became the chairman of Reform UK.*

Third, the fixers are part of a wider picture: the 'butlers' collectively produce what is known as a 'cluster effect'. This means that a cluster of enablers in different fields – banks, lawyers, accountants, PR firms, estate agents, private wealth managers, consultancy firms, concierges, private security operators – can combine as an ecosystem to provide what is collectively a compelling environment for kleptocrats and oligarchs: the offering

---

*Zia Yusuf of Velocity Black.

becomes more potent because every need can be taken care of. More and more clients are thus attracted to the UK, and there is an increasing interest in making sure the laws and regulations suit them.

The use of such fixers to facilitate political donations with the expectation of receiving access and influence is described as 'access capitalism' by Mohamed Amersi, a controversial Conservative Party donor who is himself no stranger to allegations of corruption and use of libel suits.[15] He has written of the party, 'Since co-chairman Ben Elliot set up the "250 Advisory Board" – known as the "250 Club" as its members have [each] donated more than £250,000 per annum – it has taken access capitalism to a new level within the party.' Amersi has described how members who are non-doms* could use the 250 Club to try to influence government policy through having the ear of those in power.

Ben Elliot was not just co-chairman of the Tories. He was also the founder of a company called the Quintessentially Group, which offers a full range of concierge services to wealthy clients around the world, including Russian oligarchs. That helped him to raise £2 million from Russian-linked donors for the Conservative Party, mainly from a range of semi-exiles who seem nevertheless to have maintained close ties with Putin's allies.[16] Elliot was well connected in classic establishment fashion: Eton-educated, the nephew of Queen Camilla and awarded a knighthood via Boris Johnson's resignation honours list.

But Sir Ben is not alone in merging the world of business, politics and foreign clients. Thirty years ago, an examination of men in suits would have zeroed in on two things: the City and Sir Humphrey. Remember him? Sir Humphrey Appleby

---

*Overseas nationals resident in the UK who receive favourable tax treatment.

was permanent secretary to the minister in the classic political sitcom *Yes Minister*. The running joke in the series was that, although the minister was elected to serve the people, the government was in reality run by a core of senior civil servants.

These days, while the professional enablers ensure the City is still on our list of men in suits, albeit with new overseas clients, Sir Humphrey et al. have been replaced in terms of influence by the so-called SpAds, special advisers appointed by each minister. The SpAds' fortunes rise and fall in tandem with their political patrons', and there exists a thriving market in people who have been SpAds and people who want to be SpAds, who keep a foot in the political world by working as lobbyists. They may be people dressed in business casual rather than men in suits, but the key point here is the revolving door that links the worlds of politics and lobbying and the clients of those lobbying firms.

One study looked at 521 former SpAds from the period between 1997 and 2017 and found that, after leaving their roles as government advisers, 31 per cent had moved into corporate lobbying.[17] An investigation by the NGO Open Democracy in 2025 that surveyed nearly 125 Conservative government SpAds in the run-up to the 2024 general election found that 50 had become corporate lobbyists in sectors including oil, banking and pharmaceuticals.[18]

We cannot precisely say whether this combination of concierge, lobbying and PR services, with political connections and establishment heritage, is corrupt, although it looks very much like the institutional corruption that some scholars believe exists in the American political system. However, we can surely see that it is unhealthy. The difference is perhaps in who they serve: the public interest, or the interest of their clients? Do we want our country's tax strategy to be set by the non-doms who will benefit, as Mohamed Amersi suggests is happening? Should the decision of whether the public has a right to know about who owns UK property be left to those who are paid advocates for the Overseas Territories, which have fiercely resisted such changes? Should the argument around Brexit negotiations be decided solely by informed public debate and a referendum, or influenced by tax exiles who want their political views to prevail in a country they no longer live in? In sum, is access capitalism through the new establishment beneficial for our democracy and society?

My view is that fixers are no more innately corrupt than traditional lobbyists or PR companies; but, if we were to conclude that our politics is structurally or institutionally corrupt, then they could fairly be seen as leading actors within a corrupt system. For all such groups, in representing kleptocrats and providing access capitalism they may act in contradiction to the public interest – but they might also legitimately ask why they should be expected to act in the public interest. However, some of these enabling groups, including lawyers and banks, do have long-standing entrusted privileges, even if not entrusted power, and this places them in a separate category in terms of what society can reasonably expect from them in return for those privileges. Others, like the concierge and PR companies, are seeking to alter public policy. When they are interacting with those who do have entrusted power, like politicians and civil servants, there is clearly a risk that decisions that should be taken in the public interest will instead be taken in the private interest of their clients because the decision-makers have in some way been incentivised by the wealth and influence of those clients. The situation is made worse when SpAds are moving so frequently between influential positions in government and the lobbying and PR industry. This system of hidden incentives is one of the key dangers of the dark quartet – lobbying, the revolving door, conflicts of interest and political donations. With wealthy overseas clients in particular, the risk that their UK representatives will not be acting in the UK's public interest is so high that the remedy must be proper regulation of both those who lobby and those who are lobbied.

Where does this leave us? Do the men in suits secretly operate a corrupt system that maintains their own wealth and power? Not exactly. We can see that the old establishment still exists, but some – perhaps quite a lot – of the power has shifted to a new establishment of SpAds, enablers and fixers. There is a chumocracy and an elite, though elites are also common in other countries and we should be wary of thinking this is a uniquely British problem. Deeper examination of the City, lawyers and fixers confirms that there is still a close relationship between them and with politics, and that, subtly, the men in suits have changed from being masters to being servants. Perhaps understandably, they have been seduced by the opportunity to make money: corrupt foreign clients are wealthy and pay well to access Britain and its old establishment. Political parties, public schools, universities, football clubs, racing stables, property developers, auction houses and others have all welcomed the cash. The drive since the 1980s to encourage foreign direct investment (FDI) as a complement to home-grown economic growth has brought with it the dirty money, the corrupt capital, alongside the legitimate FDI of Japanese car companies and Norwegian investment in clean energy.

The new establishment make their living from foreign – and often corrupt – wealth, but that has been made possible because they have also changed in attitude from the old establishment. A few decades ago, it would have been inconceivable for the nephew of the queen, an Old Etonian, to be anything as 'common' as a fixer for foreign plutocrats. Yet that is what the modern establishment has become. As we can clearly see with the legal profession, there is an overriding inclination to self-interest. Their role may be in facilitating kleptocracy overseas rather than in being corrupt themselves, but the underlying amorality is troubling.

What we have seen in the past two decades in the UK should act as a warning. When approached by corrupt foreign kleptocrats, Britain's men in suits did not fend them off – they were welcomed with open arms: remember the NCA's estimate that over £100 billion a year is laundered through the UK, with the help of the professional enablers. Despite their attempts at secrecy, couched as 'privacy', these cases are often hiding in plain sight. When the government introduced a new, but barely used, legal instrument called unexplained wealth orders to help plug the gap in the anti-money laundering regulations, Transparency International published a useful list of people who were candidates for a UWO.[19] They included a Libyan general from the Gaddafi era who owned a million-pound house in Surrey despite a notional army salary of around £4,000, and the ruling family of Azerbaijan, who owned £41 million of London real estate including an £18 million mansion in Hampstead. All those on the list had been traced via open-source information.

You may believe that there is an unwritten compact between the men in suits and the rest of society and, when push comes to shove, the public interest will prevail. If you believe that, the establishment has failed in recent years. The UK's own national security strategy cites 'kleptocracy and corruption' as a threat to national security,[20] and yet the UK's enablers and fixers have given them a warm welcome. If you are more cynical and believe the establishment was always out for itself, that view will have been reinforced. Either way, with self-interest to the fore and a degradation of the cultural norms that provided checks and balances, the door is open for corruption.

Just as inbreeding would weaken a bloodline, so we can see that the chumocracy, the changing establishment and butlering have reduced the UK's resilience to corruption. Corruption is not spotted when it is heading our way; when it is taking place we deny it; and when it has happened we do not know how to deal with it. And so even if the men in suits syndrome is not fundamentally corrupt, it gives this country a fundamental vulnerability to corruption.

8

MEN IN UNIFORM: POLICE, PRISONS AND BORDERS

If you've ever been arrested, you will know that an adult wearing a uniform provided by the state is a compelling symbol of entrusted power.* Most people do not try to resist arrest: we accept that the uniform represents an authority that has been delegated by the state.

Who do we put in such uniforms, granting them power over us? Typically a police officer, a prison officer or someone working in border security. In this country we seldom see the uniformed military on our streets, except on ceremonial occasions. So this chapter will focus on those whose uniforms represent authority (or entrusted power) in a domestic context.

Surveys such as the Global Corruption Barometer reveal that, in many countries around the world, it is the people who are in uniform who are most often corrupt. They are well positioned to abuse their power for private gain. The police are a particular problem in many countries. They frequently demand bribes just to allow ordinary people go about their daily business without arrest, and they also take bribes to help those who have been investigated or arrested to get off the hook. Sometimes

---

* Of course, the uniform can be worn by a woman as much as a man, though it is more usually worn by a man in each of the areas that this chapter examines.

they are on the payroll of organised crime groups; sometimes they run protection rackets themselves. In 2013, the last time this was measured, some 31 per cent of people across the world who had come into contact with the police over the previous twelve months reported paying a bribe.[1]

The police have powers that we do not grant to anyone else in our society. They can take away freedom and exercise violence on behalf of the state, and these powers extend over all citizens. Prison officers and border security officials are in an even more powerful position over inmates and immigrants; they are also subject to less scrutiny, and deal with groups who are less able to make their voices heard.

In many countries, it is quite normal for the police to demand bribes from innocent people with the threat of fine or detention. The police officer may have a daily target for income that needs to be raised through bribes, a proportion of which is passed up the chain to more senior officers. In order to become a police officer in the first place, they may have paid a large bribe to the police academy, which they must earn back through extorting members of the public at checkpoints or by stopping them in the street for a made-up infringement of a law. A detailed study of police corruption in Mexico, for example, provides dozens of cases studies, such as drivers paying bribes to get out of greater penalties after being pulled over, often at a cost of around £5.[2] One scheme that came to light in 2025 in Odisha, India, showed that candidates for the police academy paid up to £23,000 – in three instalments – for help passing the recruitment exam, which included advance sight of the test papers.[3] Just think what a new police officer might need to do, throughout their career, to pay back such a sum.

While surveys show that this kind of transactional bribery is relatively uncommon in the British police, that does not mean it does not happen – and, as with other British institutions, there are different forms of corruption at play which can be equally damaging. In this chapter we will look in depth at specific areas of British life where people in uniform are involved in corrupt practices, alongside a worrying tendency towards systemic and structural corruption. But we will also encounter strong institutions, checks and balances, and high levels of integrity from people who are not paid very much and sometimes work in considerable danger.

We will start by looking at the way in which relatively straightforward forms of corruption take place in our prisons. Then we turn to the border agencies, the country's gatekeepers, who should only be letting in people and goods that have a right to cross the border. Finally, we will look at the police, for whom the question of corruption is more complicated. It has become common for London's Met Police to be accused of having fundamental 'institutional' problems: racism, misogyny and homophobia. The phrase 'institutional corruption' is also frequently applied to the police in this country; we will examine what it really means – and whether it is merited.

Prisons

I've only spent a day in a prison, as part of a programme to familiarise community leaders with what life inside was like. But even one day was enough to verify what the academic theory suggests: the possibilities for abuse of power among a criminal population make prisons the ideal environment for corruption.

First of all, to state the obvious, everyone there is a criminal. Second, there is a high demand for illicit goods, particularly drugs and mobile phones. And finally, the prison staff are people in positions of power who control access to the outside world and to 'privileges', which may be the allocation of jobs or even prison transfers; a bribe of £5,000 can be enough to secure a transfer to a softer facility.[4] In other words, any corruption analyst would conclude that prisons have a high-risk profile for corruption.

We should be aware that this discussion on corruption in UK prisons exists in the context of an ongoing prisons crisis. This refers to a rise in violence, drug abuse and squalid conditions, usually ascribed to the government's cuts in funding, coupled with a rising prison population.[5] Corruption may not be the cause of the prisons crisis, but it amplifies the problems and makes them harder to solve, for example through increasing drug-fuelled violence in prisons and the tightening grip of organised crime within them. Moreover, the incentive structures and performance targets that the system has used over the last three decades prioritise inflexible key performance indicators for managers over addressing underlying risks, meaning that it is easy to neglect a second-order issue like corruption.

Should this unusual environment be considered anything other than an outlier that is entirely untypical of corruption in the UK? Well, I think prisons show us what we are at our core. They are the most extreme version of ourselves – both as individuals and as a nation – and show what the UK might be like if the rules were stripped away and a society were constructed in which corruption is the norm. Far from being some overseas test-bed, this is regular corruption happening on our own shores. Corruption in our prisons tells us that, in the right conditions, we can be just as corrupt as any other nation – but before we get too philosophical, let us have a look at what corruption really means in the prison system.

Our prisons are full of two types of contraband that should not be there: drugs and mobile phones, both of which are closely associated with organised crime groups and with the prevailing atmosphere of intimidation and violence. HMP Wandsworth was widely known as the 'Carphone Warehouse' due to the widespread availability of mobile phones. But how does this contraband get in?

There has been an upturn recently in the use of drones, used by those on the outside to transport goods to those inside, and for a long time the most frequent suggestion by His Majesty's Prison and Probation Service (HMPPS) has been that visitors – family and friends – are responsible. But recent evidence has demonstrated that prison staff are also involved. This does not just mean the prison officers, but also the ancillary staff who come in to help make a prison function – corruption cases have involved nurses, teachers, probation officers and catering staff who work in prisons. One example was Sara Kachach, ironically a drug rehabilitation nurse at HMP Manchester, who smuggled Class A drugs in her bra to her inmate lover, as well as providing him with mobile phones, SIM cards, tobacco and other drugs. The nationwide lockdowns during the coronavirus pandemic provided a natural experiment on the extent to which family and friends were complicit in providing contraband: despite the visiting ban, the supply of drugs did not dry up – and in some prisons, drug availability actually increased. More and more evidence in the form of cases coming to light has indicated that prison staff are a key part of the problem. The prison authorities have just started to cotton on to this, and between 2022 and 2024 the number of prison and probation staff dismissed for misconduct doubled – from 181 to 397.[6]

This looks like a straightforward abuse of power: people turning a blind eye or even smuggling in goods themselves – and getting paid to do so. Those in charge of running the system are actually corrupting the system; as one ex-inmate recently told the BBC, 'On one hand you have a prison service that's meant to be rule-abiding and strict and uphold British values, and in reality you have corrupt officers.'[7] A former prison officer said in an interview: 'There's a power dynamic, and prison officers can feel like they can do what they want ... They can make life difficult for those inside, and they know that.'[8]

In Scotland, Michael Stoney, the governor of HMP Barlinnie, Scotland's largest jail, has campaigned for tougher laws targeted at corrupt prison officers. He claimed, 'Staff corruption has always been a problem.'[9] But sometimes the problem is more complicated. Getting contraband into prisons, and distributing it, is the work of organised crime groups. They are ruthless in intimidating, blackmailing, grooming and coercing prison officers into corrupt behaviours – and the situation has been made worse by cutbacks and underinvestment. John Podmore, a former prison governor who also spent time as the head of the prisons' Corruption Prevention Unit, told the BBC in 2024 that corruption was 'a greater problem than it has ever been': 'There is a perfect storm of young inexperienced staff with poor vetting and inadequate training being thrown into a dystopian environment ... where violence and organised crime dominate a failing prison system.'[10]

Moreover, the abuses of power are not simply at the lower level. At HMP Liverpool, the chair of the prison monitoring board was charged with helping to smuggle drugs into the prison; while the governor at HMP Kirkham in Lancashire became so embroiled in a relationship with a jailed crime boss that she herself became a drug dealer in the prison, and ended up sentenced to nine years. But these cases pale into insignificance beside the corruption of Russell Thorne, the former governor of a high-security prison in Surrey. He conducted a three-year relationship with a female inmate and would instruct her to perform intimate sex acts because 'It's an order'.[11] There was a quid pro quo of perks and privileges, but the imbalance of power makes this nothing less than sextortion. We are left to ask how this was not spotted over three years in a high-security prison. Perhaps other prison staff were complicit in allowing it to happen.

That was certainly the case at Medomsley Detention Centre in County Durham. It was closed in 1987, but the inquiry into the abuse was only commissioned in 2023 and published its report in 2025.[12] The case tells us both how deep the abuse of power can go, and how long it can take for victims to be recognised. Medomsley was a juvenile detention centre, with inmates – ironically known as 'trainees' – typically aged between seventeen and twenty-one, but sometimes younger. There was serial psychological, violent and sexual abuse, including all varieties of rape. A particular focus was the kitchen, where the prison officer Neville Husband was the chef. He operated a regime of fear, excluding other warders and doing what he felt like to the boys under his care. More than 2,000 boys and young men were abused and assaulted between the 1960s and the 1980s, and some only felt able to speak out when Husband died in 2010, such was the lack of confidence in the system for reporting abuse.

Astonishingly, the same failed system for reporting still exists today as when Medomsley was operating in the 1980s. The inmates could effectively only report the abuse to those who were part of it. The Prisons and Probation Ombudsman who wrote the 2025 report on Medomsley said, 'Either staff in leadership roles were aware of the abuse, in which case they were complicit, or they lacked dedication and professional curiosity to such an extent as to not be professionally competent.'

*

In the Medomsley case, we can see the corruption was systemic within one institution in the relatively recent past, which brings us to the question of whether such cases have been systemic through the prison system more widely, and whether that continues today. The risk profile for corruption in prisons, as we have seen, is exceptionally high; our default assumption should be that there is likely to be a lot of corruption. In 2024, 23,613 prison officers in England and Wales were responsible for the care of 85,867 inmates. With a high level of risk, we might expect high numbers of corrupt prison staff, and therefore a correspondingly high annual number of investigations, convictions and dismissals. But it is very hard to get numbers about even simple things. For example, a request for information on how many staff were in the HMPPS Counter Corruption Unit (CCU) yielded the response in 2023: 'Due to the highly sensitive nature it is not possible to confirm or comment on the number of staff within the CCU.'

A House of Commons question in 2024[13] revealed that an astonishingly low number of staff members have in recent years been dismissed for transporting drugs into prisons – there was an average of around seventeen cases each year between 2019 and 2023. Even with so few cases, the data seems uncoordinated and sporadic. The BBC reported that in 2024 a record 165 prison staff were sacked for a variety of types of misconduct over the previous year, citing HMPPS data – though a government spreadsheet suggests this number may actually have been 167.[14] A separate analysis by Spotlight on Corruption found sixty-eight convictions of prison staff for misconduct in public office in the decade up to 2024, which is an average of around seven per year. So are 7, 17, 165 or 167 prison staff dismissed or convicted each year, how many of these cases relate to corruption, and are they the tip of the iceberg? Nobody appears to know. Back in 2006, a leaked Metropolitan Police report estimated that there were over 1,000 corrupt prison officers in the UK. It speaks volumes that this is the latest available figure.[15]

It is worthwhile reflecting that data only tell part of the story. Dismissals and prosecutions for misconduct tell us who has been caught, but the true picture may be better obtained from other sources, such as the stories of prisoners themselves. Often, prisoners have a profound mistrust of authority and fear of being let down by the system, and so will not use established reporting or data-gathering channels. But there is plenty of anecdotal evidence from ex-inmates, not least on several impressive websites of groups that aim to help former offenders.[16] Two recent examples are former prison officer Lee Davis, who found himself inside after smuggling drugs into a young offender institution, and Beatrice Auty, who spent a year in HMP Bronzefield in Surrey after a conviction for money laundering; she had carried suitcases of cash on multiple journeys from Heathrow to Dubai as a courier for a drugs gang. Davis reported that he had been paid £400 to £500 per package he delivered to inmates when he was a staff member between 2006 and 2010, yet he was only searched twice in three years. Auty reported a continuous pattern of sexual advances and harassment from prison staff aimed at herself and other female prisoners, as well as prison staff regularly providing drugs for inmates.[17]

Confusion over data regarding corruption often reflects the reality that an institution has not given much priority to establishing the basics of a coordinated anti-corruption response. There are many priorities in HMPPS, and in the face of violence, overcrowding, short-staffing and crumbling infrastructure it is easy to see why corruption might not feature on the list. In fact, it has long looked like 'The prison service is most definitively in denial'[18] about corruption, as John Podmore wrote in 2012.

The Ministry of Justice by contrast has consistently claimed that there is only a 'small minority who break the rules'.[19] Examining the cases that come to light, alongside the data that are available, the only plausible conclusion is that there has indeed been denial, about both the scale of the problem and who is responsible.

The UK's prisons are a microcosm of how bad things can get – and how quickly. From the availability of drugs and phones, we can deduce that petty corruption is rife. The known cases, anecdotal evidence and misconduct dismissals indicate that some, perhaps many, staff have lost their way and are too easily corrupted by the criminals inside and their associates from outside. The system is weak, unsafe and hardly able to do the job that is required.

Worryingly, our prisons might tick the boxes for all the various definitions of corruption. There are plenty of cases that meet the four-step test, and enough of them for the problem to be considered systemic. And the behaviour is so deep-rooted, covering staff at all levels, that it could also be considered to be structural in the sense that it is deeply embedded.

Might we even go so far as to describe prisons as being institutionally corrupt? This is a good example of where academic and popular definitions differ. The structural corruption we have seen in a place like Medomsley looks like what most people might describe as institutional corruption. In academic terms, Lessig's definition is 'influence which is legal, or even currently ethical, that undermines the institution's effectiveness by diverting it from its purpose or weakening its ability to achieve its purpose'. This is principally aimed at institutions like a parliament, but the concept of 'diversion of purpose' is relevant here, to say nothing of lack of effectiveness – although the influence is hardly 'legal'. The job of HMPPS is, according to its own strategy, 'to protect the public and help people lead law-abiding and positive lives'.[20] At a certain stage, when a prison becomes dominated by gangs and organised crime, when bribery is systemic and illegal drugs are widely circulated, and the culture inside means that inmates face constant violence, we might ask whether the prison has been diverted from its intended purpose. The available evidence does not allow for a definitive judgement – but of all institutions examined in this book, prisons are one of the closest to meeting the criteria for institutional corruption.

However, we can end our examination of prisons on a more positive note. Most writing on the subject, especially by former governors, emphasises that there are many individuals of high integrity within HMPPS. They want to help root out rotten apples rather than turn a blind eye, but they need support to enable them to do so. A further positive development is that the prison service's Counter Corruption Unit has been reinforced with additional staff over the last couple of years, and has started taking a more strategic approach. More data are available (if you spend long enough analysing the Ministry of Justice spreadsheets), there has been a gradual acknowledgement that prison staff are part of the problem, and the increase in the number of dismissals for misconduct almost certainly reflects better systems and more vigilant enforcement.[21] Similar reforms have also happened in the past, and things have then slipped backwards with a new minister in post or some new initiatives diverting resources and energy elsewhere. But there is enough to suggest that tackling corruption in UK prisons, though a mountain to climb, is by no means a lost cause.

Borders[22]

When you pass through an airport, you may barely notice the official who is checking your passport. But for any illegal immigrant, this person is someone to fear because of the power they have to make life-changing decisions. That is perhaps as it should be: the job of the Border Force staff is to keep out illegal immigrants and goods. They are the front line of our defences against people traffickers, drug smugglers and organised crime groups trying to penetrate the UK's borders. We rely on them to be doing a good job. But behind the uniformed officers in the passport booth are many others who have extensive discretionary powers. And just like the situation in our prisons, it is tailor-made for corruption.

Research from across the world tells us that corruption is one of the reasons why people who do not have the right to do so are easily able to cross supposedly secure national borders, gain the right papers, or speed up the processing of an application. For example, David Jancsics looked at 156 cases in which there were prosecutions for corruption among the US Customs and Border Protection Agency, and found that the extensive bribery ranged from opportunistic demands by officers who would then turn a blind eye, to full-on infiltration by organised crime groups smuggling people and drugs with the help of corrupt border officials.[23] We do not know with any certainty how much of a problem this kind of corruption is in the UK, or to what extent illegal immigration might be reduced if corruption were tackled effectively. However, a growing body of evidence suggests there may be a problem. This is much as you would expect: the risks of getting caught are low, while the rewards are high. It is rational choice theory in action. Let us look at a few examples.

*

In 2024, the BBC reported on the case of a Brazilian asylum seeker who was contacted by a Home Office official processing his claim. The official apparently suggested that 95 per cent of similar cases were refused, but a successful application could be guaranteed with a payment of £2,000. It would have been a rational choice for the asylum seeker to find the money and pay the bribe, but he reported the approach to the police and the official was arrested. We might assume this was not the first time the official had tried such a thing.

Meanwhile, at Gatwick Airport, a Border Force officer working in an anti-smuggling team was discovered to be passing confidential documents to an organised crime group to assist them in drug smuggling. The financial arrangements were not clear, but the police investigation showed that money was moving through her bank account on behalf of the drug traffickers.

In Portsmouth, a Border Force officer helped a London-based member of an organised crime gang to pass through his booth with fifteen kilograms of Class A drugs, showing how easily penetrable borders can be with the right inducements.

All three cases involved public officials acting corruptly, and organised crime was involved in two of them. For these criminals corruption is simply a means to an end, with a calculable risk–reward ratio. In most cases, we can assume that the risk of getting caught is fairly low.

We must remember that this sort of corruption is not just about asylum seekers desperate to establish a new life. Corruption across borders also has a link with human trafficking – people who are abused and exploited, often as modern slaves. A UNDP report in 2021 concluded, 'Of contemporary forms of slavery, cross-border trafficking is most prone to corruption ... Trafficking networks tend to build layers of protection within the institutions they are more likely to need.'[24] In other words, wherever we see modern slavery in this country, we should assume that border corruption is involved. But this is barely visible, in part because the parts of our system that deal with borders and modern slavery are not joined up.

In reality, the situation has been further complicated by part-privatisation. An analysis by the think-tank RUSI (Royal United Services Institute) reported that 'The range of personnel targeted speaks to the diversity of public and private sector actors with access to port information and infrastructure. Of relevance here are the changes witnessed over two decades in the form of deregulation and privatisation.'[25] Whatever benefits the involvement of the private sector may have brought, it seems to have muddied the waters in ways that make it harder to address borders-related corruption. There are blurred lines of accountability, creating gaps in the overall system that present an opportunity for OCGs and increase the risk of corruption. Different units with different ownership are not always required to liaise with each other, and it is harder to instil a public service ethos when the employees are employed in the private sector. As we have also seen in prisons, this can be reinforced when key performance indicators require one thing and good anti-corruption practice would require the opposite. Such KPIs are familiar in the private sector, and have been gradually introduced into the public sector since the 1980s in an approach called new public management. An example of the dichotomy they may reveal is where faster processing of an asylum inquiry would help meet the monthly targets, but slower processing would allow the immigration officials to determine whether there was an element of human trafficking or modern slavery.

How much of this corruption is actually going on in UK borders and immigration? Putting together figures from official reports and via a freedom of information request, we can see that the UK's two borders-related anti-corruption teams investigated about 100 cases of staff corruption in 2023, of which the majority were not progressed. By comparison, an anti-corruption hotline operating at the Metropolitan Police received 3,000 allegations of police corruption over sixteen months.[26] Border Force's official numbers for corruption seem worryingly low, and suggest that the systems in place are not picking up what is going on.

What we can see overall is a nexus of corruption vulnerability, organised crime and incentives for both paying bribes and demanding them. There is no reason to believe that the cases that have come to light regarding UK borders and immigration are exceptions or one-off rotten apples. As with the prison system, the default assumption should be that corruption is likely to be happening at a level commensurate with the risk. Think about it: if you are willing and able to pay up to £4,000 for a place on a small boat crossing the English Channel, why would you not pay slightly more to bribe a border or immigration official – or pay an all-in fee to the traffickers who can bribe or intimidate the officials on your behalf? In fact, the Home Office itself has described this as an optional 'sub-service' offered by OCGs.[27]

We are left with an unsatisfactory picture. This is a high-risk area, with proven cases of corruption and a response that looks distinctly inadequate; but the only data available suggest surprisingly low levels of corruption. It is almost inconceivable that this could be correct. We might reasonably expect that there are much higher levels of corruption, and possibly extensive collusion, as well as infiltration by OCGs, even if it has not yet been uncovered.

Police

We have so far looked at the risk of corruption in two uniformed services; the evidence suggests that corruption may be more widespread than is acknowledged. If we look at the police we see a slightly different picture, because corruption is much more widely acknowledged. Several books have been written about police corruption in the UK,[28] and there is plenty of research from both the UK and around the world. In fact, the problem is of sufficient concern that the Met's Department of Professional Standards has some 500 staff, to which were recently added over 100 more in a specialist Anti-Corruption and Abuse Command.[29]

Police corruption is so well documented that there are well-established descriptions of different types. The Knapp Commission, which investigated systemic corruption in the New York Police in the 1970s, coined the terms 'grass-eaters' and 'meat-eaters'. The latter were the corrupt officers who deliberately set out to find situations they might exploit for financial gain, while the grass-eaters were more opportunist, grazing on whatever chances for a bribe or pay-off might come their way. The police are also associated with so-called 'noble cause corruption', in which they break the rules by abusing their power to do something they think is beneficial for society – for example, planting evidence on someone they are certain is guilty of a crime. Another US police commissioner, Richard Pennington of New Orleans, coined the 15-70-15 rule.[30] He concluded that 15 per cent of cops were the driving force of corruption, while 70 per cent went with the flow and 15 per cent were clean. The percentages may vary, but there is a consensus that these categories reflect an average police force anywhere in the world. The key point is that police everywhere have a track record of corruption; indeed, police forces attract individuals who want to act corruptly; and those individuals have enormous entrusted power that can easily be abused.

The existence of police corruption in the UK is well established, but three big questions remain. First, are we talking about rotten apples or a rotting barrel? Second, are we only considering bribery or are we also looking at wider definitions of corruption?[31] Finally, given that most investigation has involved the Metropolitan Police, how typical is the Met of other police forces in the UK?

Ever since the A10 anti-corruption unit was set up by Met Commissioner Sir Robert Mark in the 1970s, there have been many cases, reviews and commissions. Operation Countryman, which investigated Met corruption in the late 1970s, remains so secret that the report has never been released. Speaking several decades later to the Leveson Inquiry, another Met Commissioner, Sir Paul Condon, said, 'Whether it's London or equivalent major cities anywhere in the world, there will always be a small number of police officers, sadly, who are drawn into corrupt criminal practice – and it can vary from relatively minor right the way up to the most serious criminal offences.'[32]

Reports from other investigations suggest that corruption involved more than a few rotten apples. The documents from Operation Othona into corruption in the Met in the 1990s were destroyed – and we do not know whether that was due to incompetence or a cover-up, or both. However, we know more about Operation Tiberius, an internal investigation launched in 2001 into the links between Met corruption and organised crime. This also remained secret until the report was leaked to the press in 2014; a heavily redacted version was subsequently published by parliament's Home Affairs Committee. It is now also available in full online.[33]

In this report, it was noted that 'The Tiberius team believes that organised crime is currently able to infiltrate the MPS at will' and the report seemed to confirm the allegations that the team was investigating 'endemic police corruption linked to major organised crime'. This story was originally written up in the *Independent* by journalist Tom Harper,[34] who recounts the many investigations into misconduct at the Met in his book *Broken Yard*.[35]

Some of these reports were into specific cases, notably the murders of Daniel Morgan and Stephen Lawrence. A secret internal report into the Lawrence investigation, which only came to light in 2023, confirmed long-standing allegations that a senior detective with links to the investigation and the subsequent cover-up was personally corrupt.[36] This was Ray Adams, who was found to have connections to the organised crime boss Kenneth Noye (who was involved in the Brink's-Mat heist, one of the biggest robberies in UK history, who went on to murder a policeman in his garden in 'self-defence' and was eventually imprisoned for life after committing a road-rage-fuelled murder on the M25). Adams and others were alleged to have used their internal influence to ensure that Stephen Lawrence's killers were not brought to book. The question of corruption swirled for years around the Lawrence investigations, and eventually a report was commissioned into 'Possible corruption and the role of undercover policing in the Stephen Lawrence case.'[37] This 2014 report, by Mark Ellison QC, found plenty of incompetence and misconduct – but concluded that 'the evidence fell short of making it sure that corruption or collusion had infected the initial murder investigation'.[38] It was controversial because the reason it reached that conclusion on corruption was that it had looked for a standard of criminal proof; whereas the civil standard of 'balance of probability' was applied to the question of racism. To a corruption analyst applying the latter standard to the Stephen Lawrence case, it is an inescapable conclusion that corruption was at play within the Met.

The report of the Daniel Morgan Independent Panel did find 'a form of institutional corruption' within the Met.[39] Morgan was a private detective who was murdered with an axe in a pub car park in Sydenham, south-east London, in 1987. The case reveals corruption at multiple levels. It was alleged that Morgan was investigating police corruption, particularly relationships between police officers and some newspapers (notably the *News of the World*), and that the murder was to silence him permanently as he got close to the truth. Subsequent reports found that the initial police investigation was deliberately misdirected and blocked internally to prevent the truth coming out. There followed a series of investigations and inquiries – six over the course of nearly three decades – which also faced non-cooperation, missing paperwork, surveillance and other attempts to derail them. Ultimately, despite sixty-seven arrests including those of eight police officers, nobody was held accountable for the murder or the serial cover-ups. The Met's official position as of 2022, responding to the report of the Morgan Panel, was 'We accept that corruption was a major factor in the failings of the first investigation, but we do not accept that we are institutionally corrupt as has been suggested. Nevertheless, we accept some officers may be vulnerable to corruption.'[40]

Unlike many of these reports, the Morgan Panel does not shy away from the subject of corruption: the terms 'corrupt' or 'corruption' occur 931 times in 1,256 pages and the report includes a 100-page chapter on police corruption. It is probably the most in-depth and insightful report into institutional corruption in the UK that has been published in the past century. Through a detailed forensic examination of documents and interviews with serving and retired police officers, the report reveals corruption both at the time of the murder and during the decades-long cover-up, and in relations between police and the press and organised criminals.

In both the Lawrence and Morgan cases, the corruption around the cover-up lasted longer and involved more people than the original corruption. The inherent cronyism of a close-knit community enabled this to thrive: confirming long-standing suspicions and allegations, the Tiberius Report noted that membership of the Freemasons was one element of this cronyism, as police officers put their loyalty to fellow Masons above their duty to serve the public interest.

Cronyism among the men in uniform does not need to involve Freemasons. Reports into scandals in both police and prisons regularly identify the risks of an internal culture where personal connections and contacts can lead to favouritism in recruitment, promotions, task allocations and even disciplinary proceedings, allowing loyalty to outweigh fairness and due process. The Casey Review of 2023 observed, 'A "boys' club" culture continues to play out across the organisation.'[41] Such things thrive in closed groups that have little accountability to the outside world.

To add further to the damning picture of Met corruption, we must consider the Spycops case,[42] a truly shocking example of the abuse of power. Between 1968 and 2010, the Met infiltrated a large number of environmental and political campaign groups with undercover officers, having decided that there was potentially a threat to national security – 140 officers infiltrated around 1,000 groups, including the Stephen Lawrence Family Justice Campaign. There may have been genuine concerns about national security, but the Met's response of mass and unaccountable undercover surveillance was disproportionate to the threats from such campaigners. The scattergun police surveillance might itself be considered an abuse of power, but what followed was even worse. At least twenty of the undercover officers had intimate relationships with campaigners; in five cases they fathered children with them, all while operating under their fake identities.

One of the most notorious was Bob Lambert, a member of the Met's Special Demonstration Squad who operated under the name of Bob Robinson and had an affair with five different women, including an animal rights campaigner known as Jacqui. He fathered a child with her, and then suddenly left when their son was two years old, inflicting lasting psychological harm on both mother and child, who were unable to contact him and never saw him again. They were left full of questions about why he had abandoned them and whether he would ever return to their lives, which were only answered when he was exposed in the press in 2012. This was fully known to his superiors at the Met, indicating there was collusion and he was not simply a rotten apple. When the son tried to gain compensation from the Met it was fought all the way, which only added to the pain and distress. Meanwhile, Bob Lambert had returned to other duties and been awarded an MBE for 'services to policing'.

Away from their undercover work, some of these officers had their own families; Bob Lambert himself was already married with children. The campaigners were entirely misled into having close physical relationships, deceived with the full knowledge of the Met's hierarchy. This was effectively state-sponsored sexual abuse. Despite this, the official inquiry (yet another one) found that it did not technically count as rape.

There are echoes of this attitude to sexual abuse in the murder of Sarah Everard in 2021 by the off-duty Met Police officer Wayne Couzens, who lured his unsuspecting victim into his car using his police ID. The tragic story of Everard, who was kidnapped and raped before being murdered, is a reminder that there are recent cases of corruption as well as historic ones – and that, despite corrective procedures having been apparently put in place, new cases of corruption arise all the time. Consider, for instance the so-called Sheriff of Soho, the nickname given to one Met sergeant who was responsible for vetting clubs and bars in London's West End between 2013 and 2015; part of his job was to recommend whether licences should be awarded, and to decide whether to prosecute when there were infringements. A corruption analyst would view it as a classic area of corruption risk; after all, this individual had a monopoly over decision-making and discretion about what decisions he would make. He was, it turned out, also eager to participate in corrupt schemes – and he was eventually jailed for serial bribe-taking. In return for ignoring breaches of licensing rules, and for helping certain security firms get lucrative contracts, he received a series of gifts including dinners, tickets for his mother-in-law to see the heavy metal band Metallica in Milan to celebrate her birthday, a made-to-measure suit, nights with call girls, a session with a dominatrix and a £7,000 family holiday in Morocco. What is perhaps most surprising in this case is that such an obvious corruption risk should have been allowed to go unchecked.

Another Met officer Kashif Mahmood (nicknamed Kash the Fed) also had a direct way of dealing. Working on behalf of an organised crime group based in Dubai, he would turn up in his police uniform at locations in London when he had been tipped off that drug deals were taking place and confiscate the cash that was being exchanged. Just like the Sheriff of Soho, luxury holidays were part of the reward from his Dubai masters, along with bundles of cash later found in shoeboxes at his house, and expensive watches. It was estimated that he had confiscated £850,000 during his fake police raids before he was prosecuted and jailed in 2021.

With investigation piling on investigation into the Met Police over the years, we come to the Casey Review. Along with the Angiolini Inquiry, this was commissioned to examine the culture that contributed to Sarah Everard's death. Baroness Casey concluded: 'Everyone within the Met also now needs to recognise that its failings go well beyond the actions of "bad apple" officers. My report makes clear that, on top of the unimaginable crimes of individuals and the shocking series of events that have hit the service in recent years, the way in which the Met has responded to them is also a symptom of a wider malaise in an organisation that has fundamentally lost its way.'[43] The message here is clear: this is not just a few rotten apples but a deep structural issue.

After so many corruption cases and lengthy reviews over the years, by the 2020s the picture of corruption in the Met was starting to look systemic, just as it had been in the 1970s. The Casey Review had little to say about corruption or organised crime, though much of its analysis was relevant to the issue. In particular, the report took as a central theme the question of the nature of police power and its abuse, and its disturbing finding was that some people apply to join the police in order to act corruptly: 'Policing needs to accept that the job can also attract predators and bullies – those who want power over their fellow citizens, and to use those powers to cause harm and discriminate. All of British policing needs to be alive to this very serious risk.'[44]

These multiple reports and investigations into the Met over the years give plenty of detail about cases like those of Daniel

Morgan and Sarah Everard, but, if you look at them all together, their conclusions on corruption are somewhat confusing. While they mostly agree that there is corruption, some say there is a rotting barrel while others prefer to follow the Met's own line that the problems are caused by a few rotten apples. The reports use a variety of definitions of corruption, some coming up with their own, and they sometimes reach different conclusions from the same set of facts. Those responsible for the reports are experts, but usually in fields other than corruption. When you comb through several thousand pages, containing plenty of contradictions and non-standard definitions, it becomes impossible to see the wood for the trees.

My own conclusion from these reports and cases is that there is plenty of evidence of systematic corruption in the Met as well as extremely dangerous links with organised crime at all levels of seniority. It comes close to structural corruption because of the scale and seriousness. This is not just about bribery; cronyism, sextortion, abuse of office and other forms of corruption are also at play. I am less inclined to describe the Met as institutionally corrupt because, although corrupt behaviour is widespread, it is usually based in criminality rather than a legal diversion of purpose as outlined by Lessig (in his definition of institutional corruption, as explained in Chapter One). If asked to choose between the description of the Met as rotten apples or a rotting barrel, I would unhesitatingly go for the rotting barrel.

What can be said in the Met's defence? Its commissioners (the person in charge) come and go, usually inheriting a legacy of scandals left by their predecessors and responding as best they can, while making tough statements about not tolerating corruption. But it is an unruly and sprawling organisation that has faced severe budget cuts while facing up to the challenge of maintaining law and order in one of the world's biggest cities.

The College of Policing launched a new 'Code of Ethics for Policing' in 2024, and the Met has expanded its anti-corruption team. Recently, the Crimestoppers hotline has introduced a facility specifically for reporting police corruption. These things make a difference, but perhaps the most important thing to realise about corruption in the UK police is that it is always there – and always will be, to a greater or lesser extent. We know that, around the world, the police are more prone to corruption than any other part of the state; we know that bad apples are attracted to the police, there are links to and infiltration by organised crime, and that in the UK previous efforts to stamp out police corruption have failed. Realistically, there is no possibility of eliminating corruption in the Met or any other police force of significant size; the best that can be hoped for is to reduce it to controllable levels.

There are well-known ways of doing this, including codes of conduct, training, whistleblowing procedures, internal investigations and the imposition of proper penalties. All those reviews were not short of recommendations; the issue is whether the political will exists to implement them. At the heart of this is the question of whether tackling police corruption is a high priority for the UK government. It means taking on vested interests, admitting that there are close links with organised crime and putting the resources and attention into a long-term strategy at a time when there are many short-term pressures like reduced budgets, low morale and staff retention difficulties. In such circumstances, it must surely be tempting to put in just enough effort to satisfy critics without going the whole hog.

These reports also talk usefully about the relevance of scale. They tell us it is important not to ignore the small things. Lax procedures and turning a blind eye to low-level acts of corruption, such as receiving a bribe for tipping off the press, create an enabling environment for a more widespread culture of corruption. So even though there is a large and continual challenge in tackling police corruption, getting the basics right is a good starting point.

Before moving beyond London, we must mention the notorious case of Derek Ridgewell, a racist detective sergeant from the British Transport Police in the capital who framed up to 100 innocent people in the 1960s and 1970s.[45] His egregious abuse of police powers ruined many lives, and he particularly targeted young Black men; many years later, as long after the events as 2025, thirteen of his victims appealed against their convictions, and in every case the conviction was overturned and they were finally declared innocent. His crimes may have occurred fifty years ago, but like so many cases of corruption have taken a long time to come to light. This case alone reveals the enormous power wielded by the police over the lives of ordinary and innocent people and the damage that can be done, literally for a lifetime, by the corruption of a single officer.

Our analysis of police corruption has so far focused on London and the Met, but how typical is it of the UK's forty-seven other forces? The police inspectorate HMICFRS has been conducting reviews of each force's anti-corruption systems, but they tend to focus on whether processes are in place rather than analysing the scale, prevalence and nature of corruption. Conveniently, there is a website called misconduct999.com that tracks cases of police misconduct – it has recorded 9,400 cases since it started in 2021. Among these there are dozens of corruption cases, and hundreds more categorised as misconduct in public office, perverting the course of justice or other offences which might also be considered as corruption.

A report on Corruption in the Police Service in England & Wales by the IPCC (Independent Police Complaints

Commission) in 2012 found that 8,542 corruption allegations against the police were recorded between 2008 and 2011, representing 5 per cent of all complaints from the public in that period. Such data must be treated carefully – these are allegations, and some will have been made by criminals trying to discredit the police who were investigating them, or from others who wanted to make a point. But there will also be genuine reports. What is also notable is that, although there were an average of thirty-three corruption complaints per 1,000 police officers/staff, these varied between forces from ten to sixty-nine complaints per 1,000 police.[46] In other words, some forces have a far better record than others.

Two recent – and randomly selected – examples from outside London are a detective sergeant from Warwickshire who abused his position of trust to have sex with a vulnerable teenage girl,[47] and a PC from Greater Manchester who sold confidential police information to a local insurance firm, which used it to create business opportunities.[48] These cases illustrate two common themes – sexual exploitation and misuse of information – which, along with financial gain (whether bribes, or profiting from misappropriating assets during searches and arrests) and colluding with organised crime, feature regularly in corruption cases both in London and beyond.

We do not know how deep or widespread the problem of corruption is across the police nationally. From the available evidence, the Met seems to be at one end of the scale, probably due to the number of personnel it employs and the strong presence of organised crime groups in London. However, forces outside London will also be vulnerable to bribery, cronyism, infiltration and the other problems that the Met has faced. Across the UK, the abuse of power by police officers for sexual purposes is a recurring theme: a 2012 report by the Independent Office of Police Conduct (IOPC) found that 'this behaviour is also a form of corruption and it should be dealt with as such'.[49] By 2024, the IOPC were referring to sexual misconduct as 'the most common form of corruption and poses the greatest threat to policing'.[50]

The Casey Review noted: 'the abuse of position for a sexual purpose is the most common form of corruption it [the IOPC] deals with. In 2020, this accounted for 25 per cent of referrals and almost 60 per cent of corruption investigations nationally. They also observe that the scale of abuse of position for a sexual purpose, and sexual misconduct, is likely to be vastly underrepresented.'[51]

This focus on sexual misconduct – a direct result of the cases from the Met and its various reviews – is one of a number of positive developments in the police anti-corruption approaches in recent years. We have been in a period where there has been a genuine attempt to do something about corruption, though only time will tell whether it makes any difference. We should also be a little wary: priorities can change according to the public mood and the concerns of the media and politicians. The threat of police corruption merits sustained long-term attention because when it takes root it can both threaten individuals and significantly undermine the rule of law, as Operation Tiberius revealed.

What does all this tell us about police forces nationwide? Well, we can see that there are rotten apples but, unlike in the Met, there is insufficient evidence to conclude that there is a rotting barrel. In some of the forces outside London, especially in areas where organised crime is prevalent or cronyism and weak oversight are part of the fabric, the situation might be more clear than in others. For the time being, we might consider the Met Police's own summary of the UK's National Threat

Assessment: 'UK law enforcement, including policing, is a high-risk sector for corruption … Corrupt insiders pose risks to the public, colleagues, the integrity, reputation and functions of their organisation, and policing as a whole.'[52] Like so many other areas covered in this book, our challenge in the UK is to make sure that the response is proportionate to the threat – and in the case of the police there is a significant and proven threat of corruption, which suggests there should be a significant response.

* * *

In this chapter we have looked at officials in prisons, borders and the police, three groups that have a great deal in common. They are all in positions of entrusted power – and when the power is abused, it has a direct effect on individuals and the rule of law. In the case of prisons and sections of the police, there is a rotting barrel; with regard to borders and other police forces, there are sufficient rotten apples to suggest there should be considerable concern.

The overall picture is of a deeply ingrained culture of cronyism and a mix of structural and transactional corruption. In borders and prisons, this is exacerbated by the fuzzy public/private sector interface, when the men in uniform serve two masters – the public interest and the shareholder – whose values may not always be aligned. However, we can also see some strong institutions, resilient checks and balances, and high personal integrity from individuals who are not paid very much and sometimes put themselves in considerable danger.

In my view, we should be concerned but not depressed. Think back to the New Orleans police chief Richard Pennington's 15-70-15 rule, in which 15 per cent of cops were the driving force of corruption, 70 per cent went with the flow and 15 per cent were clean. In the UK we might seek to change that to a 1-84-15 rule, in which just 1 per cent are driving corruption (they will never be entirely eliminated), 84 per cent are going with the flow and 15 per cent are clean (those with high integrity are always in the minority). The many reviews and investigations cited in this chapter are all at pains to point out that the majority of people in uniform want to do a good job and act in the public interest, although this has tailed off markedly with the three most recent reports on the Met.* All such reports do agree on one thing: we need an environment in which those in uniform are empowered to act with integrity, rather than one that ignores or even encourages corrupt behaviour.

____

*The Morgan, Angiolini and Casey Reports.

9

TWO SIDES OF THE COIN: THE INFLUENCING SECTORS

We have so far looked at several sectors and institutions in an attempt to build a picture of how and where corruption is happening within the UK. Politics, police and the private sector are fairly standard areas to include in such an analysis, and places where corruption might be found in any country. In this chapter we will look at something that is more particular to the UK: six 'influencing sectors', by which I mean sectors that have a significant influence on our society. When they use this influence positively it can promote integrity; when the influence is used negatively it can open the door to corruption. They are the media, social media, sport, religion, charities and academia.* And of course each of these sectors is vulnerable to being corrupt itself, which also sets a tone or a norm that can be damaging. These sectors or institutions are not exclusively British, but in several cases what goes on in them has a particular flavour or importance here.

It's perhaps a bit old-fashioned to talk about setting the moral

---

* My academic colleagues will fairly ask what research or methodology has been used to select these six; the answer is that as a professor of practice I have used the observation and practice of several decades to select them, but they are offered as a starting point for discussion, not a definitive framework.

tone for a country, but in my view that is what these influencing sectors can do. So when there is corruption within one of these sectors it has a ripple effect; and if the influencing message the sector transmits to society lowers the moral tone, then that can contribute to raised levels of corruption. Consider, for example, a newspaper that constantly supports a corrupt politician, over-looking or excusing their corruption while playing up other actions that the newspaper's owner views favourably. In such a scenario, corruption within politics gradually becomes normalised; opposition parties conclude that it is no longer politically worthwhile pointing out the corruption; and as standards get lower, so does their own behaviour. This has a knock-on effect in society. People become cynical about all institutions, assuming they are all more or less corrupt and can no longer be trusted. And if you assume everyone else is being corrupt, that is how you are more likely to act yourself.

There are two interesting strands of academic research that support this conclusion: on collective action and anti-corruption messaging. The literature on collective action – for example, from Bo Rothstein and the research team at the Quality of Government Institute in Sweden's Gothenburg University – suggests that individuals are usually reluctant to be the only one to call out corruption, because they themselves may then be targeted or inconvenienced – it's far easier to go with the grain.[1] So everyone may end up colluding in the corruption, not because they like it, but because they feel they have to. That means that, if some or all of the six influencing sectors in this chapter are normalising corruption, we can expect society's collective response to be that more people will act corruptly themselves or tolerate corruption in others.

The work by Nic Cheeseman and Caryn Peiffer has been transformative in how anti-corruption specialists think about the language of campaigns. Through studies in various parts of the world, they have found that talking about how bad corruption is does not tend to make people think they should help improve things; it actually encourages 'resignation rather than resistance'. A recent study in Albania looked at the link between corruption scandals and the rise of populism. It found that exposure to messages on the theme 'corruption is widespread' is associated with 'greater agreement with populist sentiments and beliefs'.[2]

The six influencing sectors in this chapter play a disproportionately important role in setting the nation's tone with regard to integrity and corruption, and where the bar of behaviour is set for both public figures and private individuals. Each of these sectors makes an important contribution to our social fabric. My underlying assumption is that any society is made up of a number of interlocking institutions and sectors. For a state to function well, a critical mass of those institutions needs to be working effectively; and for corruption to be kept in check, a critical mass needs to be operating with integrity. At any one time, some may be inefficient or failing, or they may be undermined by corruption; this matters less if the overall picture is healthy, and as long as there are mechanisms to address those bits that are underperforming. We can describe that ecosystem of parts working together as a 'national integrity system'.

For the influencing sectors outlined in this chapter, in each case the balance of influence could tip in either direction. It is as though a coin were spinning in the air for each sector, and it could fall showing either the healthy or the unhealthy side. There is no single controlling force that determines on which side the coin will land, but if a critical mass of those influencing sectors are unhealthy, we will have a problem.

The Media

We start our story of influencing sectors with the media, and look first at Fox News in the US. Owned by Rupert Murdoch and his family, it strongly promoted the candidacy – and subsequently the presidency – of Donald Trump. Fox News makes no pretence of offering objectivity or balance, because this has not been required by US broadcasting rules since that restriction was lifted in 1987. So are Fox News or its presenters corrupt, a claim frequently heard on social media? If we apply the four-step test, we can see private gain and arguably harm to the public interest – but no abuse of entrusted power. That is an important point to note because, as we look at both the media and other influencing sectors, we will see that they have power but not usually entrusted power – and so, despite the temptation to describe them as corrupt, it becomes hard to link that to any substantial definition of corruption. However, this does not mean the media is free of corruption; and, more importantly, it can play a central role in influencing the country's approaches to integrity and corruption – for example in normalising corrupt behaviour by politicians, as Fox News has done with Trump.

The Murdoch empire also has extensive interests in the UK, where ownership of the media is concentrated within a small number of powerful individuals or influential groups. Many of those owners use the platforms they own to promote their own viewpoints – none more so than the right-wing GB News, which is owned by a hedge-fund millionaire. These organisations certainly have power, even if not formally entrusted power: they have power to influence us, financial muscle, power to bend politicians to their will, and often the power of a monopoly over messaging. This itself rings some anti-corruption alarm bells.

A free and independent media is widely regarded by anti-corruption experts as being a key bulwark against corruption because it means those in power can be held to account. If they act corruptly, there is a greater chance that they will be exposed, and the sense of scrutiny is a deterrent to doing so. Looking over the pond to the way that the highly partisan approach of Fox News has failed to hold Trump to account for abuses of power, the UK is faced with a question about whether the concentration of ownership, and interventionist owners such as Rupert Murdoch or Paul Marshall of GB News, constitutes corruption. In my view, while this is bad news for society, it is not in itself corrupt. However, it does set up a potentially corrupt relationship with politicians.

Because they want to secure favourable media coverage, politicians may be incentivised to abuse their power by granting special favours or access to sections of the media. For example, they may try to neuter public broadcasters like Channel 4, which have long been disliked by the Murdoch empire. Politicians may also be tempted to relax rules on impartiality when they think this will win them support, or they may create an environment in which it is difficult for regulators to impose rules on impartiality – such as when MPs host current affairs programmes. Ken Clarke noted this power of the press when he said of Boris Johnson in a 2023 radio interview: 'The only people he was accountable to were the *Daily Mail*, the *Daily Express* and the *Daily Telegraph*.'[3] In the same vein, the journalist Anthony Hilton recounted a conversation with the notorious owner of the Fox media empire: 'I once asked Rupert Murdoch why he was so opposed to the European Union. "That's easy," he replied. "When I go into Downing Street, they do what I say; when I go to Brussels, they take no notice."'[4]

The relationship between our media and the police also has the potential to be corrupt. News organisations like to gain quick access to information others do not have, and the police are an excellent source. It is completely illegal, so sweeteners need to be paid or favours exchanged. And when newspaper editors or journalists do other illegal things, like phone hacking, they prefer their friends in the police not to look too deeply.

Paying bribes to the police for information or to overlook illegal investigative techniques used by reporters is out-and-out corruption. That has long been the charge against the Murdoch newspapers in the UK, and others such as the *Mirror*, particularly after the phone hacking scandal of the early 2000s. The scandal was such that a judge-led inquiry was commissioned to look into press behaviour. Lord Justice Leveson's 'Inquiry into the culture, practices and ethics of the press' reported in four volumes in 2012, and found 'there can be no doubt that, on occasion, there has been a significant failure of standards within and across parts of the national press'.[5] It was originally intended that there would be a second part of the inquiry, the remit of which was specifically to examine corruption, and especially the relationships between Rupert Murdoch's *News of the World* and the police.

But Leveson Part 2 never happened. Successive governments placed it on hold – accompanied by speculation that they had been persuaded to do so by the desire to retain the support of the Murdoch media empire. In 2018, Theresa May's government announced it would be too costly, and the final nail in the coffin was put there by Keir Starmer who announced in 2024 that, after so many years, Leveson 2 was no longer a priority. By any definition, many of the relationships highlighted by the Leveson Inquiry were corrupt; bribery of the police seems to have been rife in parts of the Murdoch empire, with unscrupulous editors and executives deeming themselves to be untouchable. One person who was eventually brought to book was Andy Coulson, former editor of *News of the World*, who subsequently worked as David Cameron's Director of Communications. Coulson was jailed for eighteen months, but other Murdoch executives, notably his long-term close associate Rebekah Brooks, managed to avoid the same fate.

As disturbing and unpleasant as that is, we should understand that this is not the norm in the UK media. The apparently widespread bribery by certain newspapers does not make the UK media systemically corrupt. The key takeaway from the Leveson Report is not that there was systemic bribery by journalists, but that media empires felt a sense of impunity because their influence was so large, which made them untouchable. But the charge of corruption will not go away, particularly in relation to the Murdoch-owned press. More recent allegations that up to 31 million emails were deleted by Murdoch's News Group in order to obstruct justice have been described as part of 'media corruption' – in this case by former UK prime minister Gordon Brown.[6] His underlying assumption was perhaps not that the media have 'entrusted power', but that the privately owned media have a duty to serve the public interest, a purpose that had been diverted towards the interests of media owners. It is a reasonable point of view, but we might also ask whether the nature of private media ownership has always meant there is self-interest in producing a newspaper or TV channel for public consumption, and that we should not expect media owners to be altruistic.

A further question is whether the influence of the media is not in itself corrupt but rather in some way 'corrupting'. For example, can the media contribute to a corrupt society if they back a corrupt politician at election time? Or, reflecting some of the academic work cited at the start of this chapter, if an outlet like the *Daily Mail* or GB News regularly implies that all politicians from mainstream parties and senior civil servants are corrupt, might that start to shift public mindsets so that people believe that the state and its representatives are basically corrupt, not much can be done, and you might as well join in and/or vote for radical alternatives?

From this we can see that there are several circumstances in which the media can be either corrupt or corrupting, particularly when ownership is exercised in a way that seems to be contrary to high editorial standards or the wider public interest. But there is another side to this coin: the media can also expose corruption and hold those in power to account. Despite the financial headwinds facing the traditional media of declining circulation and loss of advertising, the UK has an excellent record of investigative journalism and press plurality. This ranges from local news provided to fill a gap left by the decline of local newspapers[7] to the continued presence of mass-circulation broadcast and print news.

The staff cutbacks that accompanied those financial pressures had led to fears that investigative journalism might soon die out. Encouragingly, this has been replaced by cautious optimism following a series of superb investigative organisations that have made use of tech skills and open-source information. Stand-out examples are the way in which Bellingcat has investigated Russian oligarchs in the UK, and the work by the International Consortium of Investigative Journalists on the Panama Papers and other similar data sets. At a local level, the lack of scrutiny and accountability following the decline of local press has been filled by citizen journalists and niche local news websites. Good examples are Yorkshire Bylines and Shetland News, which give news coverage and editorial opinion in their local areas. These, of course, pale into insignificance compared to the scale and size of the BBC, which explains why it is so often attacked by media owners who want to challenge its dominance – and by politicians who want to challenge its narrative. To be clear, the BBC has also faced integrity problems and scandals – but unlike private media companies, it is fundamentally a public-interest organisation. From public-service broadcasting and impartial news to crowd-funded and volunteer-based citizen journalism, the public-interest media represent a very different face to the corruption of the *News of the World*. It is the other side of the coin: perhaps a bit fragile, but one of our success stories.

Social Media

Like the traditional or mainstream media, social media platforms are often regarded as having power as well as influence. If we take the abuse of power as central to our interpretation of corruption, then it follows that we should try to work out how that applies to social media. American political scientist Francis Fukuyama has succinctly identified a key aspect to this problem:[8]

> Many people have come to see the internet as one of the chief threats to contemporary democracy ... There is, nonetheless, a great deal of confusion as to where the real threat to democracy lies ... The real problem centers around the platforms' ability to either amplify or silence certain messages, and to do so at a scale that can alter major political outcomes.'

The concern is that social media acts as a conduit for those who lack integrity – like politicians and influencers who are peddling fake news or distorted realities – to reach out to a wider public, while at the same time undermining public confidence in institutions whose legitimacy relies on public trust, including those that form an important part of the country's anti-corruption defences. This gives the impression, sometimes stated explicitly, that such institutions, from MPs and judges to the royal family or the BBC, are corrupt. Meanwhile, politicians and others who are corrupt can use social media platforms and influencers to deny that they have acted corruptly while smearing their critics and building a platform of political support. As Fukuyama points out, this may not be new, but the scale at which it operates has allowed a merging of business and politics, and one effect is to give new impetus to political parties that are both smaller and more extreme. The effect on trust in democracy and the political status quo is not just speculative: a recent study in Canada, based on a survey of 4,018 respondents, found that people who get their news from the new media are more likely to think the state is corrupt than those who access news from the traditional media.[9]

Of the many concerns relating to social media in the UK, few have had anything directly to do with corruption. But the Brexit referendum came close to this, when Vote Leave, Leave. EU and Facebook were all fined for misuse of data – although Cambridge Analytica, which had been accused of much greater attempts at manipulation of the results, was found not to have done so. What this does tell us is that the UK is not immune to electoral interference linked to social media. This may not be corrupt in itself (though it breaks electoral laws and rules), but it can open the door to those who are corrupt and who will not refrain from using unscrupulous techniques in the pursuit of power.

The skilful use of social media by the MAGA Republicans in the US, which helped bring about a second Trump presidency, demonstrates this relationship. A US-based website tracks some of this, illustrating how MAGA supporters created a MAGA media ecosystem of podcasts, blogs, TikTok videos and other forums and platforms to amplify Trump's own messages, cast perceived opponents as enemies and normalise far-right thinking.[10] The US has also seen the politicisation of corruption on social media: the willingness on both sides to accuse political enemies of being corrupt on almost any grounds. Trump, for example, frequently uses his Truth Social platform to accuse perceived opponents of corruption, such as the 'crooked and corrupt prosecutors and judges' involved in legal cases against him, and the 'corrupt' Manhattan district attorney Alvin Bragg, who was leading an 'Election Interfering Witch Hunt.'

In sum, social media can facilitate and legitimise those who are corrupt, as well as undermining a country's institutional defences against corruption, and at times can participate in corrupt activities.

The flipside of social media is that it also enables greater transparency and accountability, which are considered key elements in the enabling environment for preventing corruption. For instance, e-government, the term applied to the use of digital technologies to deliver government services and engage with citizens and businesses, has provided plenty of data for individuals and organisations to scrutinise. Often such platforms increase transparency by giving citizens greater access to government information, and the results of such scrutiny are widely disseminated via social media. A good example in the UK is Companies House, where for a fee of £100 you can register a new company from anywhere in the world using an online form.

Extensive research has shown that UK companies are frequently set up as shell companies, with the sole purpose of disguising the corrupt origins of the funds. Campaigners have used social media to highlight where the Companies House rules have been broken, and this has created pressure to improve things. Global Witness and Spotlight on Corruption, for example, have highlighted serial mis-filings at Companies House over the years, and this helped persuade the government to tighten up the law in 2023 through the Economic Crime and Corporate Transparency Act. Graham Barrow, a financial crime investigator who runs a podcast called *The Dark Money Files*, has been a prolific poster on social media, sometimes exposing dozens of fraudulent company registrations in a single weekend. One of the strange anomalies he has highlighted is the registration of seven Hungarian zoos at an address in Anglesey, where the occupiers knew nothing about it.[11]

Social media has proven extremely useful in empowering 'citizen journalists', ordinary people who report on events, which has the effect of moderating the behaviour of those in authority or holding them to account when they have overstepped the limits. For instance, the death of Ian Tomlinson after he was beaten by the police at a G20 protest in London was captured on video, and suggested an entirely different version of events to the official police version of death by natural causes. Tomlinson was a passer-by, not a protestor, but was pushed to the ground from behind by a police officer targeting him with a baton and died of a heart attack after staggering away. The Met's initial response was that the police had no contact with him until the paramedics tried to save him; the police role was revealed shortly afterwards when the video emerged.[12] In a similar way, protest movements such as Black Lives Matter can gain traction that may be denied to them when they are not fully covered elsewhere in the media; and the shootings in early 2026 by ICE agents in Minneapolis were captured by citizen videos and posted online, allowing a record of events to emerge that differs from the official version. In general, social media has amplified the voices of anti-corruption campaigners, allowing information and opinions to be distributed with low levels of resourcing, and making cover-ups more difficult.

Sport

The highs and lows of watching sport give it an outsized influence on how people feel and behave. Just look at the sales of branded football shirts: when the footballer Lionel Messi moved to Paris Saint-Germain, over 830,000 club shirts were reportedly sold within twenty-four hours. This also illustrates how sport is more than just a competition played for fun; it's also big business, and gives profile and power to those associated with it. Some sports attract shady characters with big wallets, some have chronically poor governance, others (like boxing) are serially portrayed in fiction as having links with organised crime. All these sports have some key things in common with regard to corruption: the players can influence behaviour in society more widely, for better or worse; those who are in charge of a sport are responsible for setting and upholding rules and standards, and the fans' confidence in this might be undermined by corruption; while the vast increase in money related to gambling, broadcasting, sponsorship and rights has increased the corruption risk in many sports.

Almost all attention on corruption in sport focuses on either match-fixing or the use of performance-enhancing drugs. This rule-breaking is on the edge of what may be considered corruption – unless you consider athletes to be in a position of entrusted power. In some cases, there is straightforward bribery to fix an outcome. If the referee or umpire is the one taking the bribe, the corruption – abuse of entrusted power – is clear. If it is bribery of an athlete, the definition in the 2010 Bribery Act of 'improper performance of duty' seems to apply; the implication would be that professional athletes have a 'duty' to play according to a set of rules. Interestingly, no players or athletes have in fact been prosecuted to date under the Bribery Act, although agents and managers – who clearly do hold entrusted power – have been.

Looking beyond the action on the pitch, a case could be made that the financialisation of sport is corrupting, in the sense that matches end up being played for financial gain and not for any nobler reason. This seems far removed both from sport's amateur days and from its community roots. To my mind, describing sport as innately corrupt due to professionalisation and commercialisation is a tenuous argument at best; but it has a grain of truth, as the large sums of money involved in modern sport have opened the door to corruption in a number of areas. Around the world, there are corrupt owners of clubs seeking to 'sportswash' their reputations, corruption in procurement and construction contracts like stadium-building, rigged bidding for tournament and media rights, and the use of laundered money in transfer markets.

This is not just happening overseas. To take an example in Premier League football, the one-time owner of Manchester City, Thaksin Shinawatra, was convicted of corruption in Thailand after he sold the club. There may be many more dodgy owners than we know: a study from Manchester University in 2024 found that the true ownership of many British clubs is obscured through dozens of shell companies: 'these conditions make it possible for some people ... to use ownership structures to obscure the source of funds (which could be from illicit activities), the nature of particular transactions (which could involve violations), and the actual investors or owners of clubs (who may be unscrupulous actors looking to conceal their illicit funds or intentions).'[13]

Perhaps the most notoriously corrupt sporting body in recent times was FIFA during the tenure of Sepp Blatter. As president of FIFA for eighteen years until he was forced to resign in 2015, he presided over myriad corruption scandals, including allegedly huge bribes from Russia and Qatar to host the World Cup. More than a dozen FIFA officials were found to be or pleaded guilty when charged by the US authorities in 2015 for bribes or kickbacks totalling $150 million, although Blatter was never personally convicted. But these scandals neither halted the tournaments nor put off the fans. While there has been nothing in the UK to compare to that, most major sports have been plagued by some kind of corruption scandal, and some sports have experienced serial scandals: snooker, for instance, has had a long series of match-fixing scandals over the past three decades, involving both UK and overseas players, which culminated in lifetime bans for two players linked to gambling syndicates in 2023. They were among ten Chinese players banned for varying periods, including the 2021 winner of the UK Snooker Championship, Zhao Xintong.

What we certainly see in UK sport is that governance is generally poor. For example, when a cricketer of Asian background at the first-class county of Yorkshire accused fellow players and the club itself of racism, the resulting scandal revealed a lack of standard whistleblowing procedures, as well as a national governing body that failed to spot that it needed to step in when a major club was floundering. It took two years to launch an investigation, and the chairman resigned after acknowledging the club's failing, but also revealing that he had fought a battle with the board, which was unable to 'recognise the gravity of the situation and show care and contrition'.[14] Such governance is amateur and inadequate in a professional world. Why does this matter? It's actually quite hard to pin down. The United Nations, which has a division responsible for corruption because it is the subject of a UN Convention, attempted to do this in 2021:

> Corruption in sport affects the financial health of federations, clubs and athletes, and erodes public trust in and saps the societal impact of sports activities. The educative and ethical values of sport and its capacity to foster positive social change depend on the exemplarity of sporting role models and the credibility of sporting institutions. Therefore, corruption in sport is a matter of public interest because countries invest in sport and rely on it to promote health, educative and social benefits.[15]

In other words, although sportsmen and women can ideally set an example of how to play by strict adherence to a rules-based system, corruption undermines the financial health of sports, the positive role that sport can play in society, and trust in public figures and institutions. And as in all other spheres, poor governance easily opens the door to corruption.

For many fans, integrity takes a back seat to success. If their team is winning, values can be compromised. Premier League football has many examples of dodgy owners whose track record is overlooked when they bring money to a club. The controversial Saudi Arabian investment in Newcastle United is a prime example. Human rights organisations opposed it and argued that it would normalise a regime with a track record that included torture, extrajudicial killings and jailing political opponents; but the fans did not stop turning up – and they have since then been able to bask in their club's renewed on-field success.

So sport is a complex picture. While a sport and its athletes can have great influence, safeguards against corruption are weak and many governing bodies focus their efforts on keeping athletes clean rather than ensuring good governance. Fans are ambivalent about corruption; if the matches are entertaining or their team wins, that seems to outweigh the corruption – our national psyche can easily set aside moral qualms when it wants to.

Corruption in sport is not just an occasional occurrence. From skulduggery within governing bodies to links with organised crime and on-field fixing, there is no shortage. There have been scandals in cricket, football, tennis, snooker, boxing, horse racing, cycling, athletics and rugby, to name but a few. A Transparency International study in 2011 found that sport was regarded by the public as the second most corrupt sector in the UK – after political parties, and just above parliament.[16] And although fans will gladly overlook cheating, rule-breaking and the behaviour of their club's owners if they are rewarded with on-field success, the irony is that sport is also the poster child for a rules-based system.

There is a widespread acknowledgement, including among fans, that for a sport to work properly it must be clean at a basic level – with two sides competing fairly and there being an uncertainty of outcome. Professor Dan Hough, an expert on integrity in football, is clear that even the most passionate managers will acknowledge that the referees, officials and rules must be respected if the game is to work. For the sponsors and broadcasters, a game played without rules would not provide the spectacle that is required for commercial success. And just as any bad behaviour by football players and managers is reflected in the way the game is played by youngsters across the country, sport can also provide good role models when people with high skill and high integrity play by the rules. As Hough concludes:

'Embracing integrity helps football be a socially constructive force for good.'[17]

This encapsulates the role sport plays as an influencer: across society as a whole, sport can reinforce good or bad behaviour; it can normalise corruption or highlight the damage caused by corruption; and, at minimum, it reminds us that playing by the rules is ultimately in everyone's interests. Yet poor governance, ineffective regulation and failures of integrity have too often nudged the influence towards the negative rather than the positive.

Religion

Most of the influencing sectors in this chapter do not have entrusted power in the same way that institutions like the police do, but religion is in a different category. In part, that's because most religious leaders regard themselves as having power entrusted to them by God or some other higher power, and society tends to accord them special status. For those people who have faith, the Church and religious leaders hold an unparalleled position of influence. And typically, most religions – at least in theory – take a strong stance against corruption. Both the Bible and the Koran are unambiguous about this; in the former, the Book of Proverbs, which probably dates from around 900 BC, tells readers that 'The wicked accept bribes in secret to pervert the course of justice.'[18] If people with religious faith trust their church and religious leaders, we might therefore postulate that religious bodies must be a force for good in promoting positive values like integrity, and an anti-corruption culture.

But what happens if people lose faith in those institutions and leaders – particularly if they themselves have acted corruptly? Might we expect to see a loosening of moral standards within society if that pillar is removed? This loss of moral authority across many religions has become a severe problem, often due to serial corruption scandals. And these have been scandals of the worst kind – child sexual exploitation, accompanied by a long-term cover-up. We should be in no doubt that this is corruption. After years of stories trickling out, the curtain was drawn back by the Independent Inquiry into Child Sexual Abuse, chaired by Alexis Jay, which reported in several dozen volumes between 2017 and 2022.[19] This contains moving stories about children who were sexually abused by figures of authority in the Anglican and Roman Catholic Churches, as well as more or less all other religious groupings in the UK, including Judaism, Islam and Jehovah's Witnesses. In all of these, institutional denial and cover-up compounded the original crimes.

These were not committed just by one-off or marginal figures. Victor Whitsey, for example, was Bishop of Chester between 1974 and 1981. When one victim came forward in 2015 to reveal how he had been abused by Whitsey, it opened the door for others, and nineteen people in all disclosed their abuse by him, primarily in the 1970s and 1980s. They had been teenagers to whom he was supposedly offering 'pastoral care'. He was notorious for 'whole body hugs', a synonym for extended sessions in which he intimately groped children of both sexes while offering biblical phrases such as 'suffer the little children to come unto me'.

Not all such cases happened in the distant past. At the other end of the seniority scale was youth volunteer Timothy Storey from the Diocese of London between 2002 and 2007. After a history of having sex with the teenage girls he was supposedly looking after, he went to theological college to train for the priesthood. During 2008–9 he raped two teenage girls who had come into contact with him via the Church. He, at least, was convicted of these and other offences in 2016, and sentenced to fifteen years in jail. In other cases like that of Victor Whitsey, perhaps because of the aura of power around the individuals who are involved, allegations often only come to light or are investigated after the death of the perpetrator. This leaves an unsatisfactory outcome for all concerned – the alleged perpetrator has no right of reply, while the apparent victims are unable to secure justice.

Figures of authority in religious settings can indeed seem all-powerful: they have a cloak of moral integrity and so victims are easily lured into their grasp, and assume they will not be believed if they speak out. At the same time, the victims have often turned to religion or the Church because they are feeling vulnerable, which in turn means they can more easily be abused and silenced. We can see from these examples that figures of apparently high moral authority can behave corruptly, placing personal gratification above duty and responsibility – all while maintaining a public face of probity.

Loss of trust is not just a problem for the various branches of Christianity. Certain strands of Islam are perceived as intolerant of values such as equal justice for all, for example in their cultural attitudes towards women. This can easily lead populist leaders like Nigel Farage of Reform UK to express scepticism about whether Islam is a moral force for good: 'We have a growing number of young people in this country who do not subscribe to British values,' he says, speaking of young Muslims. 'In fact, loathe much of what we stand for.'[20] This has been exacerbated by the association in the popular press and social media of 'Muslim gangs' with child rape. In Rotherham, for example, gangs of predominantly Muslim men groomed over 1,000 teenage girls for rape and other abuses between 1997 and 2013. There was no evidence in the subsequent reports by Baroness Jay and Baroness Casey that religious leaders in the Asian communities had turned a blind eye to what was going on, but that narrative has taken hold on right-wing media platforms. However unjust it may be, the Islamic faith and its institutions have been tarnished by association.

We can see from the many volumes of reports into all religious groupings and denominations that religious leaders have acted corruptly, often with the complicity of their religious institution or community. The point here is that it is not just believers who feel let down by this corruption. It weakens the moral authority of religion, meaning that religious leaders who call for integrity are viewed more cynically and are more easily ignored, and people have lost trust in the role of those institutions in promoting good moral conduct. By their creed and codes, the UK's religions and religious bodies should be a bulwark against corruption, but the proven corruption from within has led to a significant decline in moral influence. Some of these institutions go back thousands of years, and have seen many ups and downs. Their ability to exercise moral authority is not irreparably lost, but recovery will be hard.

Charities

Charities – also known as non-profit organisations and NGOs (non-governmental organisations) – have played an important role in the global fight against corruption. They have provided research and campaigning, and groups like Transparency International – with around 100 national chapters, and responsible for producing the annual Corruption Perceptions Index – have become well known. Charity Commission surveys show that charities regularly rate among the sectors with the highest levels of public trust (doctors are generally higher, while politicians are at the bottom of the list).[21]

However, a few years ago there was a dip in this trust; a series of scandals within charities led to concerns that putting them on a pedestal may mean insufficient scrutiny and accountability. Such a lack of transparency and accountability can open the door to lax or unacceptable behaviour, and as a knock-on effect leads to public scepticism about the sector and charitable works more widely, combined with a concern that charitable funds might not be used as intended.

Perhaps the most emblematic recent instance of corruption within a charity is the Oxfam Haiti sex abuse case. The scandal broke in 2018, when public trust in charities was already in a period of steady decline. A team of aid workers had been deployed to Haiti by Oxfam after the terrible earthquake of 2010. Survivors were desperate for food, medicines and shelter, and Oxfam was among the organisations that sent teams to provide emergency relief – it had 230 staff and a budget of £70 million on the island. So far, so good – but some of those Oxfam staff were not so good. With little other means of earning a living, some of the desperate Haitians turned to selling their bodies for sex, and a few of the Oxfam workers proved to be eager customers. Even more shockingly, some of the 'prostitutes' were allegedly as young as twelve.

Although this scandal first came to light in 2011, it was not until *The Times* ran stories in 2017 and 2018 that the Charity Commission looked into the matter. The Charity Commission subsequently reported that nine Oxfam staff had been dismissed or resigned. The reports in *The Times* – not fully substantiated by the Charity Commission – were altogether more disturbing. One source said: 'They were throwing big parties with prostitutes. These girls were wearing Oxfam T-shirts, running around half-naked, it was a like a full-on Caligula orgy. It was unbelievable. It was crazy. At one party there were at least five girls and two of them had Oxfam white T-shirts on. These men used to talk about holding "young meat barbecues".[22]

Some of this had been covered in Oxfam's own internal report, conducted in 2011. However, just as the Church of England and the Catholic Church have found it painful to admit publicly to sex abuse scandals, the full story of what had happened in Haiti was covered up by Oxfam. Its CEO at the time thought it was better not to draw 'extreme attention' to it[23] – a huge misjudgement. I have always admired Oxfam, and the Haiti case seems to have been an aberration – but it reminds us that even those who are apparently on the side of the angels can act corruptly, especially when governance and oversight procedures are not sufficiently attuned to the risk. In fact, the word corruption is not mentioned once in Oxfam's or the Charity Commission's reports. It is cast as a problem of safeguarding rather than an abuse of entrusted power.

A final reflection on the Haiti case is that very little in the reports and press coverage focused on the victims. What happened to them? As in so many cases of corruption perpetrated overseas by organisations from the developed world, we do not seem to know.

Corruption in charities does not just take place overseas, as one recent story illustrates. The Captain Tom Foundation was set up in the name of a military veteran who, at the age of ninety-nine, won the nation's hearts during the coronavirus pandemic by raising money for the NHS through sponsored walks around his garden with the aid of a walking frame. This and subsequent publicity continued to generate funds, which went to the foundation. However, two of the charity's trustees, his daughter and son-in-law, manipulated the charity so that they could receive large personal gains; his daughter was paid a salary, and they awarded themselves a number of extra perks, including £18,000 for judging a competition run by the foundation. Even more lucratively, they kept for themselves the £1.47 million advance from Captain Tom's memoir and other books, despite their having been promoted on the basis that people buying the books were contributing to the foundation. They also applied to the local authority to erect a 'Captain Tom Foundation Building' in the grounds of their house, from which they would run the charity. This was subsequently discovered to be a spa for their personal use, and the local authority required it to be demolished on the grounds it had been built without planning permission. A Charity Commission investigation into all these issues found them guilty of misconduct, and they were banned from being charity trustees.

The relationship between charities and corruption goes beyond corrupt individuals or acts. The moral authority of charities means they can wield great influence, and this can be co-opted to support ideologies or causes that might otherwise lack credibility. The charge of exercising such an amoral and undemocratic influence is often levelled, for example, at the Tufton Street think-tanks.

When you stroll between St James's Park tube station and Parliament Square in central London, you are in the heart of the British political establishment. The route takes you past the grand townhouses of Tufton Street, and at number 55 you will find a series of organisations dedicated to promoting a right-wing view of the world. Organisations such as The TaxPayers' Alliance, the Adam Smith Institute, the Institute of Economic Affairs and the Global Warming Policy Foundation are associated with climate change scepticism, small government and free-market ideologies. Some of them are registered charities, which has proven controversial; their critics portray them as lobbying organisations on behalf of right-wing figures who exercise an undue influence on politics, the media and public discourse. But is this accurate?

It is hard to find out. Through meetings, donations and other connections that are known about, we can see close links between the Tufton Street organisations and a number of right-wing politicians, but effective lobbying usually goes on behind closed doors.[24] So perhaps if we look at where the money that funds these think-tanks comes from, that might help reveal what the intentions and motivations are. Who funds the Tufton Street organisations? Here, we draw a blank – they very rarely disclose who gives them money, irrespective of the amounts. These are secretive organisations, exploiting loopholes in charity law such as the use of offshore financial structures to hide their true donors while exerting a large influence on the public discourse. The US has demonstrated how well-funded right-wing think-tanks can shape policy, while also providing a roadmap for what happens when one of their favoured politicians comes to power. The best-known example is the Heritage Foundation, which in advance of the second Trump presidency produced an 887-page plan for many of the actions that he has subsequently taken, entitled Project 2025.[25] Many of those who have analysed the short-lived Truss government have concluded that British government policy at the time was effectively directed by a group of shadowy, and in some cases foreign, donors.[26]

Just as with the private sector, we may reasonably ask whether charities have 'entrusted power' and therefore whether these wrongdoings are corrupt. I would argue that charities and their trustees do have entrusted power – by virtue of being registered charities they are given specific responsibilities under charity law, which include being required to operate for 'public benefit', and they are often placed in a position of power over their beneficiaries. I think we can see two things going on in the cases of Oxfam, the Captain Tom Foundation and Tufton Street. First, it is clear that there can be corruption within charities and charity workers. This causes a loss of public trust in an area of society whose role is, in part, to hold those in power to account. Second, particularly with think-tanks and campaigning organisations, these can exercise influence on politicians, decision-makers, the media and the wider public. At best, this influence can help to create a more cohesive and fairer society; at worst, the influence of such organisations can spread messages and policies that suit the personal or ideological agendas of donors that are far removed from the public interest.

Academia

In a healthy society, there must be a group of people who have the role of questioning and analysing the policies, actions and assumptions of how the state is run. In the UK, these people are often found in our universities. Most academics are fiercely independent – and potentially dangerous to those who are in power. They can provide arguments and evidence that may demonstrate that a policy is failing, or that an alternative might be better. They can hold politicians accountable for decisions or statements they have made.

In the UK, we generally view universities as important in providing objective evidence, based on independent thinking. The other side of the coin is that they may be neutered or captured by those who fear independent thinking and do not want to be held accountable. This happened in Hungary, where Viktor Orbán gradually tried to tame the universities – to the extent that the Central European University was forced to move from Budapest to Vienna. In the USA, Donald Trump launched an assault on the university system within 100 days of returning to power. Ironically, he has used the notion of 'capture' as an argument for bringing US universities to heel. Many critics feel that his threats to withdraw federal research funding unless universities implement policies of his choosing represents an effort to capture them. He views them as having been already captured by woke-ism, and argues that he is liberating them from this capture. The US is not alone; in every repressive country, from China and Russia to Iran and Turkey, universities are tightly controlled.

In the UK, concern about another type of capture relates to where research funding comes from – and how that may influence the independence we need from our universities. There have been long-held concerns in the scientific community that medical research is being distorted by funding from pharmaceutical companies, which have a vested interest in certain types of research being carried out, and also in outcomes that support their commercial objectives. Likewise, the creeping influence of the Chinese-funded Confucius Institutes on campuses across the UK has caused concern. The institutes are notionally Chinese cultural centres, which offer services like language teaching and assistance with research collaborations. The Conservative MP Tom Tugendhat has asserted that they 'pose a threat to civil liberties in many universities in the UK'.[27] They have been accused of spying on Chinese students to keep them in line while they are studying in the UK, suppressing academic research into subjects like human rights abuses of the Uighur population and promoting Communist Party propaganda on subjects like Taiwan. Yet those universities that host Confucius Institutes have been reluctant to react to such abuses, for fear of jeopardising funding and the flow of students from China.

A team at Exeter University has looked into the question of how universities are funded, as they are concerned about the anonymity of donations to institutions and programmes. In addition to identifying the obvious propensity for reputation laundering, epitomised by attaching a donor's name to a grand project like the Blavatnik School of Government in Oxford, they found that £1.3 billion of donations to UK universities was of unknown origin. Although much of this will have come from alumni and UK-based philanthropists, universities are not obliged to reveal the source of their funds. The Exeter team estimated that, by 2020, one-third of UK university overseas funding came from China.[28] The secrecy, of course, creates opportunities for malign forces to exercise influence through the back door. Just as with the Tufton Street think-tanks, we are unable to find out who is trying to influence the influencers.

In other words, our academic institutions are becoming compromised. Their job in society is to question and analyse with independence and integrity, while teaching such values to each new generation of students. But we also see that anonymous overseas funding, particularly from China, has risks attached to it: the independent advancement of knowledge and understanding through research and teaching that should characterise university academics can be co-opted, chilled or captured.

* * *

Much of this book is looking at the notion of entrusted power, which naturally means shining a spotlight on traditional institutions such as the police or the monarchy. But the influencing sectors discussed in this chapter are also important.

Sometimes – as in the case of charities or religious bodies – they also hold entrusted power; sometimes they do not. When these influencing sectors themselves become corrupt – through either condoning or permitting corruption – the public loses trust in them and their messaging. The effect can be to normalise corruption, so people are no longer shocked by it; and to shift society's norms so that individuals and organisations may feel that corruption is the most sensible way to get something done, especially if everyone else is at it.

In all these influencing sectors, we can see the importance of good governance. For historical reasons, this is often absent or lags behind good practice – for example when amateur sport morphs into well-financed professionalism. But these six sectors are a key part of our national integrity system, and we need them to function well. It is equally important that regulators make sure these sectors are fulfilling their roles. We should in turn make sure that those regulators are fit for purpose and able to resist the culls on quangos that are periodically announced by all governments.

We must also recognise that, in all these influencing sectors, the situation is not static. To return to my earlier analogy, the coin is flipping through the air. Sometimes it takes a long time to land, while the tussle between integrity and corruption continues. Whether the coin lands on the side of integrity or corruption is not always a matter of chance. These sectors therefore represent both a challenge and an opportunity. If they are a positive force in society, that will help to keep a check on corruption. If they act corruptly themselves, or are a negative influence, they will normalise corruption, shifting the social norms and acceptability of corruption. While improved governance could increase good practice, vested interests often prevent this from happening. What strikes me is that in most cases the leaders

and key players in these sectors seem to be broadly unaware –
or unwilling to accept – that they may have a responsibility to
wider society. Plurality and integrity in the media, good sports
governance, religious groups that act with and promote morality, charities that act in the public interest, academics who are
able to exercise free speech – these are fundamental building
blocks of our national integrity system. As a nation, we have
often got much right in these sectors: but we need to be constantly vigilant that things do not go wrong.

10

LIFE BEYOND LONDON: LOCAL GOVERNMENT

In London, power is visible almost everywhere you look – from the grand public buildings of Westminster and Whitehall to the private empires of the City. Now it is time for us to take a look at life beyond London, to see where else power lies – and how it is abused. In particular, we will look at local government across England and Wales.

Let's start in Sussex, where I work at the university in the hills outside Brighton. This is in the Diocese of Chichester, a small city that can tell us a great deal about power dynamics and corruption in this country over several millennia.

Due to its harbour, Chichester was an important power base for the Romans, and the nearby palaces at Fishbourne and Bignor still give a glimpse of the wealth and luxury enjoyed by the Roman upper classes who settled here. The Normans, who came next, built the cathedral that dominates the view of the city from the South Downs. The highest point of those hills is an Iron Age hill fort known as the Trundle, which overlooks the rolling Goodwood estate of the Dukes of Richmond, who are descended from Charles II and one of his mistresses.

Thanks to these historical circumstances stretching back thousands of years, a small town of 35,000 people with no right to be a modern centre of power is the headquarters of West

Sussex County Council as well as the centre of the diocese. This, in turn, has led to the establishment of a world-renowned theatre, an art gallery of national importance, a military barracks and even the headquarters of Rolls-Royce. In microcosm, Chichester represents all the manifestations of power in Britain: a combination of military, Church, feudal, industrial and civic power, along with the soft power of the arts.

Was there corruption accompanying this power? Of course. A search of the County Record Office gives a snapshot of what local corruption in Chichester has looked like over the centuries. Just like in the UK of today, there are very few direct historical references to corruption in the county archives – but there are clues as to how it manifested in the provinces.

In elections, before the nineteenth-century Reform Acts, by long tradition two candidates from the two main parties were fielded for the two Chichester seats: a family member of the Duke of Richmond for the Tories, and a Whig candidate representing the interest of the city. They would each freely dispense alcohol and other 'treats' to buy votes; in the 1826 election, £6,800 was spent to persuade the 800-strong electorate – around £1,000 per voter in today's money. In the 1830 election, Charles Cullen, a Radical candidate, stood against them on a platform of 'Purity in Elections'; he refused to give out gifts and lost the election while being accused of 'saving his pocket'.[1] A memorial plaque to him in Chichester Cathedral remembers him for 'energy in the cause of freedom and the most inflexible integrity'.

A few yards away on the cathedral wall, a memorial from 1802 remembers a local lawyer, Alderman Francis Dear, who 'acquired the enviable reputation of unspotted integrity'. In his will, among numerous bequests to servants and family, he left money to Robert James of Selsey, 'well knowing him to be an honest man incorruptible'.

In these sketches of Chichester life we can see the contrasting themes of some individuals with high personal integrity and others content to go with the grain of political corruption. This did not entirely vanish with the clean-up of public life in Victorian times. After the Second Reform Act of 1867 Chichester had just one MP, and the seat was held continuously by the Conservatives until 2024 (apart from a year given up to the Liberals in 1923). Then, in the general election in 2024, the theme of corruption made a comeback: the Liberal Democrat candidate Jess Brown-Fuller won the seat with a big swing, promising to make 'tackling corruption' one of her priorities – a riposte to the Conservative governments of the past few years.

This glimpse of a single prosperous city in southern England tells us a great deal about current and historical corruption in the shires and the power centres outside of London. We can see the same path dependency here – how those who have power and money retain it, supported by long-standing traditions and institutions. There is a tolerance of corruption, which would later be controlled by legislation. And there are some individuals who stand out for their integrity, supported by a minority of their fellow citizens.

Chichester is only a medium-sized town, called a city because it has a cathedral – and in the big cities, the corruption risks are magnified. There are vast amounts of public funds at play – Birmingham City Council, for instance, has an annual budget of £1.2 billion. Historically, some of the UK's most widespread corruption has been in our large cities. Historian Peter Jones has concluded that in many of them there has been 'a diffuse complicity between politicians, businessmen and public officials that created a culture of secrecy and collusion. In such circumstances, public goods can often be regarded as private property ... and the cultivation of loyalty and support is derived from the exchange of favours which may be gifts disguised as loans or may be bribes or tribute'.[2]

In particular, the long-term dominance of a single political party in local government can create a culture of impunity. This is what seems to have happened in Liverpool under the tenure of Joe Anderson, the mayor of the city between 2012 and 2020 – and a councillor since 1998. We know a bit more about this case than usual; the police launched Operation Aloft after allegations of fraud, bribery and corruption, and the government commissioned a statutory inspection, which reported in 2021.[3] This report noted a culture of intimidation in the Regeneration Directorate, the council unit responsible for urban development that was a centre of the allegations, and media reports quoted staff as saying, 'you did what you were told'.[4] Such situations often arise when dominant local figures have been in power for a long time and come to believe that they should be allowed to do whatever they want – often while at the same time believing they are doing it for the public good.

Anderson was arrested in 2020, alongside his son David, well-known local figure Derek Hatton and a local property developer. Eventually, twelve people in total – all of whom pleaded not guilty or protested their innocence – were charged with offences related to bribery and misconduct in public office. The government report examined historic property transactions and highway and building maintenance tender appraisals, particularly in the Regeneration Directorate; it found a litany of poor governance, bad record-keeping, staff turnover, sidelining of internal audit processes and transactions that did not represent value for money. Even without any proven corruption, it is a story of things having gone badly wrong. But where was the corruption? Several people were charged with bribery, and press reports have suggested that there was bribery and cronyism in the allocation of maintenance and construction contracts, and in the buying and selling of council property. This affected some of the city's larger regeneration projects, including the Liverpool Waterfront. It was alleged that councillors, council officials and property developers had all gained a financial benefit from these corrupt deals. The press reported that at one point Anderson and Hatton were also arrested for witness intimidation.

For several years, Anderson – who resigned as mayor in 2020 – had the charges hanging over him. His defenders claimed that he had been good at getting things done, implying that cutting a few bureaucratic corners was a worthwhile trade-off. This case tells us a great deal about the potential for corruption in local government. The fact that it is hard to investigate and prosecute corruption even after a highly condemnatory independent report suggests that the anti-corruption laws are not fit for purpose; it is difficult to reach the evidential threshold required for proving corruption has taken place even when there is evidence of other wrongdoing. In addition, the length of the police investigation suggests they are not well equipped to investigate corruption – and intimidation can both make corruption more likely to happen and reduce the likelihood of witnesses being willing to turn whistleblower or testify. We can also see that the relationship between councils and the private sector creates scope for cronyism, while big budgets create big temptations. And we should not ignore a factor that has seen corrupt leaders being re-elected around the world: if they seem to be getting things done, voters will be happy to forgive them.

Those themes of intimidation and corruption also feature in the notorious case of Lutfur Rahman, the mayor of Tower Hamlets. After a hearing at the election court in 2015, he was found guilty of corrupt and illegal practices including bribery of voters, treating (giving out treats to win votes, like in the Chichester election of 1830) and 'general corruption', as well as bribery and electoral fraud.[5] This was combined with intimidation, smearing his white opponent as racist while himself exercising 'undue religious influence'.[6] In fact, anyone who spoke against him was branded as racist, and some of them had their businesses attacked and their vehicles damaged.

The successful silencing of criticism was carried out by an unpleasant henchman. Commissioner Richard Mawrey QC was particularly unimpressed by him: 'He was arrogant, indeed cocky, and did not hesitate to tell bare-faced lies in the smug assurance that the mere lawyers listening to him would not have the wit to see through them.'[7] This intimidation enabled a culture of impunity to spring up. Rahman embedded his power and exercised it ruthlessly. As the commissioner noted, 'To a large extent, the criticisms of Mr Rahman as an autocrat are well founded ... This power is consolidated by the fact that his cabinet has been chosen from his close cronies, some of whom, it must sadly be said, have little to recommend them beyond blind loyalty to their leader.'[8]

Among the examples of bribery, Commissioner Mawrey noted Rahman's payments to the media to gain favourable coverage – in one case he paid £20,000 to a journalist from a TV station that broadcasts to the Bangladeshi community in the UK. The report described how this worked: 'Mr Rahman caused the Council to pay public money by way of "fees" for broadcasts which were ostensibly about the Borough and its administration but which were in fact personal political broadcasts on behalf of Mr Rahman, promoting him to the Bengali-speaking electorate of Tower Hamlets. In the context that Mr Rahman fully intended to stand for re-election when his first term of office expired, the broadcasts cannot be regarded as other than intended to promote his political career ... It was undoubtedly corrupt ... Mr Rahman was guilty of bribery.'[9]

Rahman was banned from holding public office for the maximum period of five years and struck off from acting as a solicitor. But he was not finished: when his five-year ban was over he stood again, and was re-elected as mayor in 2022. His strong power base among Bangladeshi and Muslim voters valued his support for their communities more than they were put off by his corruption. In fact, through the handing out of grants and favours, many had benefitted from that corruption. Commissioner Mawrey's ruling revealed: 'enormous sums of public money had been paid ... in many instances, to organisations that had not even applied for grants ... [for] example, grants totalling just under £100,000 were handed out to ten organisations, all Bangladeshi or other Muslim organisations, for lunch clubs when none of them had even applied for a grant.'[10] Meanwhile, as millions in council funds were channelled to organisations personally selected by Rahman, often against the advice of neutral council officials, other organisations, like the local branch of the Alzheimer's Society, had their funding reduced or withdrawn.[11]

Rahman's reputation among those who supported him was for getting things done, sorting out problems like housing and being their strongest advocate in the corridors of power. But by 2024 he was in trouble again: the government had ordered a special inspection as allegations of new corruption arose. The resulting independent report did not paint a pretty picture: a toxic culture of patronage, a lack of transparency, weak governance and the exclusion of women. In fact, it found that Rahman and his cronies were trying to turn the clock back: 'We consider there is a culture of patronage in the Council. We have reviewed a series of case studies relating to several officer appointments and procurement decisions which in our opinion can only be described as being based on patronage and a desire to return the Council to the arrangements in place in 2014.'; 'We believe that there is evidence of weak governance in the Council.'; 'A number of female councillors raised concerns about being shut down, or not being given the opportunity to speak.'; 'The council must strive to work in a more open and transparent manner.'[12] The government responded to the report by appointing three special envoys to monitor the situation. By December 2025, little seemed to have changed; an audit by Ernst & Young found ten governance deficiencies and reported the 'absence of an effective internal controls environment to safeguard public money'.[13]

The case of Lutfur Rahman, who was re-elected as mayor in May 2026, is one of a local politician with a strong power base using corruption to gain and consolidate power. He was held to account because the courage and persistence of a small number of local residents forced a hearing by the election court, but we should not count on that happening everywhere. What other mechanism might have done this?

We end the story on a melancholic note. The Mawrey Commission mentions a whistleblower, Deborah Cohen, who was one of the council officials responsible for ensuring grants were properly awarded. She gave a full account of how Rahman and his cronies had overruled the advice of council officials and broken the rules. Her identity was kept anonymous at first, but it was soon revealed by someone who felt more loyalty to their ethnic group than to the principles of whistleblower protection. Mawrey reported: 'Though Ms Cohen, as a whistleblower, could hardly be sacked, her life was made intolerable and, in September 2014, having assisted the inspectors to the best of her ability, she left for Cambridgeshire.'[14] It takes guts to go up against people who hold power; and too often we let down those who display such courage.

* * *

I first met Derek Elliott when he visited the offices of Transparency International. He was an imposing man with a passion for local government audit – not something many people find interesting, but Derek thought it was part of what makes this country great. I might have stifled a yawn as he told me about it – but as his story unfolded, I began to think it might be more important than I had realised.

Derek had worked for several decades at the Audit Commission, the government body responsible for auditing the UK public sector, including local authorities. Such audits provide a neutral, objective opinion about whether public money has been properly spent. The mission statement was simple: 'The Audit Commission's role is to protect the public purse.' It also had an unrivalled remit to look for corruption, and Derek had been in charge of its Governance and Counter Fraud unit.

Looking closely at cases of fraud and corruption sometimes made the Audit Commission enemies. Derek himself had many years before been involved in the clean-up at Conservative-run Westminster Council after the party grandee Shirley Porter was found to be rigging the allocation of social housing to gain votes. This was exposed and pursued by the Audit Commission.

When David Cameron's government decided in 2010 to abolish this body as part of his so-called 'bonfire of the quangos', it found few friends to speak in its favour – although one witness before the parliamentary committee noted the 'suspicions of score settling and lobbying', and the decision was opposed by the ACCA, a leading accountancy trade body.[15]

It was Derek's deep concern about the plans of the Secretary of State for Communities and Local Government Eric Pickles to abolish the Audit Commission that brought him to the offices of TI. He freely admitted that the Audit Commission was not perfect but told me, while trying to hide his emotions, that public audit had existed in the country since Victorian times, having been established by Gladstone in 1866. This country's system was the envy of the world, and now it was due to be split up and privatised.

Even if the Audit Commission itself was to be abolished, Derek could not see why the system of public sector audit needed to be weakened. His worry was that, if audits were carried out less thoroughly, fraud and corruption would thrive. The specific remit of the Audit Commission to investigate corruption would be made optional. This did indeed seem serious, and a TI report at the time reached a damning verdict: 'Overall, we conclude that the corruption risk for local government in the UK has increased ... We may not see the consequences for a decade. However, a lesson Transparency International has learnt across the world is that it is better to take notice of emerging risks and to act early, because once corruption takes root it can be very hard to eradicate.'[16]

After being rapidly wound down, the Audit Commission closed in 2015, shortly after the Standards Board for England, another quango that was also culled to save money. A decade on, we are able to assess whether the warning from TI proved correct – and it is a depressing picture. It is very hard to know definitively whether corruption has got worse, because nobody is now looking for it. Along with the loss of the Audit Commission's investigative function, there is no longer any centralised data collection, nor any organisation whose remit is to look for corruption. The entire system that was designed to protect the public purse lies in chaos. By 2023, hundreds of local authorities had not even managed to have their accounts signed off – the process by which the auditor agrees that nobody has cooked the books. There were 520 council audits outstanding in 2023, and even cases with the reddest of red flags, like the Teesside Development Authority – examined in more detail later in this chapter – were not being probed by the auditors for corruption because it was not within their remit.

A report in the *Financial Times* on the new era of privatised audit noted: 'this market failure, which has been worsening for five years, eliminates a vital check and warning system on the £100 billion that local authorities spend each year'.[17] The consequence of the lack of basic oversight over local government finances was not just a rise in corruption, but in weakened financial management overall – symptomised by the bankruptcy of Birmingham City Council, followed shortly afterwards by several others. When Eric Pickles abolished the Audit Commission, he promised parliament that 'an army of armchair auditors'[18] would use the power of inspection to look over local authority accounts, helping keep everyone honest. Yet research by Ben Worthy of Birkbeck College has shown that 'most councils get zero inspections'.[19]

Each council, at least in theory, has a monitoring officer (MO) whose job is to check that standards are being upheld. Yet again, it is a picture of inadequacy and decline. A 2023 report from Lawyers in Local Government and the Local Government Information Unit found 'some have reported a steady undermining of their status and position within their local authority … MOs often find themselves in difficult situations whereby they are exposed to personal intimidation or other forms of unprofessional behaviour if they take a stand on enforcing legal norms within the council. Many report stress and absence from work while some have even left the sector altogether as a consequence of poor behaviour that has gone unchecked.'[20]

The lesson here is simple. We have some strong institutions, but we weaken or abolish them at our peril. Corruption thrives in the absence of transparency and accountability. It was a mistake to abolish the Audit Commission, which will have cost the country many billions of pounds in fraud, corruption and inefficiencies over the course of the past decade – perhaps several tens of billions of pounds in total,[21] compared to the Audit Commission's annual budget of £210 million.

There is a further lesson, which we have seen elsewhere: if you do not look for corruption, you will not find it. There are many people and companies who would prefer corruption to remain hidden; the Audit Commission was unique in its remit to investigate local authority corruption – and it is sorely missed.

A recent example of this concerns the Teesside Development Authority. This centres on the redevelopment of a huge piece of land on the banks of the River Tees into a freeport (an enterprise zone with lower taxes, an idea introduced by the Johnson government). The 4,500-acre site, which had previously been home to the Redcar Steelworks and other industrial plants, was awarded over £560 million of government funding, and the private developers pocketed around £51 million in dividends and fees while the project's risks and liabilities were left with the public sector. Most unusually, the developers were also granted an option to buy the land in future at a cost of £1 per acre, which meant they could make huge profits if the value were to rise off the back of the freeport's success, but would have limited liabilities for things like clean-up or site maintenance if the plans were to fail. The developers had no obligations to make investments. Both *Private Eye* and the *Financial Times* rang numerous alarm bells about secret deals and the closeness of the local mayor to the property developers; it was, by any standards, a huge amount of public money to be transferred to private developers, while it was unclear what value the public were getting in return.[22]

This all prompted the local MP Andrew McDonnell to claim in parliament (under the convention of parliamentary privilege, meaning that he could not be sued for slander) that there was 'industrial-scale corruption'. The pressure mounted and Michael Gove, the relevant government minister, felt obliged to launch an independent review in May 2023, following – as the terms of reference (TORs) stated – 'allegations of corruption, wrongdoing and illegality'.[23] The results of the rather shoddy investigation are examined in a later chapter, but even that brief and inexpert investigation was strongly critical of the project's governance and produced twenty-eight recommendations for improvements around governance and transparency.

What we can see at Teesworks is symptomatic of much corruption in local government – there is secrecy, poor governance, conflicts of interest, the revolving door and barely restrained cronyism. By any measure, it is offensive to notions of fairness that wealth on such a scale, particularly in one of the poorest parts of the country, should be transferred to private developers from the public purse. The investigation commissioned by Michael Gove unsurprisingly failed to find direct evidence of corruption because it did not look very hard. But clearly on display is a systemic unfairness, and a gaming of the system to favour certain vested interests, that looks to many people like corruption. The Labour government decided to have another look at it and issued a 'best value notice' in April 2025, enabling monitoring from Whitehall about future dealings. But it held back from launching a proper investigation into past dealings by the National Audit Office, apparently because it was concerned this would deter investors. This is a conundrum: the area certainly needs investment, and investors tend to be put off by corruption investigations; but if there was corruption it will now go un-investigated and unpunished.

There are many lessons to be learned from the Teesworks case, not least about the complete lack of local authority audits on corruption since the abolition of the Audit Commission. Without such a body, looking for cases of corruption in local government is hard work. It requires trawling through the local press, court cases and council records, often for offences that have been mislabelled; more often than not, even well-founded allegations go nowhere when the police or Crown Prosecution Service decide there is insufficient evidence to justify a prosecution. Corruption that is harmful but not provably illegal simply slips through the net.

A further complication for those trying to work out how much corruption exists is that the government generally lumps fraud and corruption together in official documents, and then focuses on fraud. For example, in a 2020 review into the risks of fraud and corruption in local government procurement, every case study was of fraud rather than corruption.[24]

In 2014, however, a report did come up with a plethora of case studies illustrating how corruption happens in local government.[25] But, as we have seen in previous chapters, the report also posed a dilemma:

A notable feature of researching this report has been the lack of agreement among the many experts we consulted about the scale and prevalence of corruption in UK local government. Some argued that the cases that have come to light represent the tip of the iceberg. Others felt equally strongly that the relatively small number of obvious corruption cases, and the fact that they had often been exposed by the existing oversight structures, was a sign that there is in fact no iceberg.

This report was published by Transparency International – and as its editor, I was dispatched to speak to the relevant government minister. We had asked to speak to Eric Pickles as Secretary of State but he was unavailable, so I met with a junior minister who was subsequently knighted and would briefly become Lord Chancellor. In our meeting, he could not have been more dismissive of the issue; he seized on the fact that we did not have hard and fast proof of widespread corruption and was firmly in the 'there is no iceberg' camp. He mounted a defence of abolishing the Audit Commission, which left me in no doubt that he felt it was a useless body and a waste of public funds. In some meetings with government ministers, I have had the feeling that good research may cause them to rethink what is being done. In this case, there was simply denial of the possibility of a problem.

Yet there are two particular areas that come up time and time again as being problematic for corruption in local government. They are not the only areas of risk, but they feature in many of the known cases of local government corruption. These two areas are procurement – when local governments buy goods and services – and planning decisions. Some of these cases reveal a great deal both about how corruption happens in local government, and the structural flaws that enable it.

Let's take first the issue of planning. As we saw with the example of Joe Anderson in Liverpool, the combination of embedded power, local networks of councillors, officials and business leaders, and the sums of money involved, means that the areas of planning, property and development carry a high risk of corruption. It is an area where the power of the public sector to make decisions that affect an entire community interacts with the power of private sector money. We have to be careful about applying the term corruption here, as everyone feels strongly about buildings being put up in places where they feel they should not go or whether new developments are attractive or ugly. So there is a strong temptation to call planning decisions corrupt whether or not that is actually the case, because it seems a sensible explanation for how the planners could have made such a bad decision. But it is also the case that fortunes can be made from property development, and decisions can be either taken or influenced by a small number of public officials – typically a planning officer or a group of councillors. That monopoly of decision-making is a corruption red flag.

Prior to the Town and Country Planning Act of 1947, you could build whatever you wanted on land that you owned. From that date onwards, planning permission was required – and if granted, the value of a piece of land could instantly increase enormously. According to a former adviser to Number 10 in the Cameron years, 'the incentive for corruption among low-paid officials and councillors is overwhelming ... lucrative planning decisions depend on back-room access to local bureaucrats and councillors.' This, he claimed, was 'a recipe for rampant corruption' – and indeed there is 'endemic sleaze'.[26] He noted that the revolving door between planning departments and developers meant that inside knowledge was used to bypass the checks and balances, leading to decisions typically being skewed in favour of large developers. It is a plausible argument, but difficult to substantiate in the absence of hard evidence. In fact, it was fiercely rebutted by the chair of the Planning Officers Society, who pointed out: 'In my long career I have not come across the conditions or types of incidents he describes. The system is set up to ensure that the person dealing with the planning application and formulating the recommendation is always different from the person (or committee) who makes the decision. That's why actual incidents of corruption in planning in this country are not a feature in our news, despite the clear potential for it to be so.'[27]

The American political scientist Robert Klitgaard constructed a formula for this kind of eventuality – and, while it was widely critiqued as being overly simplistic, it is very relevant in circumstances such as this.[28] The Klitgaard formula was $C=(M+D)-A$, meaning 'Corruption equals monopoly (whether one person or a small group of decision-makers) plus discretion (being in a position to make a decision based on their own judgement) minus accountability (the absence of transparency and scrutiny that may temper their decisions)'. Applying the formula allows an assessment of the corruption risk, even in the absence of hard evidence.

The formula suggests that, if we want to reduce corruption in planning, we should increase accountability while trying to reduce the number of monopoly decision-makers and their reliance on discretion. The problem is that those things can result in good judgements as well as bad ones, and they can increase the speed with which decisions are made; while it is important to get the basics right, we need to be wary about adding so many institutional checks and balances that nothing gets done.

In 2020, Transparency International ranked fifty councils according to how well their systems stacked up compared to good practice.[29] TI was assessing the 'corruption risks in local government planning', and the councils were placed in six bands labelled A to F, though no council was good enough to be in band A or band B. Eight of the fifty made it to band C, and thirty-eight others scored less than 50 per cent. It paints a grim picture of how well prepared local councils are to head off corruption in planning.

And indeed, the system sometimes goes wrong – someone accumulates too much discretion and at the same time accountability is lacking. This can happen very easily at a local government level, when everyone knows everyone, people can occupy influential positions for many years, budget cuts have reduced staff capacity and theoretical checks and balances such as the public turning up to watch council meetings simply do not happen in reality.

A particular feature of corruption risk in local government is conflicts of interest, which happens when someone in a position of power – say, a council planning committee chair – is placed to make a decision from which he or she or someone associated with them will benefit. While that would seldom mean something as blatant as granting themselves permission to build their own house, they might have a business relationship with a property developer who would later give them a contract for some unrelated work, or it may be that a planning officer nearing retirement could later be employed as a consultant by the construction firm they helped while at the council.

This all means that there can be some real abuses of power. One of the best-known happened at Anglesey Council in Wales. It looks like a classic corruption case, but we should describe it with frequent use of the term 'alleged' because a police investigation failed to find evidence of misconduct and no prosecutions resulted. It did, however, result in councillors being stripped of their powers in 2011 after an investigation by the Welsh Audit Office, when a special commission was appointed to run the council.

What happened was a conglomeration of bad practice in several areas, which allowed the personal enrichment of many of those councillors – and it shows how easily powerful local individuals can manipulate the system in their own favour. Apart from the ploy of voting to give themselves a 'special responsibility allowance' worth around £10,000 per annum, one of the many scams the councillors had in operation took place in the planning committee. It was alleged that the committee would deliberately reject planning applications, with the intention that the councillors would then buy the rejected land for a low value and grant themselves planning permission to develop the plot. Other councillors granted themselves permission to build houses on green belt land, despite rejecting similar applications from the public.

Interestingly, part of the picture in Anglesey was a breakdown of local democracy, which is supposed to provide the ultimate accountability backstop. Most of the councillors had been elected as 'independents', so there was no overarching framework of party rules and discipline. In addition, many of them held seats that had been uncontested, which meant that voters played no role in the accountability mechanisms: in the 2008 local elections, seven of the forty councillors were elected unopposed. A small group of people held the reins of local power for many years, and bit by bit the (alleged) corruption increased. In such circumstances, those people in positions of power often develop a sense of impunity, which both encourages them to further acts of corruption and deters people from attempting to speak up.

The government department that oversees the planning process is meant to be a further backstop to prevent corruption, but what if that is itself compromised? The danger can be seen in the Westferry affair, which involved the former Secretary of State for Housing Robert Jenrick and a 2020 planning decision that would have allowed the millionaire Conservative Party donor Richard Desmond to develop the old Westferry Printworks in London. The timing of the decision was crucial;

if it was taken before new rules came into force, the developer would have saved around £45 million in taxes. As the deadline for a decision approached, the planning application was rejected by the local council, but then referred upwards to Jenrick; he approved it soon after sitting next to Mr Desmond at a Conservative Party fundraising dinner, at which Mr Desmond showed him a video of the planned development and then sent Jenrick a text message urging him to approve the application. A donation to the Conservative Party of £12,000 followed shortly after the approval was granted. Jenrick denied any link between the events, but he later quashed his own decision saying it 'would lead the fair-minded and informed observer to conclude that there was a real possibility' of bias, although he said that this had not been the case.

Then there was the case of Graham Brown, a Conservative councillor in East Devon who was also a planning consultant – a rather obvious conflict of interest.[30] In 2013, he ill-advisedly told undercover journalists from the *Daily Telegraph* that he could secure planning permission in return for a payment. His actual words were, 'If I can't get planning, nobody will ... I don't come cheap. If I'm turning a greenfield into a housing estate and I'm earning the developer two or three millions, then I'm not doing it for peanuts – especially if I'm the difference between winning and losing it.' He claimed to charge up to £20,000 for this service, though would later vehemently deny the claims before resigning from the council.

Even so, this is small beer compared to the alleged £2 million bribe demanded in 2018 by a 'businessman' who told the developers of a tower block at Alpha Square in London that with such a payment he could persuade councillors in Tower Hamlets to grant the planning permission that was required.[31]

The same *Daily Telegraph* team that had interviewed Graham

Brown also found a Liberal Democrat councillor in Newcastle working for a lobbying company whose clients included Tesco, Barratt Homes and Taylor Wimpey. Their approach was more subtle than Brown's but amounted to much the same thing. The councillor told the reporters that, due to the access enjoyed by the company he worked for, there was 'a good chance that via our network someone will know someone who knows somebody' at any given council – and that his lobbying firm could use 'tricks of the trade', which included making sure the right committees had 'friendly faces' on them.

You might be thinking that surely these individuals were held to account, but no. People offering such services tend to know the planning rules very well. They can write off a boast to an undercover journalist as bravado; they will have declared their conflicts of interest to the council, and any conversations or rewards are off the record and untraceable. So there is almost no chance of prosecution, and rarely any censure from the council or their political party. However, we should be in no doubt that these cases would fit within all standard definitions of corruption.

PR and planning consultancy firms play a particularly prominent role in this grey world. In 2020, Transparency International found that hundreds of people move between those firms, elected council positions and roles in council planning departments. This revolving door is to all intents and purposes unregulated. While there is a sensible argument that such movements can allow the transfer of expertise between the public and private sectors, it also results in a system that is open to abuse.

One of the more egregious recent cases of (alleged) local government corruption was at Westminster City Council. In 2018, the *Guardian* reported that councillor Robert Davis – who was also deputy leader and chair of the Planning Committee – had over the course of three years accepted 514 gifts and instances of hospitality, including from 58 successful planning applicants in 2016 alone. This had all been declared in the right places and so, remarkably, did not breach any rules. Of course, you might reasonably ask whether it's ever right for someone with such an obvious conflict of interest to accept gifts or hospitality, even if they are declared; to do so more than 500 times suggests someone who is eager to reap the material rewards of being in a position of power.[32]

We have seen a number of cases that look very much like corruption, but where no rules have been broken. It is not all bad news, however. Sometimes a corrupt council official is caught and punished, though it generally requires them to have been foolish enough to break rather than bend the law, or to have left a sufficient evidence trail. For example, in 2004 the former leader of Lincolnshire County Council Jim Speechley was imprisoned for eighteen months for misconduct in public office. He had tried to influence the council's decision about the route for the new A1073 Spalding to Eye bypass, without declaring his interest in the matter. The decision would have diverted the route through his own land, increasing its market value for development due to the proximity of a main road. Although this prosecution was a rare case, it shows that the system can be good – when it works.

The same could be said of the system of local government procurement. The term procurement covers everything from outsourcing contracts for refuse collection to deciding who fixes the local roads, running the leisure centre, appointing contractors to run care homes, buying vehicles for council use and paying the utilities bills for council offices. These are large amounts of money. In 2023/24, local government spent around £84 billion on procuring goods and services from external providers in England alone.

The procurement process is vulnerable to the same weaknesses and pressures as planning. Cronyism, conflicts of interest and embezzlement can prevent money being spent in a way that gives the best value for the public purse, or they can allow people to cream a bit off the top along the way. Bid-rigging and bribery are particularly high risks. A government report published in 2020 found that 23 per cent of council respondents had experienced 'fraud, bribery or corruption' in relation to public procurement in the past year[33] – a big figure, and certainly enough that we should be worried. Like many government stats in this area, it does not distinguish between fraud and other types of economic crime or corruption. Though they are often related, they are subtly different – a conflict of interest that has been declared, for example, may lead to a corrupt decision, but that would not be considered fraudulent. However, it is safe to assume that corruption forms a part of this picture – even if we cannot determine precisely how much. Survey evidence certainly suggests this, even though specific cases of bid-rigging and bribery are not often discovered or prosecuted.[34]

Researchers are faced with a question in such circumstances. As we have seen in this chapter, there are high levels of corruption risk, low levels of transparency and accountability, poor monitoring and weak enforcement. These are the conditions for corruption to thrive, yet there are many fewer known cases than we might expect – especially given what anonymous surveys tell us is happening. So has the UK just been exceptionally lucky to avoid the corruption that happens elsewhere? To my mind, it is inconceivable that the UK is an exception to the global rule. Council officials – not to mention the police themselves – are often frustrated about how hard it is to investigate and prosecute such cases. Even though the police have dropped the charges in several of the cases mentioned in this chapter, one of the UK's most senior police officers in charge of investigating local government corruption told me that the extent of corruption was 'massive'. A partner at a leading London law firm with experience in this area described local government as 'a horrifying mix of rank amateurism and corruption'.

In case this chapter has not been depressing enough already, there's a further aspect to consider: the links to organised crime. As we saw earlier with borders and trafficking, corruption and intimidation are standard in the toolkit of organised crime groups. OCGs do not just deal in drugs and prostitution: they are always on the lookout for opportunities to use their techniques to make money – and the closer it is to the real economy, the easier it is to appear legitimate. Construction, development and specific areas such as waste disposal are well-researched areas for OCG activities,[35] while local authorities and police forces lack the resources to respond.

So what does all this add up to? It comes down to the question of whether or not there is an iceberg – are the small number of prosecuted cases all there is, or just the tip? I have a fair degree of confidence that when you add up the different cases, data and risks in this chapter, there is an iceberg waiting to be uncovered.

Beyond local government, we can also see what this tells us about the country's approach to corruption more generally. Official reports tend to be euphemistic: investigations in Liverpool, Teesside and elsewhere have preferred to pinpoint weak governance rather than corruption, which remains a subject that makes us squeamish. There is plenty of cronyism and patronage, and many conflicts of interest, but they tend not to be caught by existing laws and regulations – and even where we have laws, investigation and enforcement is rare. In addition, penalties are insufficient – the five-year ban for the corrupt mayor of Tower

Hamlets seems extraordinarily low for the most notorious case of local government corruption seen in modern times. We can see cases that involve every political party, and they take place all over the country. It happens at all levels: from mayors to mid-level officials. Planning, development and procurement are particularly vulnerable.

There is a gleam of hope, which suggests that the sustained campaigning by a small number of people and organisations over the past decade, combined with some of the cases in this chapter, many have been heard. When the government launched its anti-corruption strategy in December 2025, there were two announcements of particular interest to local government (though relating only to England): the creation of an independent Local Audit Office and introduction of a mandatory Code of Conduct for elected councillors. We can only hope that they are made to work.

The cases in this chapter illustrate what we might look out for as early warning signs for corruption: individuals and groups who accumulate power, intimidation, secrecy and the interface between the private sector and public officials. But the monitoring system is at present not working, and the decade since the abolition of the Audit Commission has been disastrous. The evidence tells us that local government is an area of high corruption risk, with weakened defences – and it has a real impact on the lives of people who feel defenceless to do anything about it.

11

THE NATIONS: LIFE FAR
BEYOND LONDON

Separate books might be written about corruption in the UK's devolved nations of Scotland, Wales and Northern Ireland. That is not because we know there is more corruption there, or because there is a treasure trove of information that is somehow unavailable for England. In fact, all constituent parts of the UK are notable for their paucity of data on corruption, but what makes them worthy of a separate book is how different they are from England. Devolution has magnified these differences. Context is vital both to understanding the nature of corruption and to proposing solutions that are likely to work; in this chapter I will look at some key areas that scholars may wish to explore in the future, as well as outlining the current state of play.

One part of the history of each of the four nations is the history of its great cities. These urban centres were not just large in national terms, but had global reach in the context of the vast trade of the Empire. The historian Peter Jones has said of Belfast and Glasgow, 'Arguably, they were the most corrupt cities in the UK during the mid-twentieth century.' He goes on to explain how local allegiances contributed to this: 'social and political antagonisms – in both cases profoundly etched with sectarianism – as well as poverty and economic dislocation can undermine civic trust and probity and foster forms of corruption rooted in group loyalty and party faction.'[1] We might reasonably conclude that political fiefdoms with a polarised electorate should be considered as high-risk for certain types of corruption, and we should ask whether those conditions still exist today.

Small countries, similar in size to the UK's devolved nations, have the best track record in controlling corruption. The Scandinavian countries, New Zealand and Singapore usually do best in indices of governance and corruption – just as the Scandis do in indices of human rights, happiness, media freedom and many other areas – and the Baltic States have made impressive progress since they left the Soviet Union and joined the EU. Lots of countries want to replicate the aspiration that Professor Alina Mungiu-Pippidi describes as 'becoming Denmark'.[2]

However, it is not inevitable that small states will always thrive in these areas – and corruption does also stalk small states, the governments of which can easily be captured by those who have no intention of serving the public interest. A well-known study of small-state corruption concludes that 'The smallness of Malta creates very close connections between politicians and business elites, increasing the likelihood of favoritism in matters like public tenders or procurement ... By increasing people's social and economic dependence on the politicians in power, clientelism diminishes the ability and willingness of citizens to hold politicians accountable.'[3]

In other words, there are several characteristics of this small-state corruption: politicians need money and support to keep themselves in power, which they secure from the private sector; in return, they allocate the state's resources to their cronies, for example via public contracts. As a result, they enrich themselves while trying to hide the fact that they are doing so, and the clients become dependent on the politicians and so vote to keep them in power. All this is more easily achievable in small states, where the accountability mechanisms might be both poorly resourced and, because there is a small talent pool, staffed by those who have close relationships with the people in power.

A characteristic 'small-state' scenario has also been playing out in recent years in the British Overseas Territory of Gibraltar, where a public inquiry was launched into the circumstances surrounding the retirement of the former police chief, Ian McGrail.[4] The final report by retired High Court judge Sir Peter Openshaw, published in December 2025, revealed a picture of cronyism, patronage, exchanges of favours, abuse of office and weak monitoring and accountability systems. This related in different ways to both the police and the chief minister's circle. The actions of the Chief Minister were described in the report as 'grossly improper', and led TI to conclude: 'These are astonishing revelations that, were they to be made of a UK minister, would surely be a resignation matter.'[5]

Governments have uniquely strong powers, including control over a country's laws, finances, military and police. The potential to abuse entrusted power is very high – and it can be even higher when the government has come to power off the back of an independence movement. In such situations, popular support for the ruling party means that much else is forgiven, including corruption and changes that remove checks and balances in the system. For an extreme recent example just look at South Africa, where the African National Congress Party of Nelson Mandela slowly slid from being a beacon of hope to being mired in corruption, capped by the leadership of Jacob Zuma – yet still the ANC won election after election.

The UK's devolved nations are similarly vulnerable to small-state corruption. The more devolved or independent they become, the more vulnerable they will be to corruption, unless they put in place strong transparency and accountability mechanisms. Let's look at each of them in turn.

Scotland

Under the Scottish National Party (SNP), Scotland has ambitions to become a prosperous 'Scandinavian-style' independent nation. It is a beguiling idea, but by no means guaranteed. One plausible scenario sees an independent Scotland instead resembling a country where corruption and state capture have taken hold, such as Hungary.

Corruption is a disproportionately important factor in determining why countries become like Hungary rather than Denmark. But complacency is one of corruption's closest allies, particularly in situations of elite capture or state capture, when countries slide from being reasonably good to reasonably bad, while at each stage in the process seeming to have a plausible explanation or claiming democratic support. For all Scotland's advantages, there are also clear corruption risks that merit close attention, whether the scenario is planning for independence, a 'devo-max' approach of maximum devolution or simply continuing to operate with the current levels of devolved powers.

The obvious starting point is to look at the SNP, whose long stretch in power started with the Scottish Parliament elections of 2007. This longevity, coupled with the drive towards independence, gave the party – and its leaders – an aura of invincibility. The SNP was often referred to as one of Europe's most successful political parties, until the party managed to have three leaders in two years, a scandal over alleged misappropriation of party funds and allegations of bullying and sexual misconduct. Central to this was a scandal involving First Minister Nicola Sturgeon and the SNP's chief executive, her husband

Peter Murrell; the two were arrested for suspected embezzlement of party funds. A visible sign of the fruits of this appeared to be a luxury camper van worth £100,000, which was kept at the home of Sturgeon's mother-in-law. Sturgeon herself was released without being charged, while Murrell was further investigated and then charged.

Was this corruption? Some of it might have been – notably any misuse of party funds for personal benefit by Murrell, but also the manipulation of investigatory processes in parliament to prevent proper scrutiny into allegations of bullying by Sturgeon. An aura of invincibility can easily tip over into impunity. In the case of Scotland, the state's accountability mechanisms – including the police, media and parliament – were just about sufficient to provide checks and balances, in the sense that the wrongdoing did come to light and some of it has been investigated. However, each of those checks and balances might easily have been compromised, and it appears that some efforts were made to do so.

Perhaps the key message is that the SNP should never have allowed itself to get into this position in the first place. It should never have been acceptable for such a blatant conflict of interest to exist such that the holders of the two key offices of First Minister and chief executive were partners. This is a case where transparency and declaring an interest are insufficient – the risk of cronyism is too high to manage down to an acceptable level. In a small state where everyone knows everyone in the political scene, and where the goal of independence trumps all other considerations, standards can easily slip.

The everyone-knows-everyone problem of elites in small states can also be seen in the world of Scottish lobbying. A recent study showed that '1 in 10 UK and Scottish ministerial engagements are with just ten companies, all of whom are either fossil fuel majors, or involved in energy generation or transmission.'[6] This reflects a pattern across the UK in which a small group of big companies have privileged access to ministers, but the problem becomes especially acute in a small state with a relatively small elite because the blurring of public and private interests is magnified.

But apart from Scotland's vulnerability to small-state political corruption, what else is going on? As with the rest of the UK, what we know about the corruption that exists is mainly through a small number of cases that have come to light. The Procurator Fiscal's Office (the Scottish equivalent to the Crown Prosecution Service) lists five 'recent bribery prosecutions' from the period 2010 to 2018 on its website, although we might assume that's just a snapshot of cases that have been investigated – and there will certainly be more prosecutions over time.[7]

Two examples in Edinburgh illustrate what we can find out on corruption in Scotland from publicly available information. The first is of standard petty corruption – the sort that might be found anywhere in the UK. This involved two employees of Edinburgh City Council whose job was to award property maintenance contracts. Like any public contracting, the award of contracts is a high-risk area for bribery; in this case, a company called Action Building Contracts paid bribes of £75,000 over five years to the two council staff to ensure it received 175 work orders. To add insult to injury, the company clawed back the cost of the bribes by inflating its invoices; in the words of the prosecutor, 'In essence, the council was being charged for the cost of bribing its own officials.'[8]

More encouragingly, a similar case was prevented when a council official asked a company to pay a four-figure bribe towards the cost of a holiday. This was reported by the company and led to an investigation and prosecution in 2012.[9] Edinburgh has an unusual system whereby for certain historic buildings, if the owners of shared buildings cannot reach agreement, the council can order repairs and appoint contractors to carry them out while the owners pick up the bill. The value of such contracts was £30 million in 2010. In this scheme, we can see that the council official had both monopoly (only he could make the decision) and discretion (he could decide which contractors to appoint): a red flag for corruption.

Edinburgh has also been at the centre of another long-running procurement scandal: the plan to build an 8.5-mile tram link between the airport and the city centre. This came in at £200 million over budget. A 961-page report was published in 2023 after a public inquiry (which itself cost over £13 million).[10] While there is no mention of corruption in the terms of reference or in the report itself, the chapter on governance concluded: 'The governance structures put in place for the tram project were bureaucratic and ineffective ... On almost every level, the governance structures were inadequate.'

As we will see in the next chapter, the focus of most inquiries in the UK is on governance rather than corruption. Yet this project seems to have plenty of corruption red flags: cost overruns, conflicts of interest, flawed bidding and contracting processes, and a lack of transparency. This is not to say that there was definitely corruption in the tram project. We simply do not know, and the question does not seem to have been examined in the inquiry. What we do know is that this was a high-risk project with lots of public money involved and very poor governance – precisely the conditions in which we might expect to find corruption if we were to look for it.

*

It is not just in Edinburgh – we see similar problems elsewhere. A high-profile case in Ayrshire involved senior NHS managers, including a head of IT, receiving bribes to the value of around £88,000 for the award of contracts worth £6.5 million to the telecoms company Oricom. This was a small company started in a shed in 2008 by two colleagues, Gavin Brown and David Bailey, who later recruited Adam Sharoudi as a company director. Oricom suddenly started receiving NHS contracts worth millions of pounds. The company was described in the subsequent trial as 'the Bank of Oricom', as Sharoudi and Brown gave gifts and cash, time after time, to their NHS contacts Alan Hush and Gavin Cox between 2010 and 2017. These bribes consisted of holidays, mobile phones, a house extension, concert tickets, a television and tickets to the Scottish Grand National – as well as £62,000 in cash seized by the police. All four of the men involved were jailed in 2025 after an investigation that involved interviewing over 250 witnesses, gathering 4,300 pieces of evidence and analysing tens of thousands of emails and text messages. The scale of police resourcing necessary to do this perhaps helps to explain why such cases are not more enthusiastically embraced by law enforcement agencies. But unlike many corruption cases, in this case the harm was clear: contracts being awarded uncompetitively usually means lower quality and higher prices, and that effectively sucked money out of the already overstretched NHS. The judge described the men as 'self-serving, arrogant and mendacious', noting that they had also 'subverted public trust in NHS management'.

Such investigations typically fall to the police, since Scotland – like the rest of the UK – does not have a specialist agency to investigate corruption. Police Scotland did, however, set up a Counter-Corruption Unit (CCU) in 2013 to investigate cases of public sector corruption. I spoke at its launch, in the forbidding grey granite grandeur of the Scottish Police College at Tulliallan Castle. I was impressed by the fact that such a unit was being set up, and hoped that as the first of its kind in the UK it would be followed by others (it was not). But the CCU was itself investigated not long afterwards for data privacy breaches during surveillance activities, in what may in part have been an attempt to curtail its operational effectiveness. The launch of this investigation is a useful illustration of a conundrum that often surrounds such units. Corruption is so hidden and hard to prove that investigators are sometimes tempted to explore the boundaries of powers such as surveillance, and may overstep the mark. But at the same time, corrupt people – whether inside or outside the police force – do not like counter-corruption teams; what better means of undercutting them than to discredit them or bog them down with unfounded and distracting allegations about the unit's own alleged misconduct?

Meanwhile, there were police officers in Scotland who were genuinely corrupt. In 2012 it was reported that prosecutors had received allegations of corruption against 145 police officers in Scotland over the previous five years ... but only six were convicted. As the *Daily Record* reported, 'They were probed over gangland links, blackmail, bribery, serious assault, snooping on secret files, perverting the course of justice and lying in statements.'[11] The convicted officers included Derek McLeod, from the Lothian and Borders force, accused of passing information to an organised crime group about Kevin 'Gerbil' Carroll, who was subsequently fatally shot in an Asda car park. In some areas of the police in Scotland, corruption seems to run deep: for example, it was revealed in 2012 that in the Northern Constabulary, which then had 715 officers, 45 officers were accused of 102 corruption charges over the preceding five-year period.[12]

One story that seems to illustrate a great deal about Scotland is the recent debacle around the contract for the ferries that the many Scottish islands rely on as a lifeline to the mainland – for access to essentials such as food, fuel, healthcare and education, as well as travel, inward tourism and selling their own products. A ferry service is a prerequisite to make island life possible; in fact, the ferries are so important that they are described as 'lifeline services'.

When new ferries were needed for the island services, the Scottish government put the contract out to public tender, inviting bids from ferry-building specialists from around the world. The winner was duly announced in 2015 as the Scottish company Ferguson Marine, even though its bid failed to meet the mandatory criteria specified in the procurement documents and was £37 million more than the lowest bid. Unusually, the contract was not announced in parliament or at a Holyrood press conference, but at the Scottish National Party's own conference in Aberdeen in October 2015. It subsequently transpired that the bidding process had – according to a BBC documentary based on a whistleblower's testament broadcast in 2022 – been 'corruptly rigged'.[13] The programme caused a furore, and the Scottish government felt obliged to commission an investigation, carried out by Barry Smith KC.[14] The terms of reference asked him simply to determine whether there had been criminal fraud. This he did not find – and the charge that the bidding was 'corruptly rigged' went unanswered.

The ferries were eventually built, but they were delivered six years late, and the cost of £460 million was quadrupled from that in the original bid – and the bill was picked up by the government. When the project was later audited by Audit Scotland, £128 million was unaccounted for.[15] Details like this have leaked out over the years, and the project seems to have been shrouded in secrecy; Scottish government ministers and agencies were accused of trying to cover up the magnitude of the failures by hampering investigations and giving misleading statements.

What on earth was going on? At one level, it is a story of rational decision-making being skewed by nationalism and political judgements. The contract was awarded to a Scottish company, which helped keep it in business and maintained a shipbuilding capacity on the Clyde, which had been in long-term decline – the political imperatives outweighed considerations of cost. But on another level, it's a story of small-state cronyism that bears many hallmarks of corruption. Ferguson Marine, the company that won the bid, had recently been bought out of administration by Jim McColl, one of Scotland's richest men. From his home in Monaco, he was a vocal supporter of Scottish independence. There was every reason for the Scottish National Party to sweeten their relationship with him, and the ferries contract provided an opportunity.

In most countries in the world, the subsequent delays and cost overruns would have immediately led to a suspicion of fraud or corruption, particularly when £128 million was unaccounted for. The supposed checks and balances such as the civil service, the ministerial codes and public procurement procedures were either bypassed or neutralised, or failed to work.

This may be a story of extraordinarily bad management resulting from a poor, politically motivated procurement decision, or it may be something nearer to corruption. The point is that in a small state, with politics driven by a campaign for independence and decision-makers prepared to overlook the rules and procedures, corruption is an ever-present threat. We do not need to prove that corruption was taking place in the ferries fiasco or the Edinburgh tram project to see that some of Scotland's strengths also make it vulnerable to corruption.

Wales

Like everywhere else in the UK, Wales has its fair share of day-to-day corruption. In Cardiff, for example, a small group of council officials ran a creative scheme that brought in bribes of some £175,000 before they were caught. The four officials operated the weighbridge at a waste disposal site in Cardiff, where companies disposing of waste were meant to pay for the service by the ton. Instead of paying the full cost, one company, called A&T, bribed the four council officials and was charged considerably less. As a result, Cardiff Council lost around £417,000 in fees and A&T benefitted to the tune of £238,000 – an especially large sum as the owner, Warren Roberts, was a sole trader. He was sentenced to twenty-eight months' imprisonment.

But the real story of corruption in Wales is not one of petty corruption. Like Scotland, it is another case of small-state cronyism that shows how a narrow elite looks after its own interests.

David Anderson is the former director general of the National Museum of Wales, having left under a cloud. Press reports suggest that he received a £325,000 settlement following a clash with the president of the board,[16] after (it was suggested) Anderson opposed the plans for greater commercialisation promoted by the president – a business leader with close links to the Welsh government, which had appointed him. The picture painted by the media of Anderson was of a man resistant to change, who perhaps wanted to get as much compensation as possible when he fell out with his boss. What is Anderson's side of the story? We may never know, because his settlement was made under a non-disclosure agreement (NDA), the kind of legal strong-arming used by powerful people and institutions who do not want embarrassing stories coming to light. But the facts that are already in the public domain paint a very different picture.

Anderson was already a highly distinguished museum director when he took up his post in Cardiff. After a career at the Royal Pavilion and Museums Brighton, the National Maritime Museum and the V&A, at the National Museum of Wales he had led a development project that won the UK Museum of the Year Award in 2019. He had also served as president of the UK Museums Association. Far from resisting commercialisation, the museum under his directorship seemed successful commercially – as a comparison, it reportedly had greater revenues and profits than its Scottish equivalent.

Anderson had started to raise governance concerns about the way the museum's board was operating – and when he resisted some proposed changes and was seen as a challenge to vested interests, it was his own motives and integrity that were brought into question. Although he was neither investigated nor suspended, and the precise circumstances of the case are concealed by the NDA, we know from press reports that he had left with a significant settlement after alleging that there was bullying and victimisation from the president. This sounds like exceptionally poor governance rather than corruption: but the point is that the closing of the ranks to eject Anderson, his forced resignation and the secrecy surrounding the case reveal exactly the kind of environment in which corruption might be flourishing.

Anyone who finds themselves in Anderson's position faces a quandary. Who should they complain to, in a small country where everyone knows everyone, and where so many people in public roles rely on government patronage? Even worse, the people who should be exposed are often political appointees, close to the politicians and civil servants who oversee and appoint them. In fact, anyone to whom whistleblowers and victims might turn to for help is likely to be part of the same networks. As one informant said of the Anderson case, 'the whole ecosystem is silenced by fear of a government that's been in power for twenty-seven years'. For Anderson, there was a sting in the tail: after being forced to resign, he was left to pick up the tab for several years of legal costs, which we might imagine were barely covered by the compensation that turned out to be considerably less than the £325,000 erroneously reported in the press.

Irrespective of the merits of Anderson's case, we can learn a great deal from it about the nexus of politics, public appointments and cronyism in Wales – not least because it was examined by both the Auditor General for Wales[17] and a standing committee of the Welsh Senedd.[18] These reports give a glimpse of how Wales had already started to show characteristics of small-state corruption after such a long period of single-party rule. Without the accountability framework of good governance, including an independent and well-functioning whistleblowing process, power can be abused. In common with the rest of the UK, there are close links in Wales between senior business leaders, politicians and public sector bodies. And as we have already seen in Scotland, in a small state the elite circles are smaller and the influence networks are more concentrated. The Anderson case illustrates how the development of clientelism can embed a status quo, which over time leads to a sense of impunity. Those who try to point out governance failings or take on the vested interests are not in a strong position: the power networks can swat away unwanted opposition. On a positive note, the continued existence of checks and balances such as the Auditor General for Wales shows that there are still some mechanisms to ensure accountability.

Just as with the SNP in Scotland, in Wales a single party has been politically dominant for a very long time. The Labour Party had provided the First Minister of the Senedd (the devolved assembly) since it was established in 1999. Although the office-holder has changed with increasing regularity, the fact that only one party had held power for over a quarter of a century has had a corrosive effect – even on those who started with the cleanest of sheets.

One recent incumbent certainly did not start with a clean sheet. Vaughan Gething, elected as First Minister in 2024, won the leadership race shortly after receiving a donation of £200,000 from a company called Dauson Environmental Group, which was hoping for a favourable planning decision from Gething's government. Moreover, both the owner and the company had previously been convicted of environmental offences after illegally dumping waste on a Site of Special Scientific Interest, which subsequently leaked toxic matter into the watercourses.

Such large donations have been unusual in devolved politics, but is this anything to worry about? After all, the donation was not hidden: the rules required that it was made transparently, and a subsequent internal investigation indeed found that no rules had been broken.[19] Yet as we have seen in relation to Westminster, we can at times determine that there has been corruption even when no rules have been technically breached.

A regular YouGov survey that asks people what maximum level of political donation they feel is appropriate has reflected growing concern about the propriety of large donations.[20] The proportion of people who feel donations of £50,000 or more are acceptable fell from 33 per cent in 2018 to 26 per cent in 2024, while those who felt that the maximum permissible donation should be less than £5,000 rose from 34 per cent in 2019 to 54 per cent in 2024.

Any government decision that was influenced by political donations and came to benefit private interests over the public interest would usually be considered corrupt. Any decision by the Welsh government that seemed to favour Dauson Environmental Group would make both the company and the First Minister vulnerable to allegations of corruption. In the end, this was not put to the test. After less than six months in the job, Gething was accused of lying to a public inquiry on a separate issue – this time about the Welsh government's Covid response – and following a vote of no confidence he was forced to resign.

What should we make of the Gething affair? While his behaviour was not at face value corrupt, it opened the door to corruption. It gave the impression that Wales's most senior politician was a black hole with regards to ethics and integrity, an aura that he could probably never shake off; but, just like when Boris Johnson was nearing the end of his time as UK Prime Minister, rather than leaving with dignity intact he ploughed on regardless, even after losing a first vote of no confidence in the Senedd. Had the perjury allegations not triggered another vote of no confidence, he might not have been prised from office. The story shows weak governance, a lack of personal integrity, an opaque nexus between the public and the private sector, the reluctance of the national Labour Party to exert control on integrity issues and a sense of cronyism and clientelism. Putting the Gething affair together with the Museum of Wales affair involving David Anderson, we can start to discern a picture in which those in power are compromised and not held to account, while hovering on the verge of serious corruption.

The Labour Party's dominance in Wales means that it is easy to overlook what happens in the other political parties, but issues relating to governance and corruption have affected them too. In the previous chapter, we saw independent councillors in an isolated community in Anglesey behaving inappropriately.

In 2023, the leader of Plaid Cymru was forced to step down after an investigation into harassment, bullying and misogyny found 'a lack of collective leadership and governance across the party which has meant that these issues have worsened over the last few years'.[21] There was no allegation or finding of corruption, but the key point here is that a failure of governance was 'coupled with inaction over many years from those with positions of power to challenge bad behaviour'. These are the conditions in which corruption thrives and, as in Scotland, the risk for a big player in a small state is that the combination of poor governance and ideological fervour fosters the introversion, entitlement and cronyism that can all too easily tip into something more harmful.

Real and undisputed corruption was on show in another Welsh political party in November 2025. The former head of Reform UK in Wales, Nathan Gill, was jailed for ten and a half years for taking bribes from a Russian intermediary. He had been given £40,000 to promote a pro-Russian agenda in the European Parliament – for example through speeches and questions – while he was an MEP for Reform's predecessor parties UKIP and the Brexit Party. This was an interesting example of Russia using what is known as strategic corruption to pursue its foreign policy interests, by corrupting overseas institutions to further its own agenda. Although Gill's crimes took place in the European Parliament, this approach is also characteristic of corruption in small states, where wealthy external interests can overpower the apparatus of the state with money and influence. We can see this in the active role being played by China in buying up politicians in small Pacific island states that it considers to be strategically important. One well-documented instance is the Chinese ambassador in Micronesia handing out envelopes of cash to politicians at embassy events to ensure their support or opposition to policies in which China has an interest.[22]

In the UK's increasingly devolved nations, we are seeing a vulnerability to small-state capture. The examples from Wales, as in Scotland, demonstrate weak governance, low levels of accountability and a culture of cronyism, as well as in some cases demonstrable corruption. It is not hard to envisage a future in which greater devolution, or even independence, is accompanied by a marked uptick in corruption, which may even become hard-wired into the system if it remains unaddressed.

Northern Ireland

One of the features of small-state corruption is political polarisation: there is generally one group that holds political power, alongside a diametrically opposed opposition. The group that holds power will do whatever it takes to remain in control. It is hard for the opposition to do anything about it when the government controls the apparatus of the state – particularly as they may well have captured the media and accountability mechanisms. Patronage and clientelism, as well as fear of the other group getting into power, fuels partisan politics; supporters of each group ignore corruption by their own leaders and condemn it in their opponents. That kind of polarisation is a constant thread running through the politics of Northern Ireland, between Catholic and Protestant factions, and therefore brings with it heightened corruption risk.

During the Troubles in Northern Ireland, Republican and Loyalist terrorist groups raised funds to bankroll their terror campaigns. They robbed banks, extorted local businesses and were variously involved in drug-dealing, drinking clubs, counterfeiting, loan sharking and frauds.[23] But after the Troubles came to an end, adept as they were at raising funds through unconventional means, they became organised crime gangs – and were backed by armouries, expertise and a long history of violence. This transformation has been mapped by two scholars who specialise in terrorism, John Jupp and Matt Garrod, who conclude that the peace settlement led to the creation of a hybrid 'crime-terror nexus' of groups that 'engage in organised crime while retaining a worrying capacity to return to terrorism'. Their principal means of revenue-raising is generally through the drugs market – just like OCGs everywhere else. This is not on a small scale. It was recently estimated that there are around 230 OCGs in Northern Ireland; former Loyalist paramilitaries control 60 per cent of the drugs trade there. These groups have also continued the practice of extortion, long a feature of the terrorist organisations. The average extortion payment for small businesses in the province is estimated at between £450 and £750 per week, with weekly payments of £2,500 reported by building contractors, and protection money on large building sites reaching £30,000.[24]

Against this challenging backdrop, Northern Ireland has for several years had a dysfunctional government, with the Stormont Assembly being suspended for years at a time because of political polarisation; parties representing diametrically opposed views consistently failed to reach agreement on how to convene the parliament, even though elections had taken place. As a young, small, fragile, polarised, post-conflict state with OCGs hard-wired into the economy, and the backstop of electoral democracy in suspended animation, Northern Ireland looks ripe for cases of corruption. This seemed to be evident in the Renewable Heat Incentive (RHI) Scheme.[25]

*

The RHI was a programme set up in 2012 by the Northern Irish government to incentivise businesses to switch to environmentally friendly boilers through the payment of a government subsidy. It was particularly popular in the poultry industry. The average cost of an RHI boiler was £38,000, and some businesses installed several of them – a total of 2,128 were fitted before the scheme was closed, for very good reason, in 2016. It turned out that the scheme had been badly set up, such that the subsidy could amount to £23,000 per year for twenty years. Far from incentivising environmental improvements, this level of subsidy was having the opposite effect: people were installing as many boilers as they could afford, just to get the subsidy. If you ran the boiler for twenty months you would start making a profit from the subsidy as the income from the subsidies would start to exceed the original cost of the boiler – and there was a perverse incentive to run the boilers all the time, irrespective of the need to heat anything. The projected cost to the government was £700 million over twenty years, although by the time the scheme was prematurely closed it had cost £30 million. The scandal was such that the NI government collapsed; due to inter-party strife the Stormont Assembly was unable to reconvene until three years later, which damaged the political fabric of the province at a crucial time for post-Brexit discussions on the border with Ireland.

A public inquiry, set up to find out what went wrong with the project, concluded in 2020 that 'The sad reality is that, in addition to a significant number of individual shortcomings, the very governance … proved inadequate.' But it also found that 'Corrupt or malicious activity on the part of officials, ministers or special advisers was not the cause of what went wrong,'[26] and the finding that there was no corruption led the headlines on the day the inquiry reported.

On detailed examination, it is not clear how or why the report concluded there was no corruption. The word was not included in the inquiry's terms of reference, meaning that the report contained no definition by which corruption would be assessed, and there was no investigation specifically into corruption. Yet viewing the report through that lens, there are some sections that give pause for thought. Why were the conflicts of interest that the report lists not considered corrupt?[27] Despite the media concerns about corruption prior to the inquiry, the words 'corrupt' and 'corruption' are mentioned just three times in 656 pages, including that conclusion that there was no 'corrupt' activity. Was this seriously examined? Who got rich, and how were they connected to those who made decisions? These questions remain unanswered.

Essentially, the report concluded that there was poor governance but no corruption. Nobody was held accountable, while lots of public money was transferred to a small number of beneficiaries; no rules or laws were apparently broken. This kind of report is typical of a British 'inquiry'. It may be true that there was no corruption, even though it looks very high-risk from the available evidence, but we simply cannot tell from this report.

There is a glimmer of hope in the RHI case. The inquiry did make forty-four recommendations, and one government body – the Northern Ireland Audit Office – has the job of checking whether they have been implemented.[28] Like its counterpart in Wales, this is exactly the dull-sounding kind of outfit that it is easy to overlook, or even abolish – as the UK government did with the Audit Commission in 2015. The Northern Ireland Audit Office had been one of the first bodies in the province to flag the possible spiralling cost of the scheme, and incidentally has had on its website since 2017 a set of good practice guidance for 'Managing the Risk of Bribery and Corruption'. Had this – and the complementary guidance on conflicts of interest – been followed, the Renewable Heat Incentive Scheme might have been able to demonstrate more clearly that there was no corruption. The lesson here is that dull-sounding institutions are a key part of our accountability fabric.

* * *

When we look at these cases in Scotland, Wales and Northern Ireland together, a pattern emerges. We can see the risk of small-state corruption taking root and the need for devolved governments to take ownership of the problem and prevent that happening. Yet at present, probably for different reasons in each case, none of them has paid much attention to the risk – and certain types of corruption may have become so ingrained that they are hardly recognised. Just like in England, there is a data gap about corruption: no government body is responsible for gathering or collating statistics or data on corruption, and so to some extent we operate in the dark. However, also like in England, periodic scandals reveal much about what goes on beneath the surface, as well as prompting us to count the blessings of independent, effective institutions.

These mini-states also reveal something about the real-world consequences of corruption. There are the effects of organised crime and drug-dealing, of vast quantities of public funds being channelled to underperforming projects, and of close connections between business and politics that are not shy of promoting private interests. Yet within the constraints of devolution or – if it happens – independence, it is possible to become Denmark rather than Hungary. Thirty years of corruption analysis might provide some ideas: make an effort to understand the national corruption landscape, including the risks of political corruption; strengthen civil society and the media, even when the scrutiny is uncomfortable; reinforce key institutions and create new ones if they are needed. At a bare minimum, the devolved governments should be undertaking a corruption risk analysis, developing an anti-corruption strategy and appointing expert advisers. Corruption can easily take root. A small investment of time, resources and political attention would head off the worst outcomes and help prepare for the best.

12

FRUITLESS INQUIRIES: THE VACUUM AT THE HEART OF PUBLIC INQUIRIES

I sometimes meet the victims of corruption through their involvement at public inquiries. They often have harrowing tales to tell of how they have been abused or ignored by those in power. They try to present their story rationally, sometimes with self-deprecating humour, knowing that may be the way to make it seem more credible. But the raw emotion of ordinary people who have been badly let down by their own country soon shows.

We have a lot of public inquiries in this country; they have become an increasingly common way of responding to crises and scandals, and range from the Bloody Sunday Inquiry (known as the Saville Inquiry after its chair, Lord Saville) and Hillsborough Panel to many inquiries into child abuse, and health-related issues like Covid and hospital deaths. In fact, there were sixty-eight public inquiries between 1990 and 2017, and many more are currently underway. In addition, there have been investigations, reviews and reports – and in only a handful of such cases did an examination of corruption play a central role. Only one of these inquiries that I have found – the Morgan Inquiry, covered in Chapter Eight – has pointed the finger at corruption as a significant cause of the problem it was examining.

Many inquiries in which a corruption analyst might expect to see a close examination of corruption ignore the subject entirely – but why? The staff I have encountered in the public inquiry teams have been almost uniformly intelligent, dedicated civil servants. We can only conclude that either this country has remarkably little corruption or we are regularly missing something. In this chapter, I will look at a number of such inquiries to see how applying the lens of corruption analysis can reveal something quite different from the official narrative.

The existence of many inquiries is, of course, symptomatic of there being many scandals. And it is not just that we are failing to analyse the role corruption plays in each scandal individually; it is that we have not stepped back and looked at what these scandals collectively tell us about corruption in the UK.

On the night of 14 June 2017, a terrible fire broke out at Grenfell Tower, a block of flats in west London, resulting in the deaths of seventy-two people. It seemed like the kind of tragedy that might be unsurprising in other countries, but would never happen in our own capital city. The burnt-out out shell of the 24-storey block was soon shrouded in white protective wrapping that 'sensitively and respectfully covers the building from view', after which it was set to be dismantled. The official approach to the tragedy is reminiscent of our attitude to corruption: out of sight, out of mind.

In most countries, one of the first questions to be asked after such a disaster would be 'Who paid the bribes?' This is because there is a widespread recognition that bribery is a common contributor to disasters. Two examples from recent years are the 2013 collapse of the Rana Plaza factory in Bangladesh, where public officials had been bribed to turn a blind eye to unsafe construction practices, resulting in 1,100 deaths; and the Turkish earthquake of 2023, where bribery of officials had resulted in substandard construction that meant the death toll of 53,000 was much higher than it might otherwise have been.

But we are not Bangladesh or Turkey, so why should we assume that there was corruption involved at Grenfell? Well, it is no coincidence that all these examples involve construction, which surveys across the world regularly pinpoint as one of the sectors with the highest levels of corruption. This is also the case in the UK, where the research summarised in Chapter Six shows that construction is the sector in which bribe-paying is most prevalent. To a corruption specialist, the red flags at Grenfell were such that it would be an obvious area to probe. This is not just because of the involvement of the construction sector: there were also conflicts of interest, regulatory failures and monopolistic certification procedures, to say nothing of the residents' safety concerns being serially ignored.

The death toll at Grenfell was enough to prompt Theresa May's government to announce that there would be a public inquiry. Transparency International wrote to the Grenfell Inquiry as it was starting up, suggesting that corruption should be within the terms of reference, but that did not make the eventual list of things the inquiry would examine.

When the Grenfell Inquiry's report was eventually published in September 2024, there was not a single mention of 'bribe', 'bribery', 'corrupt' or 'corruption' in its 1,700 pages. There is one lone but important mention of a 'corrupting' influence (plus a couple of references to corrupted data in Part 1 Volume 3), although this is not followed up by further corruption analysis that might naturally derive from the point being made.*

Even though the inquiry did not examine corruption, the

---

* For this inquiry report and others in the chapter, for ease of reading, where quotes or information are easily found through searches within the relevant document, references are given to the overall report and not individual page or paragraph numbers.

Grenfell Report provides a substantial amount of information to allow such an analysis. The picture is damning. In essence, the cladding and related materials that were used for the tower block at Grenfell were recognised to be unsafe for a building of this type (twenty-four storeys high and with one staircase); this was known to different degrees by many parts of the chain for supplying and accrediting materials and signing off that they were appropriately and safely installed.

Among those at whom the report points the finger of responsibility are former government ministers, officials at the Royal Borough of Kensington and Chelsea (RBKC), building and fire safety regulators, and cladding and insulation manufacturers including the companies Arconic (the US external cladding supplier) and Celotex and Kingspan (insulation suppliers). Yet those companies' materials had passed a number of accreditation and certification procedures, run by bodies permitted by the government to say whether any given building process or material is safe or not. These included the Building Research Establishment (BRE), the British Board of Agrément (BBA) and the National House Building Council (NHBC). Each of these functions had at some stage been state-run, but they were privatised in the 1980s and 1990s. In terms of our test for corruption, we can see that these bodies had entrusted power: they are private organisations that have been entrusted with power by the state to make sure we live and work in safety.

The power of these bodies was abused when safety certificates were issued where they should not have been. The cladding and insulation companies, which knew their products to be unsafe, cosied up to these accreditation bodies, which liked to be seen as industry-friendly. Even worse, since the companies were paying these bodies for safety certificates, there was a clear conflict of interest; worse still, the certification bodies had business arrangements, including membership programmes, that predisposed them to grant safety certificates without proper checks. We can see that both the companies and the certification bodies had private gain – and it was clearly at odds with the public interest. Thus all four boxes in our corruption test are ticked.

The inquiry found that the cladding installed at Grenfell was unsafe and should never have been certified. Once fire took hold, the deaths were inevitable. The inquiry did a good job of unpicking these problematic relationships; its report is damning, albeit in the polite language of a judge-led inquiry, as the following extracts demonstrate:

> We saw evidence [at BRE] of a desire to accommodate existing customers and to retain its status within the industry at the expense of maintaining the rigour of its processes and considerations of public safety ... [there was] a desire to put BRE's status in the industry and commercial position ahead of considerations of public safety.
>
> The BBA demonstrated an inappropriate desire to please its customers ... In our view all those failures reflected an ingrained willingness to cultivate customers, certainly those of any commercial value, rather than insist on high standards and compliance with a contract that was intended to maintain them.
>
> The dishonest strategies of Arconic and Kingspan succeeded in a large measure due to the incompetence of the BBA ... [which had] an ingrained willingness to accommodate customers instead of insisting on high standards.

The inquiry's verdict on the NHBC was that it 'was unwilling to upset its own customers and the wider construction industry by revealing the scale of the use of combustible insulation in the external walls of high-rise buildings, contrary to the statutory guidance. We have concluded that the conflict between the regulatory function of building control and the pressures of commercial interests prevents a system of that kind from effectively serving the public interest.'

In each relationship between the accreditation and safety bodies and the dishonest cladding and insulation companies, the inquiry is pointing out the inherent tension between at the same time being a commercial outfit and having a regulatory function. Their entrusted power is abused for commercial purposes; there is private gain through the commercial benefits; and the harm to the public interest is clear in the devastating consequences of the fire. But if this passes the four-step test for corruption, can we be more specific about what type of corruption is going on? I think we can.

The most commonly understood form of corruption is straightforward bribery, which can be prosecuted under the Bribery Act of 2010; to my mind, it is particularly worth exploring in the context of the Grenfell tragedy as it could provide a route to prosecution. Might the BRE, the BBA or NHBC, who were responsible for the certification and accreditation of the unsafe materials, and their relationships with the 'dishonest' companies, be examples of bribery? As the report notes, 'Approved Inspectors had a commercial interest in acquiring and retaining customers that conflicted with the performance of their role as guardians of the public interest';[1] this was deliberately exploited by the companies. But, frustratingly, there is a scarcity of detail that would nail down whether this might be considered bribery, even though the inquiry team must have looked at these commercial relationships in some detail in order to reach such strong conclusions. If this was indeed a case of those in positions of power having effectively been bribed, then the companies themselves would also be guilty of paying bribes.

If what happened at Grenfell were happening in Bangladesh or Turkey, campaigners would say that it looked very much like a bribe and should be investigated as such. Unfortunately, the Grenfell Inquiry did not look for bribery, so we cannot say whether there is potential for prosecution under the Bribery Act, but the report presents sufficient evidence to suggest that it could be an avenue the police should explore. On other aspects of corruption, it might be suggested that any or all of those who held public office in relation to Grenfell, the building's unsafe refurbishment and fire safety – specifically certain officials at the Department for Communities and Local Government and at the RBKC and its tenant management organisation (TMO) – had committed misconduct in public office. The report is scathing about the government's neglect of cladding fire safety risks over a number of years and accuses the RKBC and its TMO of 'a persistent indifference to fire safety, particularly the safety of vulnerable people'. Does this qualify as a 'serious wilful abuse or neglect of power' that could lead to prosecution? The truth is that we simply do not know – the report does not tell us.

A corruption analyst would also be looking for other things that might have allowed the tragedy at Grenfell to occur: regulatory capture, cronyism, patronage, lobbying and the revolving door, to name but a few. But with the marginal exception of lobbying, the report is also silent on all these things. That is without even delving into the somewhat philosophical question of whether the provision of public goods by the private sector has increased corruption risk to an unacceptable level.

Where does this leave us? The purpose of the inquiry was to look into 'the circumstances leading up to and surrounding the fire at Grenfell Tower'. The report, mainly by omission, suggests that corruption was not one such circumstance – or perhaps that it was considered insufficiently important to be a focus, given the many other important subjects covered in the 1,700 pages. It seems bizarre that, while the circumstances have so many of the hallmarks of corruption, that label is nowhere to be seen. But this may also reveal an important truth: we have in this country been so complacent about corruption for so long that we lack the skills, tools and mindset to apply the lens of corruption analysis even where it seems so evidently merited.

A postscript to this are the strikingly analogous events of the Wang Fuk Court fire in Hong Kong in November 2025. This was also a fatal tower block blaze, in which an initial fire seems to have become an inferno due to unsafe building practices and materials, and after the authorities had ignored the concerns of residents. But the response in Hong Kong did assume that corruption may have had a part to play. Within two days of that tragic event, Hong Kong's Independent Commission Against Corruption (ICAC) had launched an investigation based – it appears – on the red flags that were evident. Unlike the cases of Turkey and Bangladesh mentioned above, Hong Kong has consistently performed better than the UK in the Corruption Perceptions Index. There is no reason why the UK should not be as alert to corruption red flags, and act accordingly.

Perhaps it is no wonder that campaigners for the victims of the Grenfell tragedy are dissatisfied. If you fail to analyse the problem properly, it is hard to identify an appropriate solution. Part of the answer to addressing the needs of victims must lie in exemplary prosecutions – fining, debarring and imprisoning those who are responsible, both corporate and individual; this provides justice for the victims and acts as a deterrent that discourages others from doing anything similar. But the inquiry into the tragedy did not examine corruption – and corruption-related prosecutions look unlikely. Even without taking the step to prosecute, an official inquiry labelling individuals and organisations as corrupt might give some sense of accountability and recourse to the victims' loved ones.

The Grenfell Inquiry may be done and dusted, but it should leave anti-corruption campaigners disappointed. If corruption was indeed a contributory factor, and one that remains unaddressed, it could all so easily happen again. Why was there no attempt by Britain's anti-corruption apparatus to insist that corruption should be included in the inquiry's terms of reference? Who will assist the police in ensuring that a Bribery Act investigation is derived from the report? Which part of UK law enforcement has the expertise, experience and resources to prosecute corruption-related cases? Does the UK currently have any anti-corruption law that allows a tragedy with so many hallmarks of corruption to result in prosecution?

These questions, and others, remain unanswered – and in this sense the Grenfell Inquiry typifies the reluctance or inability of public inquiries in Britain to do anything to tackle corruption. When I started this research, I had assumed that public inquiries would provide a rich source of evidence of corruption. But, having read tens of thousands of pages of reports, I have realised that the amount of detail on the subject is disappointingly thin. Even inquiries where you might imagine corruption would be central, such as the Edinburgh Tram Inquiry and the Northern Ireland Renewable Heat Incentive Inquiry, seem to ignore the subject. In each of those cases, corruption is simply unexamined. The Edinburgh report – 961 pages – contains zero mentions of bribery, corruption or related terms.[2] The NI RHI report – 694 pages over three volumes – mentions corruption just once; and that is only to state that 'Corrupt or malicious activity on the part of officials, ministers or special advisers was not the cause of what went wrong with the NI RHI scheme (albeit the Inquiry has identified some instances where behaviour was unacceptable).'[3]

One of the biggest inquiries in recent times, the Independent Inquiry into Child Sexual Abuse (IICSA), mentions in its final report (468 pages) the words 'corruption' twice, 'corrupt' once and 'corrupted' once – all peripherally.[4] But its conclusion on the abuse of power states: 'Adherence to a particular grouping, often of long standing, led to an abuse of power and lack of accountability, and compromised child protection. This was particularly evident in religious organisations and political parties.' To a corruption expert, that sounds very much like corruption.

In some of the cases of child sexual abuse being investigated by the IICSA, the crime was directly committed by a person in a position of entrusted power – a priest or a teacher, for example. But the inquiry goes beyond that, to those who should have acted but failed to. In the case of the Rotherham child grooming scandal, there have been allegations that senior police officers colluded with the rapists to allow the abuse to continue. A separate report by Baroness Casey concluded of the South Yorkshire Police: 'They had been incompetent at best – sometimes turning a blind eye but often actively enabling abuse – and corrupt at worst.'[5]

Yet such institutions – police, social workers, schools, Church hierarchies, mosques and others – had a duty to act when faced with such systematic abuse. Turning a blind eye is a constant institutional failing that is exposed in such inquiries. This, in itself, can at times be akin to corruption. Inquiries often do a good job of uncovering the facts of an event and analysing institutional failings. Yet their predisposition not to imagine that corruption might have been involved means that corruption is not looked for – and therefore not found.

A further example of a case where corruption looks to have been present is the infected blood scandal, which was also examined by a public inquiry. Over the course of two decades, NHS patients were given transfusions and treatments using blood plasma that should never have entered the health system. The plasma was imported from the US, where it had often been donated or commercially obtained in high-risk situations such as prisons, and the US authorities themselves issued advice in 1983 that it should no longer be used.[6] But it continued to be imported to the UK, where medical researchers found the ready supply useful. In many cases it was infected with viruses including hepatitis and HIV, and so the very operations that were intended to be life-saving would prove fatal. As with what happened at Grenfell Tower, much of this scandal was not related to corruption, but some aspects were clearly corrupt. Yet in the 2,555 pages of the seven-volume report published in 2024, bribery is mentioned three times and corruption does not appear at all.[7]

One heart-rending section in the report, which would give a corruption analyst most cause for concern, relates to the deliberate testing of blood products, for research purposes, at Treloar's School in Hampshire, a special school for children suffering from haemophilia. Of the pupils who participated in the research, 70 per cent died. As the inquiry found, 'There is no doubt that the risks of viruses, in particular hepatitis, being transmitted through blood or blood products were well known to Treloar's clinicians. Moreover, practice at Treloar's shows that the clinical staff were well aware that their heavy use of commercial concentrate risked causing AIDS.' Yet the research continued, without permission from the parents or the children – some of whom were never told that they had been infected with the HIV virus. This was more than unethical – it was corrupt.

Doctors are in a privileged position of entrusted power, and in this case it was abused to administer high-risk – and indeed life-threatening – treatments motivated by research curiosity, while the welfare of patients was entirely neglected. It is not clear whether there was any commercial gain, but we can assume that producing groundbreaking research would come with professional benefit, or at the very least a sense of personal gratification. This scandal ticks most of the boxes for our definition of corruption, but more than anything else it exemplifies the 'diversion of purpose' laid out in Lessig's description of institutional corruption: a medical institution that was meant to cure children ended up killing them. Don't get me wrong: this was a thorough, detailed, necessary report into a complex situation that was some time in the past, which did not hold back on pointing the finger at guilty parties. But the thing that stands out to a corruption analyst is that the lens of corruption was not applied to circumstances where it would seem to have been appropriate.

And this pattern of corruption being overlooked by inquiries looks set to continue. There are several ongoing at the time of writing, including the Spycops Inquiry into undercover policing and the Covid Inquiry.[8, 9] In both cases, there are grounds to suspect that corruption played a part – but yet again, in neither case does it feature in the terms of reference.

Another ongoing inquiry is into the Post Office Horizon case.[10] The facts that have come out so far already tell us something important. Sometimes, a significant crime or injustice may not itself be corrupt, but the institutional reaction compounds the original problem by adding a layer of corruption. In these cases, it is the cover-up that constitutes the corruption. Those who have the power to investigate or to hold the wrongdoers accountable instead turn on the victims or whistleblowers in order to protect themselves or their institution. The Post Office Horizon scandal is a good example of this.

It is plausible that the original investigators employed by the Post Office believed that a number of sub-postmasters were committing fraud. That could explain the initial aggressive approach to investigations, in which community Post Offices were raided and sub-postmasters treated like criminals. Likewise, it is plausible that the Horizon computer system was believed to be fault-free for a while, both by the Post Office hierarchy and the IT system provider Fujitsu.

Over time, the approach of senior Post Office employees to the unfolding crisis began to change. It gradually became clear that the Horizon system itself was faulty, and that there was therefore a good chance that the sub-postmasters were not defrauding the Post Office but were themselves the victims of a faulty IT system. But admitting this would have been deeply embarrassing to the Post Office; in the absence of rock-solid evidence that the sub-postmasters were innocent, the senior managers combined their aggressive approach to prosecutions with a cover-up about new evidence. They ended up withholding information that could have provided a defence in the prosecutions that followed, and indeed should have prevented the prosecutions happening at all. This meant that many innocent sub-postmasters including Alan Bates and Jo Hamilton were convicted, jailed, bankrupted and shamed in the communities they served. The miscarriages of justice seem to have continued for years after the original investigations, with a ratcheting pressure on those doing the covering up to be ever more dishonest because, as is common with a cover-up, the longer things go on, the greater the disaster if it is found out. It is not yet clear who in the Post Office management was in denial, who was deliberately hiding things and who was consciously looking the other way. The official inquiry, set up in 2020 but yet to report, should help to reveal this. But, putting it all together, it is already clear that there was a serial attempt at covering things up, from the very top.

The victims of this scandal were the sub-postmasters and their families. Throughout the managerial hierarchy at the Post Office, those who held power were using their positions to perpetuate the cover-up. It was an abuse of their entrusted power that harmed the public interest – and there was a gain both to the Post Office (which avoided having to admit it had procured a dysfunctional computer system) and to the individuals who both escaped censure and sometimes even received performance-related bonuses. These were substantial sums – in total, the CEOs are reported to have earned at least £19.4 million during the years in which the events unfolded. Paula Vennells, the CEO at the time of the cover-up, earned £5.1 million between 2010 and 2019, of which around half was performance-related bonuses.

The installation of the computer system and the misguided original investigations were not corrupt – but the cover-up was. It is not a uniquely British form of corruption, but many inquiries have demonstrated that it is a type of corruption at which Britain excels. Cover-ups are highlighted in the Daniel Morgan Report on the Met, Spycops, Hillsborough, infected blood, and so many other public inquiries and investigations.

There is a clear message from studying the reports of various inquiries: when it is merited, we should not shrink from labelling the cover-ups themselves as corruption, even if what they are covering up was not itself corrupt. It is a kind of secondary corruption. This is easily overlooked by the inquiries, since they are usually charged with looking at the original wrongdoing. We have seen that these inquiries are already poor at identifying corrupt behaviour in the original scandals; the secondary corruption of the cover-up may be even further from their scope, and yet from the perspective of the corruption analyst it may be as significant as the original misdemeanours. This is therefore important territory to examine.

One of the reasons why institutions like the police, the NHS and the Post Office have these scandals in the first place is that the structures strongly predispose them to putting the interests of those who hold power above the interests of victims. That makes it easier for managers and boards to ignore or victimise whistleblowers and protect their own organisations, rather than rock the boat and examine an issue that could bring them all sorts of unwanted problems. A second strong message from such inquiries is that it is hard to hold individuals to account for turning a blind eye, even if they have done so knowingly and other people have suffered as a direct result. Applying the corruption label to those who have been complicit in exacerbating or prolonging the harm to victims may be a stronger and more useful label than terms such as 'turning a blind eye' or 'institutional inertia'. The Bishop of Liverpool felt so strongly about this in his Hillsborough Inquiry that his report to the government was entitled 'The patronising disposition of unaccountable power.'[11]

In many of these cases the original wrongdoing has been compounded by a cover-up, but what about an inquiry where the specific remit was to look for the possibility of corruption? Let's consider the Teesworks Review of 2024, one of the few corruption-specific inquiries that have taken place in recent decades.

*

In May 2023, following 'allegations of corruption, wrong-doing and illegality', Michael Gove (as Secretary of State at the Department for Levelling Up, Housing and Communities) commissioned an 'Independent Review into the Tees Valley Combined Authority's oversight of the South Tees Development Corporation and Teesworks Joint Venture'. It was unusual for this to be an independent review rather than a more formal inquiry; and, although this meant it could report more quickly, it lacked the support apparatus of a big public inquiry. Indeed, it came in at a slender ninety-six pages.[12]

As we saw in Chapter Ten, when the old Redcar steelworks had been selected for development as one of the Boris Johnson government's new freeports, the land was sold at a very low price to two local developers – while the local authority picked up the lion's share of the bill for the clean-up and restoration of the land. The developers made tens of millions of pounds, while the taxpayer, having put in more than £560 million, was left with the ongoing liabilities. At face value, it looked as though large amounts of money had effectively been handed to two local businessmen who carried very little risk, justified by the promise of future investment in developing the site. The situation was compounded by secrecy, poor governance, and complex and unusual financial arrangements, all overseen by the local Conservative mayor Ben Houchen. This sparked allegations of 'industrial scale corruption' from the local Labour MP Andy McDonald, after long-running coverage in *Private Eye*.

There are some things that we might admire about the independent review's insights and recommendations on governance and transparency but, surprisingly, it failed to answer the central question of whether there was merit in the allegations of corruption. Once again, we can apply the lens of corruption analysis – and in this case we might identify half a dozen things that experts would typically look for in an investigation into this kind of project to assess whether it could ever produce an insightful report into corruption. None of these six gets a tick in the box – and there is a big question mark over several of them.

These include terms of reference that were not exactly independent; they were given the premise that 'The department has seen no evidence of corruption, wrongdoing, or illegality', which might reasonably be viewed as a less than objective framing of the panel's work. The ToRs then proceed to list seven specific questions to explore, but there are two problems with this: first, none of the seven questions is 'Is there evidence of corruption or a high risk that corruption has occurred?' and second, they are all about process and governance rather than actual wrongdoing. It is hard to think of any inquiry, review or investigation with ToRs of this nature that has ever succeeded in uncovering corruption.

Furthermore, we might expect the members of the review panel to have had some known expertise in the subject of corruption – but none of their online biographies indicate that they had any prior interest or expertise in this field. Gaps like that might theoretically be filled by having expert advisers, but there is no information or evidence that such advisers were called upon.

The report states, 'we have found no evidence to support allegations of corruption', but it very clearly does *not* state that there was no corruption. That may not sound unusual, but since this review's remit was specifically – and unusually – to examine the question of corruption, the finding of 'no evidence to support the allegations of corruption' of course begs the question of what evidence the panel did actually review – as well as what sort of corruption the panel was looking for, and where it sought evidence. The report tells the reader that 'we have reviewed over 1,400 documents'; this may sound like a large number, but compare it to the Serious Fraud Office where, according to an interview with the former director, 'The SFO deals with "many millions" of documents, including "complex digital data across many different devices", which in any given case "could fill up twenty-two London buses" if they were printed out.'[13] Moreover, the much more thorough Covid Inquiry has revealed the importance in today's world of examining WhatsApp messages, text messages and emails in order to gain a full picture of what is happening. Yet WhatsApp is mentioned only once in the Teesworks Review; it looks like there was no systematic scrutiny of the kind of material where the evidence of corruption is most likely to be found.

Astonishingly, the only mention of 'corruption' in the report occurs in the statement that the inquiry failed to find any evidence of it – and nor is there a single mention of cronyism, bribery or misconduct. This reinforces the impression that the Teesworks Review did not really cover corruption in any standard or recognised way. The report simply does not tell us whether the irregularities and poor practice that were identified, including the passing of millions of pounds of public assets and subsidies to the developers, were due to carelessness, fraud or corruption.

Unsurprisingly, Rishi Sunak's government seized on this flimsy review to claim complete exoneration of its freeport – not to mention the Conservative mayor at the heart of the scandal. A ministerial statement on the report to the House of Commons claimed: 'Today we have the answers to the primary question about the extremely serious charges of corruption and illegality – they are not correct; they are untrue. For the avoidance of doubt, let me repeat that: no corruption, no illegality.'

The minister erroneously concluded, 'it has been proven comprehensively through an independent review that there was no corruption and there was no illegality.' This ministerial statement was entirely incorrect. In my view, parliament was misled. It was another cover-up.

The sense of the government offering a protective veil to the Teesworks project and its controversial chair, the Tees Valley mayor Ben Houchen, is strengthened by his treatment during the review. Many figures in the public and private sector who are under corruption investigations are suspended from their roles pending the outcome – for example, there have been several recent cases of chairs of parliamentary select committees who have stepped down or taken leave of absence while under investigation for alleged misconduct. Houchen, by contrast, was awarded a peerage even while the investigation was ongoing.

The flimsy review into the Teesworks project reinforces a lingering sense of uncertainty over the question of how the UK should handle an investigation or review into the possible existence of corruption in a public body. The Grenfell Inquiry demonstrates that, even when red flags point to corruption, the UK finds it institutionally hard to factor this into a public inquiry. The review in the Teesworks case confirms that, even when it is apparently an inquiry into corruption itself, we lack the institutional wherewithal to set it up in a way that will get real answers.

These examples – Grenfell, child sexual abuse, infected blood, Spycops, Post Office Horizon and Teesworks – are cases where inquiries did actually happen, even if corruption was overlooked. But there have been many other instances in which a public inquiry might have been called to look at corruption but did not happen at all. Perhaps the best-known of these in recent times is Leveson 2, the proposed second part of the 2012 phone hacking inquiry by Lord Justice Leveson 'into the culture, practices and ethics of the press'. As detailed in Chapter Nine, what might have been the UK's most significant public inquiry into corruption in recent decades was postponed by successive governments and then cancelled.

The investigations by the 'Covid Corruption Commissioner' have suffered a similar fate. The creation of this post was promised at the 2023 party conference by Rachel Reeves while the Labour Party was in opposition, a pledge that was repeated in the party's election manifesto. By the time the post had been filled in December 2024, it had been subtly rebranded as the 'Covid Counter-Fraud Commissioner' – corruption, it seemed, was no longer a headline part of the remit. Moreover, this role would be three days per week, and for a fixed term of just one year. It was hardly a surprise when he published his report in December 2025 and explained that he had not looked at corruption at all: since corruption had been excised from the terms of reference, the report 'does not address allegations of corruption or cronyism in PPE procurement. These important allegations have understandably led to high levels of public interest. My core focus as Covid Counter-Fraud Commissioner has been on the pressing and distinct issue of fraud against the public purse.'[14]

Transparency International had meanwhile done some research into what kind of cases the commissioner might look at. Using solely publicly available information, 135 high-risk contracts were identified as having three or more corruption red flags – with a total value of £15.3 billion. If the part-time commissioner were to have only looked at those, many of which would be opaque and complex, he would have needed to get through more than one per day – to say nothing of investigating the many other cases not listed by TI. The Serious Fraud Office can take several years to investigate a single case. It was implausible to think that corruption could have been uncovered by a part-time one-year Counter-Fraud Commissioner, even if corruption had remained within the post's remit.

What on earth is going on with these inquiries? Of course, the depressing reality is that, if anyone should be finding corruption, it is them. They have teams of researchers, lawyers and officials, with the power to call witnesses, and they take place over many years. Yet even those meant to be looking for corruption seem to find it hard to mention the word in their reports.

Such inquiries and reviews are complex and, as with the Grenfell tragedy or the infected blood scandal, they are often not primarily about corruption. This might be a good reason as to why they should concentrate on what they view as their core business, which is usually establishing the facts and highlighting institutional weaknesses. But the point here is that, in some cases, corruption would also prove to be part of their core business if they were to consider its role in allowing unsafe cladding to be put on a high-rise building or failing to prevent unsafe blood products from being tested on children.

It is worth reminding ourselves why it might be useful to add the analysis of corruption more explicitly into the scope of these complex inquiries. There are five reasons, the first of which relates to legal recourse. As in the Grenfell Inquiry, there may be aspects that an inquiry would not otherwise consider, such as offences under the Bribery Act or misconduct in public office. The police have historically been reluctant to investigate these without a compelling reason. Initial evidence-gathering by an inquiry, and a recommendation that the police should consider prosecution, would increase the likelihood. It would be nice to think that if someone's corrupt actions had contributed to the Grenfell tragedy, they would have been prosecuted.

The second reason is individual accountability. Far fewer prosecutions or firings result from an inquiry than one might expect, despite the fact that individuals are often shown to have acted dishonestly or negligently. If they were also found – where justified – to have been acting corruptly, that label would be attached to them and their behaviour. They may not end up in jail, but victims would have the satisfaction of knowing that those individuals have been censured with a damning label. That might be enough to require their resignation from current positions of power or exclude them in the future. Importantly, this label could also be attached to an official or perpetrator who has died (not uncommon, given the length of these inquiries), in cases where evidence exists for what would have been a successful prosecution.

Another reason relates to institutional accountability. As in the case of individuals, it may be helpful to victims if an institution responsible for their harm can be labelled as corrupt – even if it is not prosecuted. This should be a stimulus to wide-ranging reform – it is not a label that can go unaddressed. For a commercial organisation, particularly one in a position of authority such as a certifying body, the commercial implications might be such that it acts as a strong impetus to change, as well as a deterrent to others from acting in the same way. In some jurisdictions, an official censure can lead to debarment from public procurement contracts, which might have a significant financial impact.

Fourth, as we have seen elsewhere, if you do not understand the problem there is a risk that the solution will not be fit for purpose. All inquiries produce lessons learned. And if corruption was part of the problem, it is important to acknowledge this and make sure that any lessons learned include proposals to address the corruption, rather than hope it will simply go away if other things are attended to.

Finally, perhaps the least tangible – but most important

– reason for labelling someone or an institution as corrupt is that it publicly acknowledges the deep harm and damage that they have done. This does not have a direct legal or financial implication, but it represents an opportunity for society to say 'what you have done is beyond the pale'. That kind of censure must be used sparingly, and only when appropriate. But at times it should be used.

Depending on how far you are inclined towards conspiracy theory, you may feel that the fruitless inquiries – from a corruption perspective, irrespective of other good work they have done – are either an establishment stitch-up, incompetence, lack of expertise in a niche field or blithe indifference. In my view, what we have is a serious malaise at the heart of our politics and institutions. The underlying assumption is that, despite the red flags, corruption just does not really exist in this country. This means we do not need to look for it, and so we do not find it. The danger is that, if and when there is a problem, we will not know about it till it is too late.

We have seen in this chapter that the very investigations that should be helping us establish whether corruption is a problem are neglecting to do so. The UK lacks the institutional self-awareness to understand that, where corruption might exist, it should be included in an inquiry's terms of reference. With nobody in charge of the national fight against corruption, there is nobody to insist this should happen.

By no means all the big scandals we have had in this country are due to corruption – but it will have played a role in some of them. Inquiries and investigations are meant to tell us what has happened. Their reports are by and large serious work by serious people, professionally put together and thorough in the areas they choose to examine. But by sidestepping corruption, they have consistently failed to uncover the full picture.

13

SEVEN THREATS TO THE BODY POLITIC: HOW THINGS MIGHT GO BADLY WRONG

So far we have looked at the current state of corruption in Britain, but in this chapter we will focus on the near future, drawing on examples from other countries where things have gone badly wrong. What are the threats facing Britain right now that might be made worse by corruption, or which might cause corruption to get worse?

To some extent there is a path dependency here: these threats are more likely to become reality because of what has happened in the past. However, that does not mean such a trajectory is inevitable. There are choices to be made, and a key part of finding solutions, and having them adopted as a policy priority, is to recognise that in each of these areas corruption is either a current problem that might get worse, or a problem that will arise if the issue is not addressed. The seven threats are: the failure of public services; decline of the public service ethos; organised crime groups; corrupt capital; inequality and disillusionment; strategic corruption; and state capture.

It is also easy to look at each threat individually and think that the situation might not be as bad as it may seem – but therein lies the danger. Each threat by itself may be manageable, but we must look at all of them together and see how they create a structural threat to the nation. The purpose of this chapter is to encourage us to consider the threats collectively and see the big picture.

Threat 1: The Failure of Public Services

I will start by looking at what I perceive to be the biggest threat: the decline in public services. There's a yawning gap between what people expect from the British state – free healthcare, education, national security, transport, benefits and pensions, a functioning justice system, housing, emergency services, secure borders, support for agriculture and business, to name but a few – and the quality of what the state is currently providing.

Research from across the world shows how corruption comes to fill the gap of poor public service provision – sometimes described as 'functional corruption'.[1] Scholars have also differentiated between corruption that is motivated by 'need' and 'greed' – in the case of need, participating in corruption in order to get something that is a necessity and to which you are likely entitled anyway, and in the case of greed getting something to which you are not entitled and which may give you a material gain.[2] The failure of public services can lead to both. You could find yourself driven to jump the queue for a necessary operation by paying a bribe; you might build a house without planning permission as a result of knowing the right people; the justice system could be tilted in your favour if you pay off the police; you could receive an agricultural subsidy because your cousin works in the right office. It is impossible to assess precisely how much of that sort of petty corruption already exists in the UK, but we can surmise that it has been kept sufficiently in check because it is not yet perceived as a widespread problem.

However, there is abundant academic research that demonstrates that there comes a tipping point at which public services are failing to the extent that people feel incentivised to act corruptly. When the system is not meeting people's needs, they naturally try to find their way round the blockages in order to get access to essential services. The action comes not just from the public, but also the officials with whom they are interacting. With a decline in salaries, morale and faith in the institution they serve, public servants feel more inclined to make life easier for both themselves and the people who want public services by introducing a bit of informality into the system.

Threat 2: Decline in the Public Service Ethos

As we saw in Chapter Three, public office changed during the nineteenth century from a means of lining your own pocket to a position of public service. That public service ethos, encapsulated in the seven standards of public life called the Nolan Principles, has been a bulwark against corruption.

In fact, the British public service ethos is at the heart of our defence against the abuse of power and the subversion of the public interest. It assumes that all public sector workers, all public sector institutions and all politicians are doing their jobs on behalf of society; but there are a number of challenges to this philosophy. Contracted-out public services, and the privatisation of companies that retain public interest obligations, have created fuzzy lines such that it is unclear when the public service ethos applies. When public services are either privatised or outsourced, Freedom of Information requests – which would normally allow the public access to information about public services – no longer apply, so it is even harder than usual to find out what is happening. The Nolan Principles may apply in theory, but not in reality. As we have seen in an earlier chapter, the water companies exemplify how a public service lost sight of the responsibilities for serving the public and instead prioritised shareholders, financial institutions and private owners: while underinvestment has led to the public suffering from polluted rivers, floods and droughts, the owners have extracted wealth.

If you are a prison officer in a privately run prison, who are you actually working for? Those who work in a prison that is operated by Serco or G4 are employees of a company, but are they also servants of the state when their incentives and loyalties lie elsewhere? A key finding from the Grenfell Inquiry was that when building certification companies had been privatised, this altered their incentives so that they prioritised serving their customers (the providers of unsafe building materials) over the public interest (being uncompromising on safety) – which, in turn, led to a breakdown in safety protocols and the tragic fire.

Even within the public sector, there are problems: the civil service has become demoralised, and this has gone hand in hand with it becoming more politicised, as well as regularly denigrated by its own political masters. The increase in politically appointed special advisers examined in Chapter Seven suggests a lack of confidence in career civil servants; and the description by senior figures in the Johnson government of the civil service as the 'Whitehall blob' can hardly be considered motivational. Of course, the civil service may very well need to change; but since it is also necessary to run the country, we all benefit if it does so with a strong public service ethos, which in turn can be reinforced or undermined by how politicians behave towards it and speak about it.

Moreover, it is unrealistic to expect public servants to stick to the Nolan Principles, from the top to the bottom, if there are serial and shameless breaches by their political masters – as happened so notably during Boris Johnson's government. It is too soon to tell what damage that has caused elsewhere in the public sector, but in most organisations a poor tone at the top is replicated further down the hierarchy. We are also seeing changing norms over what behaviour is acceptable after leaving public service; and the lack of investment has led to a high turnover of inexperienced, poorly trained staff, helping to deplete further the public service culture.

Combined with austerity and under-delivering service provision, this weakening of the country's defences is a significant red flag for corruption. The UK has traditionally had a strong public service ethos, but that requires a supportive environment in which to thrive. What should be a strength may instead become – by its absence – a threat.

Threat 3: Organised Crime Groups

Into this fragile state of public services we must introduce the threat of organised crime. Corruption can be used to co-opt, subvert or intimidate public officials and institutions to facilitate organised crime. There has been a rise in organised crime, which exerts ruthless and relentless pressure on the state, probing for weakness and using any method necessary to achieve its ends. When circumstances permit, organised crime moves from the fringes to the mainstream, becoming involved in legitimate companies and politics while remaining under the control of the criminals.[3]

In 2023, the government stated in its Serious and Organised Crime Strategy 2023–2028 that there are 'a minimum of 59,000 people in the UK known to be involved in serious and organised crime', including 11 per cent of the prison population (9,300 people) and 4 per cent of people on probation (around

10,000 people). An earlier report from 2020 had said there are 4,772 known organised crime groups in the UK[4] – and those, of course, are just the ones we know about.

Research on the relationship between corruption and organised crime, especially in Italy and the USA, has revealed that OCGs regularly use bribes and other forms of corruption to achieve their own ends – for example, bribing a border official or prison officer to allow in drugs. OCGs view laws and enforcement as obstacles to be avoided, not as rules to be adhered to. So when an OCG sees a law or an official in their way, corruption is an obvious way round it.

But there is a second – and increasingly dangerous – approach taken by OCGs. Why wait for an obstacle to arise when they could instead infiltrate key institutions and corrupt them from within? This ranges from placing OCG members in recruitment processes so that they become employed by the target body, to identifying key individuals who might be co-opted in order to provide a more favourable operating environment. You may recall the Operation Tiberius Report on the Metropolitan Police, which found the institution could be infiltrated by OCGs 'at will'.[5] The report also noted similar infiltration in HMRC and the criminal justice system (especially by nobbling jurors).

There is a third, even more worrying aspect to the threat that organised crime groups pose: the infiltration may not stop at low- to mid-level officials. Why would they not aim to place their members or affiliates at the very top? When OCGs have an influence on the levers of political power, a country is in deep trouble. We have already observed the beneficial shift in Britain away from government run in the private interest to government run in the public interest; this progress can also be reversed.

*

A new breed of populist politicians in mature democracies, including Silvio Berlusconi in Italy and Donald Trump in America, have taken steps on that reverse journey. In a definitional sense, both their acquisition of extreme wealth and their behaviour in office have strong similarities with an OCG – for example, being unscrupulous in the methods they use, intimidating opponents and making blind loyalty to the leader a determinant of political fortune among their followers. With their business backgrounds, they have been described by Fieschi and Heywood as representing a new sort of 'entrepreneurial populism': 'The entrepreneurial populist is trusted because they do not claim to be trustworthy and nor are they perceived as being so; the system is seen as generally corrupt enough that it deserves to be "played" rather than respected.'[6] These entrepreneurial populists both bring their business skills to politics, and use politics to strengthen their commercial power and wealth.

It may seem like an exaggeration to describe such characters as being similar to OCGs, but the point is not that they are criminals themselves (although they may be), but that they change the norms of what is acceptable in politics and government, and this itself opens the door to figures who are comfortable being more recognisably like OCG bosses, such as Vladimir Putin, or are close to OCG bosses, such as the government of Joseph Muscat in Malta.

Having OCGs of any sort run a country is never the kind of politics likely to benefit the public interest. In countries where oligarchs come to power – such as Georgia, or Ukraine prior to the Maidan Revolution of 2014 – it can be hard to draw a distinction between a businessman with inexplicably large assets and an organised crime boss. In other countries, like Mexico and Guatemala, the links between politicians and OCGs are all too clear.

The National Crime Agency's National Strategic Assessment of Serious and Organised Crime 2025[7] for the UK paints a bleak picture of the damage done by OCGs: 'There have been continued increases in child sexual abuse, drugs, and illicit finance. And last year's decreases in fraud and organised immigration crime have been reversed.' On the positive side, these types of strategic assessments from the NCA now more regularly recognise corruption as a cross-cutting threat. But by the time the UK's fight against OCGs reaches the regional level, through the Regional Organised Crime Units,* corruption is barely to be found on their website – and there is no mention of a strategic approach to it. That may not be surprising given the multiple threats posed by OCGs, but it symptomises the lack of recognition of their links to corruption.

While we may console ourselves that we do not live in a state where organised crime is dominant – like several countries in South and Central America, for example – we must recognise that Britain and a few other countries are so far the exceptions. The Global Organized Crime Index of 2023 revealed that 83 per cent of the world's population live in conditions of high criminality, which is significantly linked to OCGs.[8] And there are countries that are more like the UK than those in Latin America which do have a serious problem with organised crime.

One well-known example is Italy, where the Tangentopoli cases of the 1990s exposed the links between government and OCGs.[9] They revealed that for many years OCGs had been winning public contracts by paying kickbacks to politicians, which were in turn partially used to fund their re-election campaigns. Italy

---

* ROCUs look set to be abolished under the latest plans for police force reorganisation.

is a fellow G7 state, with a similar population size and GDP – much more similar to the UK than to Mexico. The deep rot of corruption that Tangentopoli revealed to be running throughout the Italian state was not all due to OCGs,[10] but the case shone a light on how in an advanced economy OCGs were able to thrive with the collusion of politicians.

We might look at Italy – and Latin America – and think, 'It couldn't happen here.' But while it would not occur in the same way, the deliberate infiltration of politics by OCGs could all too easily happen in this country – just as it is already happening in other sectors of public life. As the section below on corrupt capital will show, the British experience in laundering dirty money, reputation laundering and allowing those with money to cosy up to the establishment is unrivalled. If we believe that the UK is too special for organised crime to be able to infiltrate our politics, we are merely leaving the door open to money and muscle influencing elections, criminals using their connections to win public contracts, and laws and enforcement that favour groups with criminal connections.

Threat 4: Corrupt Capital

We saw in Chapter Seven how the UK is tainted by dirty money – in politics, the professions, in the distortion of the property market, and the country's global reputation. The term 'Londongrad' encapsulates how over the past twenty years the UK has become a magnet for corrupt capital.

My colleague Dr Daniel Haberly has analysed the Panama Papers data to demonstrate the importance of the UK as a centre for corrupt capital flows, and the centrality of the Crown Dependencies and Overseas Territories, such as the British Virgin Islands and the Channel Islands.[11] The National Crime Agency states that 'It is a realistic possibility that over £100 billion is laundered through and within the UK or UK-registered corporate structures each year'.[12] When such funds are derived from state capture, in which governments and their cronies parcel out the spoils of the state, the means of accumulating wealth can become indistinguishable from organised crime.

The UK's reaction to such funds has been ambivalent – partly because it can be easier to see the benefits (described as 'overseas direct investment') than the harm. As a result, foreign money has often been welcomed with no questions asked, with a targeted crackdown happening only when the government or regulators have felt pressed into doing so by incidents such as the Russian invasion of Ukraine. Many of these corrupt capital flows into the UK have been brought to light by campaigners and journalists – for example, in 2021 Finance Uncovered found that a £50 million, ten-bedroom flat at One Hyde Park Place had been owned by the family of former Pakistan prime minister Nawaz Sharif. This level of spending was way beyond his notional wealth and reinforced the findings of his conviction for corruption in Pakistan in 2018, a case that itself had used evidence of his ownership of other London properties as revealed by the Panama Papers.

Even though a great deal is known about these global flows of corrupt capital into the UK, both the City and the government have been reluctant to do much about it. As mentioned earlier, I realised while I was an adviser to the Lord Mayor of London that little progress was being made regarding money laundering: it was a time of grand white-tie dinners at the Livery Halls, while there was a resolute belief that money laundering was not a big problem – or at best, a much lower priority than other issues such as negotiating the market turmoil following the departure of the UK from the European Union.

For some people, there is a moral case as to why being open to corrupt capital is a bad thing. It is effectively announcing to the world's kleptocrats that the UK does not mind where people get their money from or how they get it – they are welcome to spend it in the UK. For others, the practical consequences are a cause for concern. The volumes of money are so large that individuals, firms and whole sectors of the economy can become dependent on corrupt capital – essentially meaning that they operate on behalf of their corrupt clients and paymasters. This phenomenon has been noted among certain professional services firms. Smaller firms, in particular, are vulnerable if they have a large client on whose business they become reliant, and it is probable that such clients deliberately seek to develop a dependency relationship. I recall the head of a boutique PR firm in London telling me that one day she realised 60 per cent of her firm's income was coming from one Russian oligarch, which made it ever harder for her to stick to her own ethical values – for example, when the Russian client wanted to use particularly aggressive PR tactics against perceived UK enemies.

The UK is gradually noticing that such financial dependency has costs. For example, the UK anti-corruption strategy 2025 notes: 'The UK is home to a thriving cultural sector and world-renowned institutions, making them attractive to legitimate investment and philanthropy. However, the sector is also a target for corrupt elites and kleptocrats seeking to secure access and influence in the UK. There is concern among the public about the impact of corrupt actors from abroad on key national institutions, including UK cultural institutions, educational institutions and sports organisations and events.'[13] It is difficult to articulate what harm this does to the UK, as opposed to the countries from which the wealth has been extracted, and this may be one reason why it has been generally encouraged by the UK.

However, over the past decade, the UK security services have started to rate corrupt capital as a national security issue. It is not just that corrupt capital has corrupt origins; it is also that the countries from which it comes are, or may one day become, enemies of the UK. This subject was examined in 2019 by parliament's Intelligence and Security Committee.[14] The Committee's resulting 'Russia Report' was not published until a year later, reputedly blocked from publication several times by the government because of the embarrassment it might cause, before it eventually came out. As it stated, Russian money was 'invested in extending patronage and building influence across a wide sphere of the British establishment'.[15] Moreover, the committee noted the view of Russia expert Bill Browder that 'Russian state interests, working in conjunction with and through criminal private interests, set up a "buffer" of Westerners who become de facto Russian state agents, many unwittingly, but others with a reason to know exactly what they are doing and for whom'.

Whether you object to the UK being a safe haven for dirty money on moral grounds or because of the risk to our national security that is presented by British institutions, politics and the establishment being infiltrated, the threat of corrupt capital working against our national interest is real.

Threat 5: Inequality and Disillusionment

Most people will agree that inequality is a bad thing, but that does not make it corrupt. The French economist Thomas Piketty has traced how capitalism tends to lead to an increase in inequality. Setting aside the argument that capitalism is intrinsically corrupt, it seems clear that the economic system in the UK does create inequality – and in doing so leads to a set of problems that seem very similar to corruption: an increasingly rich elite separating from an increasingly impoverished population, while opportunities for advancement are diminishing and public services declining. So while the inequality itself may not be corrupt, the consequences look very much like the outcomes of grand corruption. It is not surprising that people equate the two.

When inequality resembles corruption, people lose trust in the institutions of the state as they are perceived to be corrupt. Meanwhile, inequality and poverty can stimulate corruption as people try to navigate a system they feel is against them. The American scholar Eric Uslaner[16] describes an 'inequality trap' in which the rich get richer and the poor get poorer. When poverty combines with a lack of trust, corruption can seem like the best means to gain wealth – or even to survive. This leads to higher levels of corruption, which leads to further poverty. Elsewhere, Uslaner and a co-author have suggested that both economic inequality and inequality of opportunity undermine social trust and social capital,[17] creating a self-reinforcing 'social trap' in which corruption generates mistrust and dysfunctional institutions, which in turn perpetuate inequality and corruption.

Ironically, the risk of disillusionment seems to increase when campaigners and governments highlight corruption that has taken place. Research in both Europe and Africa has shown how anti-corruption campaigns, rather than deterring people from acting corruptly, can encourage people to do so by engendering a sense that the system is irreparably broken.[18] In the UK, too, the more noise that is made about corruption that goes unpunished, the more it risks sending the message that this is the way to get on.

Rising inequality in Britain thus creates twin vulnerabilities. On the one hand, it may cause people to lose trust in political and economic arrangements under which the rich are getting richer and the poor are getting poorer. On the other hand, it may encourage ordinary people to take shortcuts. This is not just a matter of economic inequality – just as damaging is the sense that the rich and poor aren't treated in the same way. Perhaps the best example is in the field of justice. Why do the wealthy seem to get away with committing crimes when poorer people are convicted and jailed?[19] Consider, for instance, the former Chancellor of the Exchequer, Nadhim Zahawi, who used an elaborate scheme to avoid paying tax. This was uncovered by some journalists, bolstered by campaigning tax lawyer Dan Neidle – who Zahawi then tried to silence with a threat of legal action, while denying he had done anything wrong.[20] He paid fines, penalties and interest of £5 million to HMRC, and was forced to resign after he was found to have demonstrated 'a serious failure to meet the standards set out in the Ministerial Code' and – in the wondrously convoluted language of the Independent Adviser on Ministers' Interests – 'shown insufficient regard for the requirements to be honest'.[21] Why was he not jailed – and would anyone else have been treated in the same way?

The point is that this is starting to resemble a two-tier system; the provable inequality is made worse by perceived unfairness – and at a political level, this can have severe consequences. It leads to disillusionment and the rise of what is known as 'anti-politics', in which citizens reject parties and institutions they perceive as being corrupt. This in turn is closely linked to the rise of populism, as we have seen both in the US with the rise of Trump, and in many other liberal democracies that have rising levels of poverty and inequality as well as an affordability crisis. Corruption creeps in all too easily: corrupt leaders elected because they promise the earth and voters think all the other candidates are corrupt or ineffective anyway; corruption as a shortcut to getting a fairer share of what the state and society have to offer.

Threat 6: Strategic Corruption

The Russian invasion of Ukraine in 2022 shone a light on an alliance of autocratic states – Russia, China and Iran – which had long been a thorn in the side of anti-corruption campaigners. Those countries, joined by a few client states, had become known as 'the blockers' in the effective implementation of the UN Convention Against Corruption. In the case of Ukraine, joined by North Korea, they supported Russia's war effort, which was characterised as the front line in a battle to defeat the hegemony of the US-led Western Alliance.

As this picture emerged of how Russia and its allies would be prepared to work together, and the anti-Western philosophy underpinning it, intelligence agencies, journalists and campaigners began to see more clearly how those countries had waged a long-term hybrid warfare in liberal democracies: interfering in elections, supporting destabilising far-right parties and spreading disinformation.

Disillusion, and what populism expert Professor Paul Taggart describes as 'unpolitics', have provided fertile ground for such hybrid warfare waged against the West.[22] Unpolitics takes things a stage further than anti-politics: citizens are not angry and voting for populist alternatives to traditional parties – they have become so disillusioned with the political system that they disengage entirely. The nature of a hybrid warfare approach is that it seeks out weak spots like this and exploits them. This has given rise to a new phenomenon, termed 'strategic corruption', where a foreign power – or other malign actor, such as an organised crime group – deliberately promotes corruption in order to weaken its adversary from within. That can involve weakening the political system or deliberately promoting activities that undermine the nation's well-being, like the drugs trade. Corruption can be weaponised and deployed to weaken an enemy state.

Strategic corruption was trialled by Russia in Ukraine before 2014, with good results. President Yanukovych was helped into power, having been enriched by favourable energy contracts arranged by the Kremlin. There was a dual benefit to Russia: it had bought the head of the government, and put into that position someone who would weaken the state through his own corruption. As things played out, the revulsion of the Ukrainian people at their own president led to the Maidan Revolution of 2014 – and then the Russian invasion of Crimea, and all that has followed since. This has given the world a glimpse of how strategic corruption operates.

Could anything like that happen here? Without wishing to sound like a conspiracy theorist, we may already see the ground being laid. For example, in the pro-Brexit campaigns, money was donated via a loophole in the Northern Ireland electoral laws designed to protect political donors from being targeted by terrorists. The origin of this dark money has never been satisfactorily explained.[23] By contrast, the donations by Russians and others to the Conservative Party are well known – but subject to surprisingly little scrutiny. Close personal relations between British and foreign elites provide another entry point: as mentioned in Chapter Four, we may never know what Boris Johnson was doing at a party in Italy where he met a former KGB agent while carrying secret documents and having dismissed his security detail, but this is the kind of situation in which corrupt dealings can be forged. At the very least, such matters show us that the UK is vulnerable to hostile foreign powers that might choose to exploit its lax rules, weak security and open society.

A good example of how easy it is for those with corrupt connections to infiltrate Britain's political establishment is the case of Mohamed Mansour, an Egyptian billionaire who served as his country's Minister for Transportation between 2005 and 2009. This was in the government of Hosni Mubarak, who was shortly afterwards overthrown and convicted for corruption. Mansour moved to the UK and at some point became a British citizen. Welcomed into the Conservative Party, he made a £5 million donation to the party and was appointed as its treasurer. Despite having retained business operations in Russia well after the invasion of Ukraine – in direct contravention of the UK's official policy – Mansour was knighted in 2024.

This is not to say that he was personally corrupt, despite having held a ministerial role in the government of a corrupt autocrat in Egypt. But such instances have started to normalise the idea of foreign involvement in our democracy, with no apparent concern about any possible connections with corruption. Each time such things happen, they become more normal. A hostile power with bad intentions could easily make use of this.

Beyond politics, the openness of the UK has been easily penetrated by other hostile powers such as China. The tech firm Huawei was the lead bidder to provide the UK's 5G infrastructure, for instance, until it was eventually banned from doing so on national security grounds. China's Confucius Institutes, as noted earlier, have similarly established a foothold in major universities, where they provide courses in Chinese language and culture. There are thirty across the UK, in universities including Cambridge and the LSE. Critics accuse them of providing propaganda and using their locations on campus to intimidate or undertake surveillance on Chinese students.[24] In a report on China in 2023, the UK parliament's Intelligence and Security Committee noted that 'China has been particularly effective at using its money and influence to penetrate or buy Academia in order to ensure that its international narrative is advanced and criticism of China suppressed.'[25]

While we should beware of appearing to be reflexively anti-foreigner, it is also easy to be too naïve. There are countries that view the UK as a rival, competitor or an enemy and, as has been demonstrated in other parts of the world, weaponising corruption is a means of hybrid warfare. People usually want something in return for the money they spend. Any of the examples cited above may indicate that hostile foreign powers are already attempting to weaken the UK from within – and if that has not yet happened, these cases show how easily any concerted effort could succeed.

Threat 7: State Capture

Where might all this end? The ultimate concern is that a combination of some or all of the threats outlined in this chapter might help move the UK into a situation of state capture via a period of illiberal democracy.[26] State capture does not just mean more widespread or systemic corruption but a concerted power grab, directed by those at the top. A glimpse into this possible future has been offered to us by the governments of Donald Trump and Boris Johnson. These two governments had one key difference: in Trump's second term he has approached government in a well-planned and coordinated way, following the 887-page blueprint called 'Project 2025' drawn up by the Heritage Foundation, which laid out clearly how areas like the civil service and the Department of Justice could be brought to heel. Johnson's adviser Dominic Cummings seemed keen to take a similar approach, while Johnson himself displayed an eagerness to dismantle or evade conventions and institutions whenever they annoyed him or got in the way. This showed the pathway towards capture in the UK, even if that was not Johnson's own intent; a more organised or malign leader could easily take it further.

The concept of state capture was developed by economists to describe the post-Soviet diversion of politics and the economy to benefit a narrow elite. Recently, the term has been applied to democracies in which the democratic process itself has been exploited to gain power. In countries where this has happened, such as Hungary, Turkey and South Africa, the governments have moved to dismantle or undermine key accountability institutions – for example, in each case the judiciary and mainstream media were pressurised or taken over by various means.

A precondition of state capture is that an individual or small group must have their sights set on doing the capture. They generally claim to be offering the answer to their country's problems, and to promise a return to traditional values. In democracies they need to be elected, which usually means they have a charismatic leader with a populist message. Typically, this does not appeal to everyone – but it does appeal to enough people to win the election.

Once in power, the person or group wants to keep hold of it at all costs. They seem not always to set out with the motive of personal enrichment – the initial motivation may be power or a messianic self-belief in being the country's saviour – but self-enrichment unfailingly ends up being part of the process. This is in part a hedge against being removed from power, but it is also a way of maintaining a support base that is both elite (oligarchs and crony capitalists who benefit from government contracts) and popular (handouts are offered, to keep enough of the electorate onside). And the ruler now needs enemies, in order to justify suspending or amending laws and breaching ethical norms in the name of national security: immigrants, the liberal woke elite, the 'corrupt' opposition, NATO, the decadent West, the EU – there is no shortage of possible enemies.

At this stage, a traditional autocrat might launch a security crackdown, arresting the opposition and beating up any protestors. In a democracy, muscle can also be at hand; that may mean creating a loyal paramilitary division in the police, as Trump has done in the US with his deployment of the National Guard and upscaling of the Immigration and Customs Enforcement (ICE) agency. Another option is to deploy thugs and hitmen from organised crime gangs. If that sounds far-fetched, think again: they are already operating in the UK and Sweden on behalf of hostile powers such as Iran.

In 2025, a Home Office minister told parliament that the Iranian secret service 'use criminal proxies to do their bidding'.[27] By this he meant that criminal gangs can be hired in the UK to eliminate enemies such as journalists and exiled dissidents. Likewise, in 2024 Russia's Wagner Group hired five drug dealers with connections to organised crime on behalf of Russian intelligence agencies to burn down a warehouse in Leyton, east London, which was storing satellite equipment en route to the Ukrainian military. They were paid around £9,000. A London-based comedian who satirised the royal family of Saudi Arabia on YouTube was harassed, stalked and eventually beaten up, apparently by proxies of the state security service.[28] This is not mere speculation: in 2026, he was awarded £3 million in damages against the Kingdom of Saudi Arabia in the High Court, where the judge commented, 'There is a compelling basis' that the assault along with other actions 'was directed or authorised by the Kingdom of Saudi Arabia or agents acting on its behalf.'

We have not, as far as I know, had a modern political leader in the UK whose lack of scruples has led them down such a path, though historically Oswald Mosley's Blackshirts show that the

UK is not immune to this. In more recent times, Boris Johnson is known early in his career to have leaked the address of a journalist to one of his friends so he could be 'beaten up', demonstrating a rare instance in which a future political leader in Britain can be directly linked to a threat of third-party violence.[29] The point here is that if a politician came to power in the UK and wanted to hire muscle to keep themselves in power, it is available – and it has already been used in this country by foreign governments.

A more likely approach by an individual or group seeking state capture in this country is to attempt to close down or disable potential checks on their power by 'disabling the accountability institutions', as Professor Liz Dávid-Barrett, the world expert on state capture, describes.[30] She lists the institutions that typically act as checks and balances to those in power, and which are systematically targeted during the process of state capture: parliament, the judiciary, the media, the civil service, the supreme audit institution, the electoral system, academics and civil society. In Hungary, for example, Viktor Orbán had taken over or assaulted each of these institutions.

Disabling the accountability mechanisms need not mean closing them down. It might mean placing party-friendly officials as the senior staff in regulators or the state broadcasting company. Institutions can be captured one by one or in a swift concerted push. A particular prize, as for example happened recently in Poland, is capturing the judiciary, which allows control over how the law is applied. Some of the capture can be achieved through market forces, for instance when oligarchs buy up the media and direct the editorial line in support of the government.

This may all seem a long way from the UK, but the Johnson government did two things to bring state capture a step closer:

first, they interfered with – and damaged – certain key account-ability mechanisms such as the civil service, the Electoral Commission and the BBC; second, they laid a clearer pathway showing how those with malign intent could move towards state capture in this country. For any future politician intent on state capture in the UK, Johnson may well prove to have been a useful idiot: in an uncoordinated and ineffective way, he showed what could be done to dismantle the UK's accountability mechanisms. By the same token, we can also see more clearly which institutions need to be strengthened and protected. This threat could still be neutralised, but we must recognise that the UK has started a journey towards state capture. It is still at the stage where it can be halted, but political will is key.

* * *

The seven threats outlined in this chapter are hypothetical, in that the worst-case scenarios have not yet come to pass. This should be encouraging, because it means that by anticipating the threat we can prevent it from becoming reality. But in each case, the threat already exists and is gaining ground; corruption can both help it along, and get worse as a result.

14

DULL-BUT-IMPORTANT: THE UK'S SPECIAL POWERS

Superheroes in films have special powers. They tend not to be immediately obvious but, when the time comes, they always prove handy in defeating the enemy. In the same way, the UK has some special powers when it comes to defending itself against corruption. They are at first sight quite dull, but all very important. The notion of special powers being employed to combat corruption is also a reminder that power is not intrinsically bad. We should be cautious about those who hold it, but in the right hands it can be exercised for the good of the country.

To some extent, the UK's complacency about corruption is understandable. Whatever the pessimists may say, the situation in the UK is not like Russia or Afghanistan – and this is, in large part, because we have had strong defences in place. These reside largely in institutions like the judiciary, a credible electoral system and an independent National Audit Office; they are not specifically designed to tackle corruption, but a strong system of such institutions helps keep corruption at bay.

Although these institutions are widely admired, both within the UK and overseas, and would generally look good on an institutional scorecard, the things we think we do well can also be folded into our national complacency about corruption. In countless conversations I've held across the country, people have told me about their pride in these underpinnings of our society, and sometimes about their relief that we have them. But the problem with pride is that it can easily turn into smugness.

I particularly remember attending a meeting at the time when the Johnson government was trampling on traditions and institutions left, right and centre – and there was real concern at what was happening. Sitting at a table in the basement meeting room of a grand Regency building were leading academics, heads of think-tanks and a group of senior public officials – particularly those with responsibility for safeguarding integrity in the public sector. A paper was to be produced setting out how to strengthen the system against such assaults in future.

The Johnson government's own assaults on integrity, as outlined in Chapter Four, included ignoring breaches of the Ministerial Code by senior cabinet ministers, rigging the public appointments system, removing key powers from the Electoral Commission, disregarding security service and other advice on appointments to the House of Lords and repeatedly failing to make proper declarations about gifts, hospitality and favours. In addition, Boris Johnson himself had breached the Ministerial Code several times, covering up law-breaking in Partygate and permitting Dominic Cummings's infamous 'eye-test' trip to Barnard Castle during the coronavirus lockdown, as well as lying to the media, parliament and more or less everyone else.

Early drafts of the paper produced by this eminent group contained sections on corruption, and acknowledged the dangers of a corrupt government. But by the time the final version was published, all the substantive references to corruption had been removed. Johnson and Liz Truss had given way to Rishi Sunak, and the political system seemed to be all right after all. No irreversible damage had apparently been done, and the mood of the group was now surprisingly upbeat: Britain's institutions of integrity had come through a trial by fire and won. Johnson had been ejected by the system. Pats on the back all round, along with minor tweaks suggested to a Rolls-Royce system, like beefing up the independence of some of the watchdogs. No need to rock the boat after all.

It was certainly true that the Sunak government seemed more calm and measured than that of Johnson – and to that extent, the period of immediate harm could be considered to have passed. But we need only look across the Atlantic to see what happens when a system full of loopholes is exploited by someone who is self-interested, malevolent and – not to put too fine a point on it – personally corrupt, and is surrounded by a circle of advisers who are either ideologically driven or looking for power and money. Strong institutions are a safeguard – albeit an incomplete one – against that day.

One way of describing these institutions is as a 'national integrity system'. This conceives of a country's defences against corruption as a series of interlocking institutions. Typically, those institutions would be seen as central to upholding democratic values and the rule of law: they would include, among others, law enforcement agencies, regulators and watchdogs, public audit functions, the judiciary, and of course parliament and the civil service – as well as laws and regulations themselves. When they are all working well, there are lower levels of corruption. They do not all have to be working perfectly at the same time, but a critical mass of them must be doing well. We have already seen how some of our institutions are either failing or highly vulnerable with regard to corruption; in this chapter we will look at how some of our strong institutions constitute a set of 'special powers' that have served the UK well.

What makes an institution work well as a defence against

corruption is a combination of how it is set up and its culture, reinforced by the presence of tradition, trust and transparency. In the academic literature, this set of circumstances is described as institutionalism. The theory is that even if individuals are inclined to be corrupt, they can be kept in check by the right institutional setting – whether that is an individual body like the National Audit Office, or a set of bodies responsible for a principle such as the rule of law.

The fate of the Audit Commission, discussed earlier, gives a taste of how one of the nation's key institutions can be casually cast aside – yet such dull-but-important institutions give the UK a strong defence against corruption. If all is going well, the six influencing sectors that we analysed in Chapter Nine might also be considered part of the UK's special powers – for each of those sectors, if they use their influence for the good, can be an important part of the national defences against corruption. For example, the strength of investigative journalism in the UK, combined with our independent public service broadcasters, is unparalleled. But at present neither of those sectors is fully doing its job to support integrity as a counterweight to corruption.

We also have superheroes who could badly do with some special powers – the heroic whistleblowers who stand up against injustice. They are themselves often victimised, marginalised and discredited. Alan Bates, one of the heroes of the campaign to get justice for those sub-postmasters wrongly accused of fraud by the Post Office, was rightly but very unusually rewarded with a knighthood. Most whistleblowers are either overwhelmed in a David-and-Goliath fight, or even if they are successful find that they have been badly scarred. We need to find better ways to support and recognise them, not least by making sure they are properly protected in law. [1]

In this chapter I will focus on four of the special powers that the UK still has, even if some of them are under threat: civil society; the rule of law; transparency; and the Nolan Principles.

Civil Society

Civil society is a term used for what in the UK we tend to call charities, voluntary organisations, community groups or NGOs, ranging from small grassroots organisations to large international NGOs. In Chapter Nine we looked at how corruption can take place within charities, and in this chapter we will focus on those sections of civil society which specifically address corruption. Such campaigners play a crucial role in highlighting abuses and campaigning for change; they have a deterrent effect on those who might want to act corruptly. But it can be dangerous work: colleagues of mine around the world were variously strangled to death by police officers, had their houses firebombed, had their faces Photoshopped onto pornographic images on social media to discredit them and were followed 24/7 by the security services.

In the UK, while civil society operates with greater freedom, the right to protest has been curtailed as the government has taken action against protestors on issues such as climate change and Palestine. The impact on the anti-corruption movement has to date been minimal because it has not tended to be a mass protest movement, although those rights are important – one day they may be necessary to protest against a corrupt regime.

The UK's anti-corruption movement dates from 1993, when Transparency International's UK office was set up. Since then a small number of anti-corruption organisations have taken root, and together they have formed a group called the UK Anti-Corruption Coalition. By 2025, the seventeen member organisations included new specialist anti-corruption groups like Spotlight on Corruption, large development NGOs like the One Campaign, smaller, single-issue campaign groups like Open Ownership and the Open Contracting Partnership, and groups with related expertise, such as Protect (whistleblowing) and Article 19 (freedom of information).

The campaign for the 2010 Bribery Act, which occupied the first few years of my life at Transparency International, shows how effectively these groups can work both individually and together. The old anti-corruption laws, which dated from the First World War and even earlier, were not fit for purpose, but there was little political will to change them; after a half-hearted attempt in 2003 that ground to a halt in parliament, the government put the idea on ice.

TI kept plugging away during the 2000s, receiving a small grant to hire legal experts who drafted a new law. After a few years, the government was forced to revisit the issue due to the massive bribery scandal at defence company BAE Systems: as part of its £43 billion deal with Saudi Arabia, BAE had allegedly paid bribes worth billions of pounds to middlemen and Saudi princes. This led to an SFO investigation, which the Blair government closed down after political pressure from the Saudis and the British defence establishment. There was a public outcry, along with legal action led by campaign group The Corner House, and TI took this opportunity to restate its message on the need for new anti-bribery legislation.

Despite concerted opposition from the Confederation of British Industry (CBI), some of whose members were unashamedly of the view that paying bribes overseas was just part of international business, a new law crept closer to the statute books. I recall, in trying to counter this influential backlash, frantic late-night calls to members of the House of Lords, visits to the Conservative opposition in parliament, meetings with CBI members at a City law firm and fierce opposition in some parts of the media. Just when things looked promising, Gordon Brown called a general election, and the Bribery Act squeaked through before parliament closed down. Though it is generally acknowledged to be a very good piece of legislation, which has provided a template for other modern anti-bribery laws around the world, it is easy to forget that the Bribery Act might never have happened – it was just a few hours away from failing to pass.

This example tells us some important things about UK civil society and the UK anti-corruption movement. First, this was not a mass movement – it was more of a think-tank-style approach, which worked through developing detailed policy ideas and draft legislation and playing them into parliament rather than having campaigners on the streets. Second, allies in the NGO movement helped support each other at key moments in the campaign: towards the end, large development NGOs like Tearfund and CAFOD put their weight behind the campaign – they could see the damage that bribes were doing in the developing countries where they were operating. Third, with a small amount of resources an NGO campaign can be mounted and won. Fourth, there was a concerted opposition from the CBI, operating on behalf of a number of multinational companies that might have had skeletons in the closet. Although our campaign was successful, we were always aware of the huge lobbying power of those who opposed us – and it seemed a minor miracle that we managed to see them off.

That think-tank-style approach to corruption has served the UK well, but equally interesting are a number of smaller, sometimes local, initiatives that have played an important role in exposing problems and holding those in power to account. Often, such initiatives are not primarily about corruption, but the local campaigners soon see corruption as part of what is going on and so incorporate it into their campaigns.[2]

An example of grassroots civil society is the Stop Aquind campaign in Portsmouth. The Aquind project is an ambitious plan to run a vast power and data cable from France that would emerge from the sea in Portsmouth and go through a series of tunnels and trenches to an electricity substation in the South Downs. The proposed route crosses many areas of conservation value, as well as public amenities like sports pitches and allotments, and various parcels of private land – not to mention its proximity to sensitive military installations. For this project to happen, multiple planning approvals are needed. Residents of Portsmouth and the South Downs villages near the route would face years of disruption, and in some areas permanent changes to the landscape.

A group of local citizens created the Stop Aquind campaign, which initially focused on conventional aspects like community disruption and environmental impacts. However, after the publication of the Pandora Papers, it became clear that the mysterious entity behind the project was backed by a Russian oligarch who was a personal friend of Boris Johnson, Viktor Fedotov. The oligarch had made his money in a highly suspicious Russian oil deal, but thirty-four Conservative MPs had accepted funding from him. The Stop Aquind campaign naturally became interested in this related set of issues – secretive foreign ownership of UK assets, the ease with which Russian oligarchs can invest corrupt capital in the UK, and the use of political party funding as a means of trying to influence development decisions. The grassroots campaign joined forces with Transparency International to gain exposure for these issues, and eventually the planning application was turned down – a decision overturned on judicial review, after which the project was once again blocked by the regulator.

Irrespective of the merits of having an energy pipeline connecting us with France, and the community and environmental considerations, there were some important corruption-related issues to highlight and address. The Aquind case shows how the energy of grassroots activists can be adopted by the anti-corruption movement to advance both local and national causes. Overall, these cases tell us that a combination of transparency, collaboration, community spirit, smart campaigning tactics and – crucially – the legal and political space to operate means that civil society is a key part of the UK's defences against corruption.

The Rule of Law

The second special power in the UK is the rule of law. Most countries have reasonably good laws in relation to corruption – at least on paper. The UN Convention Against Corruption (UNCAC) has provided a template, and specialist help has been available for drafting the detail. Corrupt governments have passed laws that are UNCAC-compliant, knowing they will not need to adhere to them. Reforming governments have passed good laws, hoping that something will stick if they are forced out of office. With the exception of a few holes that need to be filled, the UK itself has good laws in the form of the Bribery Act and the various laws on economic crime and transparency. But the best safeguard against corruption is not anti-corruption laws: it is the rule of law itself. In other words, having in place a set of fair and just laws that govern the state, which are broadly adhered to and effectively and impartially enforced.

Lord Bingham, a distinguished judge who wrote the definitive modern book on the subject in 2011, determined eight principles for what constitutes the rule of law.[3] At their core is 'that all persons and authorities within the state, whether public or private, should be bound by and entitled to the benefit of laws publicly made, taking effect (generally) in the future and publicly administered in the courts'. A central concept here is that the law applies to all persons and authorities within the state. Nobody is above the law. The good administration of good laws can be a block to those who want to act corruptly or with impunity, which means that corrupt governments often try to reinforce their position by putting in place a corrupt judiciary, or persuading judges to act corruptly. When the judiciary are corrupt, those in power can use the law as a weapon against their enemies and as a shield for their friends.

Try to guess how much it costs to bribe a judge in the UK. A High Court judge is paid around £225,000. As we saw in the Introduction, bribes in the UK tend to be relatively low, especially in comparison to other countries. But a judge is in a monopoly position and has a lot of discretion over certain cases. So how much would you offer them? £100,000, £500,000 or £1 million?

Thankfully, we don't know how much it costs to bribe a judge in the UK because there seems to be no market for doing so. In all the cases I have researched, I have only come across one serious allegation of judicial corruption. The lawyer who told me about it was convinced that a judge had been bribed, and the circumstances certainly made this look plausible. The judge was holding a hearing in the Family Courts for a Russian oligarch and his wife. The ruling would determine who had custody of their children, and how his considerable property would be divided. The judge ruled in favour of the oligarch. As a High Court judge in the Family Division, his salary would have been around that £225,000 mark – a good income, but not riches for life. The allocation of hundreds of millions of dollars of assets rested on his decision. A few million paid in a bribe

would represent peanuts to the oligarch – and a sound investment – but considerable wealth to the judge.

That (alleged) case stands out because it is so rare. More
usually, people are inclined to see bias or arrogance or discon-
nect with social realities or political leanings in judgments they
do not like. There are allegations of cronyism and, as followers of
TV's Judge John Deed will recognise, some colourful fictional
accounts of government interference, but on the whole the UK
judiciary has had an enviable record for being uncorrupted for
nearly two centuries.

This does not mean all is rosy. The next generation of judges
will be recruited from a much more commercialised legal
profession, among whom are some professional enablers of
kleptocracy, as we have already seen. Will they import to the
judiciary a different set of ethics? And the Johnson and Sunak
governments made periodic noises about the need to bring
judges to heel, perhaps by having an appointments process
with more political involvement.[4] This confrontational attitude
towards the judiciary was most prominently on show after the
Supreme Court ruled that Johnson's prorogation of parliament
– to force through a hard Brexit in 2019 – had been illegal.

In general, though, the UK is well off in this regard. On the
Rule of Law Index produced by the World Justice Project, the
UK is a respectable fifteenth place – though it was in the top ten
as recently as 2018.[5] The rule of law – having robust laws that are
enforced effectively and impartially – is a key defence against
corruption, supported by an independent judiciary and law
enforcement agencies. It is one of the things that distinguishes
the UK from a kleptocracy. As Lord Bingham put it: 'The hallmarks of a regime which flouts the rule of law are, alas, all too
familiar: the midnight knock on the door, the sudden disap-
pearance, the show trial, the subjection of prisoners to genetic

experiment, the confession extracted by torture, the gulag and the concentration camp, the gas chamber, the practice of genocide or ethnic cleansing, the waging of aggressive war.' Bingham was not specifically talking about corruption, but he could very well have been: as he argues, the rule of law is a defence against precisely those wrongs. And despite many challenges within the criminal justice system, a fundamental commitment to the rule of law remains one of the UK's special powers.

Transparency

For many campaigners, it will be a surprise that transparency is listed here as a special power; they might be more used to pointing out the government's poor record on its legal obligations in this area. For example, the transparency on lobbying is pitifully poor, and there has been a deliberate campaign within government and the civil service to block the proper implementation of the Freedom of Information Act (FOIA). Campaign group Open Democracy has noted there is in operation 'A cynical tactic for avoiding FOI', having uncovered an 'Orwellian' unit within the Cabinet Office that monitors requests from journalists and campaigners.[6]

Yet these things are comparative, and the UK has more transparency than many other countries. Several of the 'new generation' of corruption indices are, in fact, measures of a country's transparency, such as the T-Index published by a Washington think-tank; this collates data from twenty-one indicators including government expenditure, the existence of a public procurement portal and Auditor General's report, easy access to Supreme Court rulings and financial disclosures for public officials.[7] The T-Index gives the UK a transparency score of 85 per cent – well above the world average of 62 per cent, and above the European regional average of 81 per cent – but also some way below France (93 per cent) and the USA (90 per cent).

The academic literature is unambiguous that transparency is one of the most effective methods of deterring and detecting corruption. Acknowledging the benefit of transparency as a means of combatting corruption has become so commonplace among practitioners that grand statements abound from world leaders – for example, former UN Secretary General Kofi Annan: 'If corruption is a disease, transparency is a central part of its treatment.' This draws on a long-standing strand of thinking that was summed up by US Supreme Court Justice Louis Brandeis in 1914, with the phrase 'Sunlight is said to be the best of disinfectants.'

There are, however, some issues with transparency. Sometimes there is a conflict with privacy or confidentiality. Most anti-corruption experts would feel that we might reasonably expect transparency from governments and companies, but that we should have privacy and confidentiality for private citizens. And when someone is unashamedly corrupt, or prepared to argue about whether what they are doing is corrupt, transparency is not a solution in and of itself. A good example here is President Trump. When offered a Boeing 747 by the government of Qatar as a replacement for the ageing Air Force One, which would be transferred to Trump's personal control once he had left office, he accepted the plane and called it 'a very public and transparent transaction'. It was, indeed, in plain view, but the transparency failed to answer the question of what he might owe the Qatari government in return. We may never find out whether there was any quid pro quo. We can see that transparency only works as a mechanism for holding those in power to account when other mechanisms are also in place to act on what the transparency has revealed. Despite this, it remains an important foundation – and the UK is fortunate to have much of that foundation in place.

It was not always like this. The big change I saw was in 2013, when the UK was hosting the G8 Summit at Lough Erne in Northern Ireland. The civil servants who were in charge of the summit began to use a phrase I had not previously heard from them: 'transparency by default', a conscious shift from any previous British government's approach. It means that governments should assume that information will be made public unless there is a good reason for it not to be. In part, this was driven by government excitement about how transparency might help tech start-ups, in the way that releasing Met Office data has helped the development of weather-related apps and traffic flow data has been used for mapping apps. For anti-corruption campaigners, it was good news.

The first item on the campaigners' agenda of transparency measures for the government to adopt was BOT, or beneficial ownership transparency, meaning that companies should be obliged to disclose publicly who are their true or 'beneficial' owners. This is important, because kleptocrats tend to hide their wealth through layer upon layer of shell companies in different parts of the world, before establishing an innocuous-looking front company in London that can purchase property, make investments and pay for services like lawyers and PR companies. BOT laws were designed to strip away this secrecy; either the kleptocrats would be exposed, or they would need to lie about being the beneficial owner – and in doing so they would be committing a criminal offence. More than a decade later, BOT has not been fully implemented, even though there has been significant progress in the UK, most notably in the registrations at Companies House.

This illustrates how transparency can be hard-won, even

when the right laws are in place. Along the way, there was an unexpected 'proof of concept' of BOT: something happened that showed how much could be revealed by putting such data into the public domain. This key event was when a series of documents were leaked, revealing a global network of transactions and ownership, and how it could be used to hide the origin of funds and launder the proceeds of corruption. In quick succession, a gold mine of information was released via the Panama Papers, Paradise Papers, Pandora Papers and FinCEN files. It became possible to see what transparency could look like and, with the help of dozens of specialist journalists analysing the data, how it can shine a light on kleptocracy. For example, it gave credence to the allegations that Vladimir Putin has wealth of up to $200 billion, through his association with a series of off-shore shell companies notionally owned by his close associates. And Nawaz Sharif, former Pakistan prime minister, was shown to have extensive international assets, which contributed to his conviction and imprisonment for corruption in 2018.

Other areas of transparency in the UK are less immediately obvious. For instance, we take for granted that we have internet freedom, which allows uncensored access to the world's plethora of knowledge, data and information. And for those who have the time, patience and technological expertise, there are obscure corners of the internet on which a multitude of government documents can be found. This ranges from every pound the UK has spent on Overseas Development Assistance (ODA) and the detail of every planning decision, to rulings of the Supreme Court and all government procurement contracts worth over £12,000. The authorities do not always make it easy. If you want to know who has been meeting government ministers, the information is all there – at least in theory – but it can be very hard indeed to access. In that instance, civil society has come to the rescue: you can visit the OpenAccess website to find the data neatly organised, searchable and cross-referenced.[8]

Public service broadcasting is another aspect of transparency in this country. The news is impartial and fact-checked, which helps to counterbalance voices in the unregulated space of the internet and social media, where news is co-opted as a weapon of propaganda or misinformation. Perhaps because they are aiming to be impartial, institutions such as Channel 4 and the BBC often find themselves under attack, whether from commercial media competitors or ideologues who would like to see a Fox News-style approach in the UK.

Finally, I should mention an obscure but important area of transparency that provides a crucial historical record of what has happened – our national system of archives and records. Although historical documents are open to manipulation and reinterpretation, they can also provide an accurate record of how those in power have acted. The Stasi files from East Germany, meticulous surveillance and detention records kept by the East German secret police, are a good example of how detailed record-keeping by a repressive regime can allow accountability – but only once that regime has been overthrown.

By contrast with East Germany, repressive regimes also try to destroy archives and historical records. After the Ukrainian city of Kherson was captured by the Russians in 2022, the archives were destroyed in a twin effort to erase Ukraine's own national identity and cleanse the records of Soviet repression. Similar damage has reportedly been done to the national archives of Iraq and Syria; but it is not only deliberate destruction that needs to be feared. Deprioritising and funding cuts can cause archives to be lost; UNESCO tracks this, and in the late 1990s it was reporting a steady decline in the quality of archiving. Though digital archiving has made a huge difference to document security and availability in some countries, others have suffered, with archives in countries such as Mali and Tunisia being ransacked by civil wars and insurrections. Of these challenges to archives, the one that has most troubled the UK has been years of budget cuts, but despite this our archive and records system has so far managed to hold its head above water.

The National Archives in Kew, west London, contains over 250 kilometres of archives, including 10 million military service personnel records and the records of many of the public inquiries mentioned in Chapter Twelve. All this information is available to any citizen of the UK who wants to access it, both in person or increasingly online. The challenges to archiving are not just budgetary, but also the sheer scale of documentation to be catalogued and stored. Digitisation of information has created a new set of problems: the National Archives' annual report tells us that 'it has taken our collection 1,000 years to reach its current expanse of around 250km; over the next ten years, we will take in half as much again.'[9] We also have an extraordinary network of county record offices that provide an exceptional resource of local information – but they are funded by local authorities, which face funding pressures, and in recent years have proven to be exactly the sort of thing that can easily be cut.

About a decade ago, the transparency revolution looked unstoppable: the combination of the internet and digitisation meant that more data and information than ever were being placed in the public domain, and being circulated by citizens without governments as intermediary. Since then, the opponents of transparency have fought back: in China, internet censorship affects two-fifths of the world's population; in many countries, misinformation is used deliberately to downgrade truth; law firms have challenged the legality of beneficial ownership transparency laws on human rights grounds – they argue that the privacy of oligarchs should be protected. Even the USA's previously sacrosanct national archive in the Library of Congress has come under assault; the Archivist of the United States and the Librarian of Congress have been fired on spurious grounds by Donald Trump and replaced by political appointees.

The UK's approach to transparency is by no means perfect. Apart from cutbacks, other changes have taken their toll – for example, the local press, which was once a terrific force for transparency at a local level, has more or less been eliminated by market forces. However, and notwithstanding the pressure from campaigners who justifiably argue that the government should do more, the level of transparency in the UK still just manages to stand out in a less-than-transparent world.

The Nolan Principles

In a lecture in 2020, Lord Evans suggested that the UK might be entering a 'post-Nolan age'.[10] It was one of the most chilling phrases I'd heard for a long time, but to most people it probably didn't mean very much. Why did I find it so disturbing?

Jonathan Evans had been head of MI5 before becoming a member of the House of Lords, Deputy Lord Lieutenant of the county of Kent and member of the board of HSBC. He knew the establishment from the inside, and his lecture expressed deep discomfort with what he was seeing in British politics under Boris Johnson's government. Speaking in his capacity as chair of the Committee on Standards in Public Life, Lord Evans listed a litany of breaches by the Prime Minister and his cabinet of the standards in public life described by the Nolan Principles; he reached the powerful conclusion that 'the perception is taking root that too many in public life, including some in our political leadership, are choosing to disregard the norms of ethics and propriety that have explicitly governed public life for the last twenty-five years'. In a later speech, when things seemed to have got even worse as scandal followed scandal in short order,[11] he warned: 'the priority that is given to this across government departments is low and this opens a door to opacity and potentially corruption'.

This is the only recorded occasion on which a former head of MI5 has issued a public warning to the government that its behaviour was verging on corruption. We can only imagine how many attempts must have been made through the usual back-channels to convey this message, and the level of frustration that led to the need to make such a public statement.

We have seen a little of the Nolan Principles already in previous chapters. The seven standards of public life are considered the bedrock of public service in this country. As Lord Evans put it: 'In their essence, the Seven Principles are there to govern the legitimate use of entrusted power in public life.' I have already outlined how a decline in the public service ethos represents a threat to this country. We might expect that the Nolan Principles would similarly be in decline. But what is encouraging is not so much the principles themselves, but their underlying philosophy. In essence, they assume that public office and services should be conducted in the public interest; a set of standards will help ensure this; and there is a reasonable expectation from both officials and the public that officials will adhere to them. In my experience, there is still a broad adherence by public officials to this set of expectations, even though the wider political environment that is necessary to support the Nolan Principles' proper operation is not one that always promotes or supports integrity.

Scholars of corruption are increasingly making the case that the opposite of corruption is integrity,[12] and that, rather than fighting a rearguard action against corruption, we should be on the front foot by promoting integrity. In other words, instead of waiting for someone to act corruptly and then trying to spot it and punish them, we should be developing a culture, backed with the right incentives, in which people do not act corruptly in the first place. The Nolan Principles embody this idea; they exemplify a social norms-based approach, in which culture and principles rather than rules and laws are seen as the prime means of influencing behaviours.

The principles were introduced by 1995, after John Major became fed up with the sleaze scandals affecting his government. He said at the time, 'I believe public confidence in parliament and politicians is essential. I care about the reputation of parliament. It matters. I worry that it has fallen.'[13] He commissioned Lord Nolan to produce a report, which went on to lay out the principles: selflessness, integrity, objectivity, accountability, openness, honesty and leadership.

The Nolan Principles might sound obvious and innocuous; moreover, they are not regulated, and there are no formal sanctions for breaching them, unless a given institution (such as parliament) decides to write some of them into its rules or code of conduct. They did not magically arrive in 1995 – as Lord Nolan himself pointed out, they had long been implicit in British public life, and all he was doing was making them explicit and codified: 'We have inherited a legacy of immense value from those who laid the foundations of a public service in the last century ... the recommendations we make are designed to ensure that public life in Britain retains the highest standards.'[14]

The last of the seven principles is leadership; as the Nolan Report put it, 'Holders of public office should promote and support these principles by leadership and example.' In anti-corruption compliance procedures this is often described as 'tone from the top'; within the academic literature as 'political will'. This recognises the critical role that those at the top of the hierarchy have in influencing behaviour lower down the tree, both by their own example and by their decisions and actions. In fact, when John Penrose resigned as Anti-Corruption Champion in the dying days of Boris Johnson's government, he explained that it was 'failures of leadership and judgement' that had led him to do so.[15] He was recognising the fact that his own role as Champion was no longer possible to carry out if his boss, the PM found guilty of lying over Partygate, was in such flagrant breach of the Nolan Principles.

This highlights how such principles rely on leaders with integrity to make them effective. The Nolan Principles were not defeated by the Johnson government, but they were severely challenged. A British government showed that, despite serial breaches by its most senior members, it could retain power on the basis of a compelling personality and other policies (such as Brexit) being considered sufficiently attractive to enough voters to maintain a majority.

For its twenty-fifth anniversary in 2021, the Committee on Standards in Public Life produced a report with thirty-four recommendations to the government on how to update the country's ethics and integrity apparatus.[16] These included, for example, that the Ministerial Code should be strengthened, that lobbying via modern communication methods not covered by previous rules – like WhatsApp and Zoom – should be disclosed like face-to-face lobbying, and that lobbyists themselves should have to make disclosures about who they had lobbied and what about.

There have been four governments since then, and most of the recommendations have been ignored. The crisis of ethical leadership that characterised the era of Boris Johnson has not gone away – the issue has been shunted to the side, while the majority of those thirty-four recommendations sit on the shelf, waiting for a government that gives ethics and integrity a sufficiently high priority.

At times, the failures in ethical leadership by the PM and other ministers have felt like an assault on the Nolan Principles, as though there were an attempt to marginalise them or normalise the notion that the most powerful people to whom they apply can ignore them when they become inconvenient. But they still exist, and they have force. Despite being a principles- and social norms-based approach rather than hard law, they are generally agreed to be the bedrock of public service in this country. I have spoken to many ethics experts in many countries and, as they compare their own situation to ours, there is a recurring theme: the Nolan Principles are the envy of the world.

To reiterate, the special power is not that they exist, but what they stand for: a set of integrity norms that there's a reasonable chance people will follow, as well as a public expectation that they should be followed. That is something that sets the UK apart – another of the UK's dull-but-important special powers.

However, before we congratulate ourselves, it is worth remembering when the Nolan Principles have failed – and not just under the Johnson regime. In those cases we encountered in Chapter Twelve that have been the subject of public inquiries – and in the cover-ups that in so many cases exacerbated the original misconduct – the inquiries found failures among board members, senior managers and mid-tier bureaucrats alike. The Post Office senior managers, the senior officers at the Met in the Daniel Morgan case and the governance failures at Teesworks are all examples of where the individuals concerned have breached the Nolan Principles; yet they have seldom been held personally accountable for the harm and distress they have caused others. The tendency of institutions where this has happened seems to be a shrug of the shoulders, an expression of mild regret and an explanation that it happened in the distant past.

Historian Peter Jones, who has studied standards in politics and the public sector of major British cities throughout the late twentieth century, has also expressed scepticism about how readily the Nolan Report would be adhered to in party fiefdoms with a long history of corruption: 'The Nolan Commission's view that it could recover Gladstonian moral virtue failed to recognise the realities of corruption in the modern and postmodern era.'[17] This points to an important issue. Standards like the Nolan Principles are voluntary and self-regulatory and depend strongly on the existence of 'social norms', which the theoretical literature on corruption suggests is a key way to tackle corruption. But an alternative way is to take a 'rational choice' approach, which incentivises and disincentivises certain behaviours through rewards and penalties. So perhaps for the Nolan Principles to be most effective we need to mix a bit of rational choice theory with our social norms; there may be occasions when there should be real sanctions attached to such breaches, such as loss of pension or being debarred from holding similar posts in future.

* * *

In this chapter, we have seen four of the UK's special powers – and there are others, too. Overall, the UK has a strong institutional set-up to help defend it against abuses of entrusted power and all forms of corruption. The central message is that our core underlying strength comes with a caveat. Just as it is a mistake to be complacent about corruption, we should not be complacent about our institutions. Cutbacks, lack of support and direct political attacks have weakened the UK's national integrity system, even though there is still much in place. As a country, we need to ensure that those institutions avoid the same fate as the Audit Commission, when the government thought it had good reason to abolish a key institution without fully understanding the consequences.

15

THE BLINDFOLD ORCHESTRA: WHO IS IN CHARGE?

You will have discovered by now that there is real corruption at the heart of some of our key institutions. We have seen this in politics, the police, prisons, the private sector and sport, among others. There are also high levels of corruption risk – places where we might strongly suspect there is corruption but do not have the evidence to prove it; we have seen this in local government, the media, cronyism in the nexus of business and politics, and in cases examined by public inquiry in each of the UK's four nations. We have seen complicity in corruption by professional enablers and fixers. And we have seen an extraordinary level of complacency; despite all evidence to the contrary, corruption is still broadly thought of as happening overseas but not in the UK.

In this chapter we will look at the gaps and loopholes in Britain's formal anti-corruption apparatus. As we will see, there is a fair amount of activity, but there is also wasted effort and resources. That is in part because, although there are lots of people doing lots of things, it is uncoordinated and without overall direction – like an orchestra playing with blindfolds, in which each musician may be perfectly competent on their own instrument but playing out of time, or in a different key to the others. We will also see that, in 2013, a rare opportunity to centralise and coordinate the diverse players was missed.

In 2016, a study found sixty-six separate 'specialist enforcement, prevention, investigative and oversight agencies involved in the policing of offences directed against corruption behaviour' – in addition to forty-eight police forces.[1] More recently, a report by the Independent Commission on Aid Impact (ICAI), the most comprehensive analysis of how illicit financial flows and corruption are tracked in the UK, identified twenty government departments, committees, agencies and operational bodies with overlapping responsibilities.[2] As an example, the Treasury is responsible for the UK's anti-money laundering system, whereas the Foreign Office is responsible for relations with the Overseas Territories, which are deeply implicated in the flows of dirty money through the UK; and the anti-corruption strategy that says these things should be dealt with together is actually owned by the Home Office. A research team from Manchester University undertook a 'network analysis' of the UK's AML regime and found no fewer than eighty-eight organisations in the public and private sectors with central responsibilities for tackling money laundering.[3]

The problem is not just that the orchestra is playing blindfold. An equally important question is: who is conducting the orchestra? Who is responsible for removing the blindfolds and coordinating all these moving parts, overseeing the UK's national well-being concerning corruption?

The nearest we have to a conductor is the post of Anti-Corruption Champion. Since its creation in 2006, there have been eight Champions – though some have been more effective than others. The role is often described as 'the government's anti-corruption tsar', an incorrect – and slightly misleading – title. This is not a government position; it is a personal appointment by the Prime Minister, and so subject to the political patronage that an anti-corruption apparatus is usually meant to combat.

Until December 2024, when Margaret Hodge, a member of the Lords, was appointed, the position had always been held by an MP. Hodge has an excellent track record of anti-corruption campaigning and is personally held in high regard by both civil servants and civil society, which somewhat papers over the cracks in the governance of the role. But the truth is that the supposed conductor of the UK's anti-corruption orchestra, as well as being appointed at the whim of the Prime Minister, has no official status and can easily be ignored if they say or do inconvenient things.

Over time, the seniority of the post-holder has been downgraded from cabinet minister to backbencher, to a senior but non-ministerial peer. There have been long gaps between appointments; after the Champion who had served under Boris Johnson felt compelled to resign, neither Liz Truss nor Rishi Sunak appointed a replacement. Keir Starmer did so eventually, but only after six months in office. It clearly was not a high priority.

Such ad hoc positions always depend on the interest and energy of the incumbent – and this has varied over time. Eric Pickles (2015–17) enthusiastically engaged with civil society; he talked a good game – and, importantly, he changed the focus of the role so that it looked at corruption within the UK and not just abroad. However, he could never shake off the tag of being the man who abolished the Audit Commission, about which he remained unrepentant, even as his new brief must have showed him the problems it had caused. Ken Clarke (2010–14) spent much of his time as Champion being lobbied by businesses to repeal or water down the newly passed Bribery Act, which resulted in a long delay in its implementation; despite repeated requests, he refused to meet with Transparency International, which had led the decade-long campaign for the new law.

A few years earlier, John Hutton (2007–8) succeeded Hilary Benn (2006–7), the first Anti-Corruption Champion. Getting access to Hutton proved hard, so eventually I asked him, during the audience Q&A of a conference at which he was speaking, what his priorities would be in his role as the Anti-Corruption Champion. He seemed rather confused, and hurried on to another question. I was left with the impression that he actually had little recollection that he had been appointed to the position, which was later confirmed to me informally by officials.

When John Penrose (2017–22) was appointed to the role by Theresa May, I was not optimistic. A backbench MP who had previously worked in the City, he had only held a junior ministerial position. As it turned out, however, he was the best of the Anti-Corruption Champions since Hilary Benn kicked things off in 2006 with a flurry of initiatives – like funding specialist units in the City of London Police and the Met that were designed to counteract the negative attention the Blair government was attracting for its role in the BAE Systems bribery scandal.[4]

Penrose launched his tenure with an event to which he invited all those with an interest in corruption in the UK; as obvious as it might sound, he was the first Anti-Corruption Champion to have done so, and he continued in this vein through his five years in the role. Although the Johnson years were not propitious for tackling the political corruption that his premiership brought to the fore, progress was achieved in other areas: the Economic Crime Act of 2022, for instance, did take some steps forward in addressing the proceeds of corruption flowing around the UK's financial system.

Penrose's time in office came to an abrupt end when he resigned, deciding that the contradictions between the integrity of the post and serving under Boris Johnson had become too stark. He had also been the subject of jibes in the press; his wife was Dido Harding, who was responsible for the costly Covid test and trace scheme. The media are never shy of calling out hypocrisy – and that was the charge against the Penrose family. To my mind, it was unfair: there was no evidence of Harding having presided over a corrupt regime, and Penrose was doing a good job in difficult circumstances. It is notable that civil society and anti-corruption campaigners did not join in the attacks. However, this did highlight the politicised nature of the role, and how it can become the focus of media attention.

One of Penrose's tasks was to oversee the introduction of the UK's first national anti-corruption strategy in 2017, which was regarded as key to giving the role a sense of purpose and direction. For campaigners, having this strategy was something of a breakthrough, even though there had been a couple of shorter national plans before then. I remember visiting 10 Downing Street and explaining the benefits of a long-term strategy to tackle corruption. The officials did not seem convinced at the time, but the introduction of a strategy was one of a raft of announcements made by David Cameron in 2016, just before the Brexit referendum that would lead to his departure from office.

Many people were sceptical about Cameron's professed interest in corruption. They questioned why such an establishment figure would be concerned by such a subject. In private, leaders like Cameron often express their dislike of sitting round a table discussing world affairs with those who are known to be corrupt. Cameron himself has publicly given two examples of events that provoked his interest in the subject.[5] First, his realisation following a visit to Afghanistan that ordinary people might prefer life under brutal Taliban rule because it was less corrupt than the alternatives. And second, the bruising experience of bidding to host the football World Cup, when he turned up to the final vote with Prince William and members of the England delegation including David Beckham in December 2010 believing that they had a fair chance of being selected as hosts.

In the end, this belief would prove hopelessly optimistic: England received only two votes from the twenty-two delegates and was eliminated in the first round. Cameron and others became convinced that there had been some skulduggery, and subsequent events proved this to be correct: investigations revealed that there was widespread corruption within FIFA, including serial bribery. It culminated in the departure of Sepp Blatter as president and the indictment or sanctioning of ten of those twenty-two voting committee members. England had been discreetly asked for bribes by four different people in the FIFA hierarchy, but had not (as far as we know) paid them. The German delegate, football legend Franz Beckenbauer, allegedly sold his vote for 3 million euros, and received an additional 1.5 million euros when Russia won the vote. The winning bid by Russia was led behind the scenes by the now-sanctioned Putin ally Roman Abramovich, whose operation swiftly destroyed all laptops and other material used for the bids, as though there might have been something to hide.[6]

From speaking to members of the British delegation and other politicians, I had the impression that this British failure on the international stage due to corruption had a galvanising effect. The government had been outmanoeuvred by people playing to a different set of rules. It was no wonder that Cameron would take an interest in corruption and what could be done about it.

The tipping point that might have convinced Cameron to take action seems to have been the publication of the Corruption Perceptions Index by Transparency International in 2013.

The UK had slipped in ranking to seventeenth place – below not just the usual high performers, but also Barbados, a developing country and ex-colony that many in the UK would believe we should comfortably outperform in matters of governance. A former senior civil servant told me that when the UK's low ranking was published 'the blue touchpaper was lit'.

A cross-Whitehall review was commissioned, led by a top Foreign Office official who had been closely involved with the Bribery Act and was very familiar with the UK's anti-corruption apparatus. His initial recommendation was to concentrate everyone who had anything to do with anti-corruption matters into a single centralised unit. This revolutionary act would have brought officials from the Foreign Office, Department for International Development, Home Office, Department of Trade, Ministry of Justice and relevant Crown Prosecution Service and law enforcement elements under a single command. But most departments did not like the idea of giving up their staff to a new central command, in part because many of those staff had combined roles and were not dedicated to corruption (itself an interesting insight). Number 10 compromised; a golden opportunity had been missed.

Even the compromises, however, represented a considerable advance on what had gone before.[7] As well as announcing that there would for the first time be a national anti-corruption strategy, Cameron created a small team of civil servants, known as JACU (the Joint Anti-Corruption Unit), based at the centre of government in the Cabinet Office. Less successfully, an inter-ministerial group was created, so that ministers whose departments had something to do with corruption could come together to coordinate and make decisions. That sounds good in theory, and it occasionally worked well; but more often than not, once there was no longer direct leadership from the Prime

Minister it was subject to ministerial apathy, lack of interest and occasional turf wars.

Despite these shortcomings, for the three years before Cameron resigned the UK at last had someone conducting the orchestra, with the players operating more harmoniously than before.

JACU, in contrast to the inter-ministerial group, was a success story. If we are looking for encouraging things about the UK's approach to tackling corruption, this small team is an example of how energy can be maintained even once the political will has moved elsewhere. Although it was unceremoniously shunted from the Cabinet Office to the Home Office after Cameron resigned – with the unconvincing argument that this was somehow a more appropriate home – JACU worked quietly behind the scenes to draft the strategy and oversee its implementation, trying to coordinate the orchestra even if there was no longer a conductor. Most impressively, the civil servants seconded to it were generally first-class. Although in many ways it was not an obvious career choice for those who wanted to get on in the civil service, the people who were attracted to it were committed and willing to build their expertise.

Similarly, other parts of the UK's anti-corruption apparatus have often employed excellent personnel. I have encountered committed, intelligent and well-intentioned people in the anti-corruption teams of the police, prisons, the NHS, sporting bodies, the military, parliament and the private sector, to name but a few. They are usually being let down by the institutions in which they are working when there are senior managers and boards for whom corruption is a low priority. Often, managers and boards would rather not hear about corruption – not because they are implicated, but because corruption demands a response, which can be disruptive or costly or cause institutional embarrassment. Even when anti-corruption teams are working well and in a supportive environment, three things impede progress.

First there is the blindfold orchestra problem; however much of a virtuoso they are in their own field, circumstances prevent them playing in harmony with the rest of the orchestra. Much of the most successful anti-corruption work across the world, particularly in law enforcement, has succeeded because there has been cooperation and collaboration between different agencies and authorities. In the UK anti-corruption teams operate in silos, both within their organisations and in relation to other such teams in other sectors. There seem to be few opportunities either for sharing good practice or for mutual support.

Second, most of those charged with addressing corruption lack data. Perhaps because there has been a long-standing belief that corruption does not happen in the UK, even the institutions with the best anti-corruption approaches tend to be operating in a data-scarce environment. Surprisingly little is known about corruption in some key high-risk areas, including borders and immigration, modern slavery, social housing, health and care provision, local government and prisons. The same data gap will exist in five or ten years if those institutions do not put in place a systematic data-gathering procedure to help find out where corruption is happening, what form it takes, how prevalent it is and at what scale. On an encouraging note, the new anti-corruption strategy published in 2025 was accompanied by new data and surveys commissioned to fill some of the gaps, and contained a section acknowledging the need to gather more evidence.

Third, there is a gap in expertise. This does not mean that the UK lacks expertise in the field of corruption analysis, or that those individuals in anti-corruption positions are inexpert.

But time and again I have seen that practitioners are narrowly focused on a specialised field, and so are unaware of the wider context. For example, designing a programme to gather data about corruption in UK prisons would ideally draw on similar exercises around the world, and in different fields where such exercises have already been successful. But many of the UK's anti-corruption specialists have come to the field as practitioners, and so have not studied corruption beyond their own sector. For instance, police anti-corruption experts will unfailingly – and understandably – be trained police officers; but they will not have had a wider exposure to the anti-corruption movement, let alone an academic grounding in corruption analysis. Jonathan Benton, who was head of the NCA's International Corruption Unit before leaving to set up his own company, describes how 'I've learned huge amounts since moving into the private sector and I've had the privilege of working with some really interesting people, from NGOs to international banks and sovereign states. It's really opened my eyes as to [...] how insular policing and law enforcement is and how it's not harnessing the expertise and the resources that are out there.'[8]

Symptomatic of the UK's approach is the way responsibilities are split for the four international anti-corruption treaties and conventions to which the UK is a signatory. JACU is responsible for the OECD Anti-Bribery Convention and the UN Convention Against Corruption; the Financial Action Task Force relationship belongs to the Treasury; and the Group of States Against Corruption (GRECO), part of the Council of Europe, is owned by the Ministry of Justice. This is not to suggest those departments are doing a bad job; my point is that, with the responsibility for the UK's fight against corruption being split and spread so thinly, it is hard to take a strategic approach. And that is only compounded when nobody is in overall charge.

One obvious question is: who is checking up that these things are being coordinated, or that the Anti-Corruption Champion and JACU are doing a good job? The answer is a blank. The Champion notionally reports to the Prime Minister, but with the exception of when there is a corruption scandal, the activities and performance of the Champion are hardly likely to be a priority for any PM. At times, it has proven very hard for those outside the apparatus of government to hold the government accountable for its anti-corruption performance given how little information had been made available. For example, campaigners have in some periods only been able to find out the name of the current Anti-Corruption Champion by persuading friendly MPs to submit a question in parliament. Transparency and communication vastly increased under John Penrose, and continued under Margaret Hodge. But overall, the governance of the UK's anti-corruption approach shows all the signs of having grown organically and disjointedly, and without a strategic vision – somewhat ironic in a field that promotes good governance and transparency as a remedy.

A small part of this accountability gap has been filled by parliament's International Development Committee. What has it got to do with them? It all goes back to how the UK has traditionally perceived corruption. Funding for the National Crime Agency's anti-corruption work, and for JACU itself, comes from the UK's overseas aid budget (because successive governments have perceived corruption as an overseas problem). So the parliamentary committee that looks at overseas aid occasionally checks whether it is being well spent on tackling corruption. In fact, that committee has done a very good job, but the fact that it is the principal accountability mechanism for the UK's anti-corruption performance reflects the old logic that corruption is a problem that happens elsewhere.

*

Related to my theme of the need for someone to take charge when it comes to tackling corruption, next we have the conundrum of UK laws and law enforcement. Not all corruption can be addressed by a law enforcement approach but, where a corrupt act is also criminal, we might reasonably expect it to be investigated and prosecuted. On paper, we have some very good anti-corruption laws, such as the Bribery Act and the provision for unexplained wealth orders. We also have, for misconduct in public office, a law that is not very good (because it is very hard to get a successful prosecution against senior people) but which is now due to be replaced by new legislation on public office (accountability). Why, then, is there so little law enforcement activity around corruption?

The answer is that, in contrast to the US, the UK has failed to use its legislative armoury effectively. Bribery Act prosecutions are few and far between. They were tracked by accounting firm EY between July 2011, when the act came into force, and June 2020, and just twenty-three cases were found.[9] Another fifty-eight were prosecuted under various other laws such as the Proceeds of Crime Act and the Companies Act, though in some cases the offences had taken place many years earlier. That is an average of around ten bribery cases per year being prosecuted under a variety of laws. Given the evidence presented in this book, can we really believe that is even a small part of the bribery that goes on in this country? If we think the laws themselves are good enough, the numbers suggest that either our laws are not being used effectively or our law enforcement is weak.[10]

In fact, both are the case. We have good laws, but they are being underused – and our enforcement capacity is not strong enough. In 2022, the researcher Helena Wood estimated that

£43.1 million was allocated annually to enforcement activity, which relates to the tackling of grand corruption, foreign bribery and related money laundering and confiscation of proceeds. Of this, around half the budget and staff were allotted to HMRC, whose anti-money laundering enforcement has been described by Transparency International as offering 'little deterrent'.[11] Some key parts of the system assigned to the task of tackling corruption and money laundering did not appear to have any full-time staff dedicated to this exercise – including the Crown Prosecution Service (CPS).[12]

Sir David Green, former director of the Serious Fraud Office, believes: 'The budget could easily double. I say that because one of the biggest problems we face and the biggest hole in our defences [...] is the slew of dirty money coming into London. That money comes from grand corruption abroad and we are helping kleptocrats to launder their money.' He also notes that the SFO is a big net contributor to the public purse, through fines, assets recovered and financial settlements; during Green's tenure, every pound invested in enforcement there generated six pounds back to the Treasury.

Of course, these figures related principally – once again – to the UK's activities to combat overseas corruption. They were collated from a number of different government sources – indeed, the fact that no consolidated figures are available for how much is spent on law enforcement to combat corruption reinforces the point that it is a disjointed and neglected field. It is inconceivable that the government would be unable to publish figures on how much national resource is allocated to tackling other significant areas of crime.

One interesting recent development has been the creation in December 2024 of a new Domestic Corruption Unit (DCU), which sits within in the City of London Police. This is significant because it acknowledges the importance of domestic corruption, but also because the government has made a public commitment to expanding the DCU. It may come to play a transformative role in the UK's policing of corruption; but this still does not answer the problem of the blindfold orchestra and lack of conductor.

If the UK's anti-corruption governance is so neglected, we might ask what other countries do. Does anywhere else do it better? Unlike the majority of countries in the world, the UK does not have an anti-corruption agency to help identify and address such problems. ACAs (sometimes, for example in Australia, known as anti-corruption commissions) are envisaged in Articles 6 and 36 of the UN Convention Against Corruption as appropriate institutions to tackle corruption within a country. Such ACAs were set up by British administrations in former colonies like Singapore and Hong Kong; and, although until recently they had been less commonly found in advanced economies, in the past few years ACAs have been created in other economically advanced democracies such as Australia, Italy, South Korea and France.

Instead of putting in place an anti-corruption agency, the UK's approach to preventing and tackling corruption has been characterised by a 'multi-agency' approach, in which the role and powers are dispersed among multiple bodies and agencies. This would be an entirely legitimate approach – if it worked. However, there is a set of standards by which a country's anti-corruption apparatus can be benchmarked: the UN's Jakarta Principles set out sixteen underlying principles 'to promote and strengthen the independence and effectiveness' of a country's response to corruption, whether via a single anti-corruption agency or a multi-agency approach.[13] This is where the

UK clearly falls short; our apparatus does not fulfil these principles in a number of important respects, including independence from political interference and being 'established by a proper and stable legal framework'.

In reality, the track record of the UK is patchy. On the positive side, we have made progress in designing and implementing an anti-corruption apparatus. There may be no anti-corruption agency, but much has been put in place that did not exist two decades ago: an Anti-Corruption Champion, a civil service team, a national anti-corruption strategy, the Domestic Corruption Unit and two cross-departmental coordinating bodies.

However, the achievements, such as they are, have come via a series of tactical decisions rather than a strategic approach. The unsuccessful attempt in 2013 to establish a centralised co-ordinated anti-corruption command was a missed opportunity. As this chapter has shown, accountability relating to the governance of corruption is, quite literally, all over the place: split between different departments, overlaid by other committees, with several ministers, and a non-minister, all seeming to be in charge simultaneously.

The UK's anti-corruption strategy, launched in December 2025, opened with the words 'Corruption harms the UK and its citizens directly. It makes British people poorer and less safe, and undermines our democracy. Corruption fuels instability overseas, increasing crime, illegal migration, and other threats back in the UK.' It sounds like this is a threat that should be taken seriously. But there is a mismatch between the UK's current system of ad hoc governance and the government's stated concerns and aspirations on a subject that it has repeatedly said is vital for economic prosperity and national security. The conclusion must be that, while it is possible for the UK's approach to work when there is political and institutional will, it is less effective when those key components are lacking. As with governance in any other sphere, the nation's anti-corruption governance should act as a backstop when other key components are weak or missing – as well as acting as a support when those other key elements are present. The UK's experience suggests that more attention needs to be paid to this if we are to be consistently effective in tackling corruption.

You might recall from the Introduction that the UK's position in all the major indices of corruption has been falling. Things have been getting worse rather than better. We need an apparatus that can do three things:

1. ensure that the current and future strategies are delivered as effectively as possible, with associated benefits for national security, prosperity, and trust in institutions;
2. demonstrate that the UK is operating to global standards;
3. increase resilience: it is not clear that the current system can withstand a shock, whether that is an attempt at capture, a significant scandal, or something else.

In sum, the UK's anti-corruption governance is not fit for purpose. There are multiple agencies with partial responsibilities for corruption, in the public and private sectors. While we have created responses to individual scandals, we have failed to look at corruption as a systemic threat. The UK has much of the apparatus in place, but is weak in oversight, accountability, leadership and overall strategic direction.

The good news is that this should be reasonably easy to sort out with the right institutional structure in place – which requires a relatively small investment of resources but a larger investment of political will. Meanwhile, the blindfold orchestra plays on without a conductor, occasionally making a lot of noise but rarely playing in complete harmony.

16

LOOK AWAY NOW: LEARNINGS AND HOW TO FIX THINGS

We're all familiar with the phrase when the day's football matches appear at the end of the TV news: 'If you don't want to know the scores, look away now.' That same phrase could be applied to our national attitude to corruption: if you don't want to know about corruption, just look the other way. And that's precisely what we have been doing for the past three decades or so.

Let me summarise the five main arguments that I've made in this book.

First, we in Britain have a national tendency to moral exceptionalism; we find it hard to believe that corruption can really happen here, which leads people in senior positions to discount it, deprioritise it or turn a blind eye. When it comes to corruption, we have a national syndrome of complacency. We happily treat as rotten apples those egregious cases that are clearly symptomatic of a wider problem and are reluctant to see when there is a rotting barrel. The lack of hard data is no excuse for inaction; in the first place because putting the evidence together provides enough to make the case for change; and in the second place because there are sensible ways of using the existing evidence to make a case for anti-corruption activity being a much higher priority.

Second, if we look below the surface we can see far more

corruption in the UK than is widely understood or acknowledged. As distinguished historians have long demonstrated, the lack of visible corruption does not mean it did not – or does not – exist. The evidence of corruption presented here in areas like local government and prisons shows that much is simmering away, and in many different places. This information is scattered and dispersed: by putting it together in one place, this book has presented an overview that should be disturbing. Even so, it is a snapshot. Much more research needs to be done, but the national picture is that corruption in the UK is relatively widespread and seems to have been getting worse over the past decade. The UK's slide on global indices of corruption, governance and transparency is not a coincidence. Former prime minister John Major confirmed this as his view in June 2025: 'Britain enjoyed a very good reputation for being as free of corruption and bad practice as any nation in the world. I think that's a little less true today.'[1]

Third, there is a particular problem at the political level: the acceleration of scandals, under governments of all political colours, has revealed an absence of leadership on issues of integrity, with significant consequences throughout the public service. It also points to a relapse of integrity standards at the heart of our politics.

Fourth, we face a convergence of threats. These are both external, such as organised crime and hostile states, and internal, such as the decline in the public service ethos, the failure of public services and rising levels of inequality. Collectively, these threaten so many areas of our national integrity that our defences against corruption seem profoundly inadequate.

Finally, the ad hoc approach to the governance of anti-corruption apparatus in the UK – the blindfold orchestra without a conductor – is not fit for purpose. We know much less than we should, and we react much less well than we should.

Public inquiries illustrate this, having serially failed to reveal corruption even when it has subsequently been shown to exist. We can only conclude that the UK lacks the institutional knowledge and expertise to conduct an investigation into corruption, except in the narrowest criminal sense.

What about those arguments that the establishment, the monarchy or the neoliberal system are inherently corrupt? Interesting though they are, the problem is that they tend to be subjective or ideologically led and so can easily be undermined or disregarded by those who wish to remain in denial about corruption. There are other things going on that by any reckoning are corrupt, and my intention has been to focus on those.

But while I have sidestepped those more conceptual debates, I acknowledge that they contain underlying truths. There is no doubt that much corruption in this country results from the long historical tussle between private and public interests, and that the private interests now come in the form of companies, kleptocrats and high-net-worth individuals supported by a new establishment of fixers and enablers rather than the aristocrats of yore. There is no doubt that we continue to have an elite, but I would not conclude that we yet have the kind of structural corruption that characterises illiberal democracy or state capture abroad. However, the four-step test for corruption reveals more than enough for us to get worried – and nor are we immune to structural corruption. State capture is a destination we never want to reach, and we need to be sure that we do not take too many steps on that journey.

What Needs to Be Done

There is some good news, however. In terms political scientists would understand, we can break the cycle of path dependency and find an approach that combines rational choice and social norms to design a better national response to corruption – as long as the problem is properly acknowledged.

There has, since the 1990s, been some progress in the UK's approach to tackling corruption: updated legislation, a national anti-corruption strategy, gradual improvement in large companies' anti-bribery and corruption (ABC) procedures due to the Bribery Act, continuing global influence for the UK on the global anti-corruption agenda, and an increase in transparency helped by more open government and social media. The UK has some special powers; since 1990 there have been copious initiatives and institutional changes, some of which have been successful. There are knowledgeable and committed individuals in institutions as diverse as the police, prisons, local government and politics, and the UK has a strong civil society.

One of the UK's go-to responses for addressing corruption has been to take a lead on the international stage. The peak of its ambition was the genuinely successful London Anti-Corruption Summit, the high-water mark for the UK in this area. But Britain also has a track record of undermining its own efforts – the BAE Systems case of bribery in Saudi defence contracts in the early 2000s was internationally condemned, as is the UK's role as Londongrad, a centre for corrupt capital from the former Soviet Union and elsewhere. Overall, our recent international activities therefore present a mixed record. However, there remains an opportunity for leadership – but if we are to have international credibility we must clean up our own backyard. Moreover, as long as the default option for addressing corruption continues to be looking overseas, our focus will never be on corruption at home.

There are also some clear ingredients for a more successful outcome. These include adequately considering victims and harm when designing national responses, properly researching the issues to provide the kind of evidence that policymakers think they need, reviving and strengthening key areas of national integrity – including the adoption of unimplemented recommendations from the Committee on Standards in Public Life and closing the loopholes exposed by the Johnson government that make us vulnerable to political corruption. The UK should acknowledge and address the threats set out in Chapter Thirteen and make sure that the coin spinning in the air to decide the fate of each of the six influencing sectors highlighted in Chapter Nine lands on the side of integrity. There are practical recommendations in many of the chapters in this book, and some of these could be taken forward when the government is next reviewing its approach to corruption. This requires a coordinated and well-planned effort from both government and citizens; it requires leadership, and someone to take off the blindfolds and conduct the orchestra.

I am generally not in favour of adding new laws – we already have a good selection, though we require better enforcement as well as more creative application of existing laws. However, I am strongly supportive of the idea that we need a general replacement for the misconduct in public office offence, akin to the corruption in public office approach proposed by the Law Commission.* The Public Office (Accountability) Bill that is currently in parliament may in due course play that role. We need to be more aware of the conflict between private interests and the public interest; we should crack down hard on abuses in the dark quartet of lobbying, the revolving door, political donations and conflicts of interest by exercising the option of long-term debarments from public contracts.

---

*The government has announced its intention to introduce a new law on public office accountability to replace misconduct in public office.

Several corruption scholars have recently emphasised the benefits of what might be described as 'tackling corruption without tackling corruption'.[2] In other words, by addressing other weaknesses and strengthening related areas – for example, by reinforcing the UK's 'special powers' as outlined in Chapter Fourteen – corruption might be prevented. To that extent, the disastrous abolition of the Audit Commission should be a warning. Just as we can fight corruption by strengthening accountability mechanisms and law enforcement, we can weaken our defences when short-term decisions have unintended long-term consequences.

Finally, the big question: does the UK need a powerful, wide-ranging anti-corruption agency? A single body responsible for all corruption in the UK could either be coordinating and educational or have investigative and prosecutorial powers like the Serious Fraud Office – or it could be a hybrid of the two.[3] ACAs have been highly successful in some countries, notably Singapore and Hong Kong, and generally less successful in countries with weak overall governance, although we should be closely watching Australia, France and Italy, which have all recently created them.

We certainly need someone to conduct the orchestra, and there are strong arguments in favour of creating an ACA that have never seriously been addressed in the UK. The feeling in government and parliament has been that we do not need one. When I have periodically raised the idea with other agencies on whose space a new ACA might impede, they have been fiercely territorial.

There are also alternatives to an ACA that should be properly explored. For example, the central anti-corruption command envisaged by David Cameron's advisers in 2013, or a new position of Anti-Corruption Commissioner, as proposed recently by former prime minister Gordon Brown. Such a role – low-cost, but designed to hold the nation to a high standard – would be akin to the Children's Commissioner, the Anti-Slavery Commissioner or the Office for Environmental Protection. It seems to me that the UK might not yet be ready for an ACA, but we have certainly outgrown the post of the Prime Minister's Anti-Corruption Champion.

Ultimately, however we go about it, the UK's fight against corruption needs strong political and institutional will in one direction and impetus from citizens and voters in the other. There is no inevitability that the UK will sleepwalk over the edge of the cliff, but lack of leadership makes that more likely, and, apart from the positive blips during the premierships of John Major and David Cameron, this has been the UK's biggest weakness since 1990.

Britain perceives itself to be much less corrupt than other countries, with a common belief that corruption is widespread overseas. Complacency and denial mean that the UK is ill-prepared to tackle the corruption challenges it faces.

In short, we have both surprisingly high levels of corruption and surprisingly weak defences against it. Since the 1950s, some things have got better – but some important things have got worse, and there has been an acceleration over the past decade. We have seen dirty money pouring in from overseas; at times a near-collapse of basic integrity standards in politics; and the deep penetration of organised crime gangs into areas of the country where the state is weak or absent.

The UK is not alone; such challenges are also faced by all other liberal democracies in an age of instability, change and populism. What is at stake is the primacy of democratic values that have served so many countries so well since the Second

World War, but where both politics and economics are going off the rails. The world has yet to see how liberal democracies can take a proactive approach to tackling today's challenge from corruption. Britain does have a chance to show leadership. But even without such a lofty aspiration, it has a need to strengthen its own defences against corruption so that it can manage current and future challenges.

For proponents of the big bang theory of corruption reform (the idea that you need a big shock to jolt a political system into a new direction), the political turmoil of the Brexit years might come to be seen as such a moment for the UK.[4] The fracturing of the national equilibrium in this period might provide the impulse for a moment of self-reflection and a spur to reform. Or like revolutions and coups in so many other countries, it could cause the UK to revert to a modernised version of the corruption from which it had slowly dragged itself between the Middle Ages and the Victorian era.

At present, the UK may be sleepwalking over a cliff edge into a deeper condition of corruption. We just need to look across the Atlantic to see what might happen. Our weaknesses can be exploited by those who prioritise private or criminal interests over the public interest. A failure to address the threats could see a further deterioration. Faced with the political and economic challenges of post-Brexit Britain, those who have the power and responsibility to create change might give in to the inevitable short-term pressures of political firefighting and business as usual, and shy away from the necessary actions. That in turn could open the door to those who are not just lacking in integrity, but are genuinely corrupt.

But things could also get better, leading to a higher standard of politics, improved public institutions and a revived meritocracy. The long-term stability and enhanced international reputation this creates would provide a platform for economic growth. It is ironic that the phrase 'Singapore-on-Thames' has become associated with low regulation. To anti-corruption experts, Singapore is, in fact, a jurisdiction with high standards, thoroughly policed, and in which corruption is vigilantly dealt with by a strong, dedicated government agency. It is a model that has helped the country on its way to becoming one of the world's richest.

I have argued that, in many areas of our national life, integrity has been gradually disappearing – and, in some areas like politics, not so gradually. That does not mean we should think of the past as a golden age – there has always been a certain level of corruption in the UK, and always will be. But at times we have been better at keeping it in check. Yet I remain an optimist. Our national integrity is disappearing, not disappeared, and it is not too late to act. Here's my top five list of things we should be doing:

1) Support and defend key institutions; of the several mentioned in this book I would prioritise the judiciary, civil society, public service broadcasters and public auditors.

2) Be active citizens – record and report incidents of corruption and do not be prepared to tolerate it, whether in the workplace or in public services or in public figures (however much we may like them for other reasons), vote wisely in elections at all levels, and follow and subscribe to those on social media who promote transparency and accountability such as investigative journalists.

3) Put corruption analysis at the core of our public inquiries, which are mechanisms that already exist to examine scandals in detail but have serially ignored corruption.

4) Act firmly on the small things, whether in the police, prisons, local government or elsewhere, since minor breaches of integrity normalise such behaviour and are a pathway to corruption.

5) Introduce thorough reforms targeted at political corruption, starting with political donations and lobbying. But this is a list of areas to start with, and by no means the full list: we need leadership with the authority to deliver a strategic approach – we need a conductor for the orchestra.

In the UK, in too many places, rotten apples are already becoming a rotting barrel. This is corruption in the old-fashioned sense. The body politic is becoming infected by what might be described as subcutaneous corruption, lurking beneath the surface and barely kept in check by institutions that have in recent years been stretched too thin. It feeds the concern of voters that democracy has failed, that our politics and economy are no longer capable of guaranteeing security, prosperity and a fair society. This underlying weakness is vulnerable to a convergence of new threats to which Britain is therefore ill-equipped to respond. In the past, we have muddled through. But the old defences were barely adequate, and faced with new forms of corruption in a globalised world, things look in bad shape. The door is open for a malign actor to exploit the UK's weakness.

This should act as a stark warning to policymakers. By ignoring the threat of corruption, we have failed to put in place the defences that many other countries have. Like weeds taking over a garden, once corruption takes hold, it progresses with great speed and is hard to undo. Britain is not invulnerable.

ACKNOWLEDGEMENTS

This book has been decades in the making, and so there are many people to thank. That also means there is not room for everyone by name, so first of all, to all who have played a part in helping me research the material or form views, very, very many thanks, and apologies if you are not personally mentioned in this list. Likewise, a large number of interviewees have either asked to remain anonymous, or were having conversations informally or off the record, and my thanks go to all of them. You know who you are.

At Transparency International: Rachel Davies, Nick Maxwell, Maggie Murphy, Jameela Raymond, Dominic Kavakeb, Duncan Hames, Juliet Swann, Steve Goodrich, Ben Cowdock, Rose Zussman, Rose Whiffen, James Sale, Peter van Veen, Peter Wilkinson, Rory Donaldson, Joe Ghandhi, Chandu Krishnan, Mark Pyman and the outstanding team of Defence specialists, John Drysdale, Laurence Cockcroft, Peter Berry, Jeremy Carver, Jeff Kaye, Dominic Martin, David Nussbaum, Fiona Thompson and fellow Board members, Claire Prescott, Kamila Przybyszewska, Kate Zechner, Jan Lanigan, Delia Ferreira Rubio, Rueben Lifuka, A. J. Brown, Frank Vogl, Robin Hodess, Finn Heinrich, Dieter Zinnbauer, Anne Koch, Deborah Unger, Paul Zoubkov, Cobus de Swardt and many, many more.

The faculty at the University of Sussex's Centre for the

Study of Corruption, which has been an exceptional academic and intellectual community: in particular, and most especially, Liz Dávid-Barrett, Becky Dobson Phillips, Georgia Garrod, Tom Shipley, Dan Hough; also Tena Prelec, Devi Pillay, Dan Haberly, Aya Eldeeb, Shahrzad Fouladvand, Dan Paget, Francis McGowan; and over the years, our universally excellent PhD students and those on our MA in Corruption & Governance, many of whom have gone on to work in this field.

In and around the UK Anti-Corruption Coalition and related campaigning and investigative journalism: Sue Hawley, Helen Taylor, Gavin Hayman, Thom Townsend, Louise Russell Prywata, Nick Hildyard, Alex Jacobs, George Boden, Anthea Lawson, Melissa Lawson, Bill Browder, Oliver Bullough, Peter Geoghegan, Tom Burgis, Robert Palmer, Josie Stewart, Dan Neidle, Tom Keatinge and the team at RUSI, Stevie Wolfe, Susannah Fitzgerald, Peter Munro.

Fellow academics have been exceptionally generous with their time and thinking: among many, Paul Heywood, Mark Philp, Heather Marquette, Matthew Stephenson, Michael Johnston, Dani Kaufmann, Roxana Bratu, Sam Power, Mark Knights, John Jupp, Paul Taggart, Paul Webb, Will McCready, Lucy Welsh, Judith Townend, Michael Macaulay, Michael Levi, John Heathershaw and his team at Exeter University, Nik Kirby and Ian Cawood. The journey started with my life as a historian, and my thanks go especially to Robert Beddard, the late Jeremy Catto and David Starkey. Among many institutions and archives, Marco Zhang of Oriel College, the staff of the Bodleian Library, the University of Sussex Library and the West Sussex County Office.

Many civil servants, officials and politicians – whom I will not name, but who may recognise themselves or their views in the text. Within the City, private sector and the legal profession,

Acknowledgements

Karina Litvack, Jonathan Benton, Leo Martin, Michael Bowes, David Green, Sam Eastwood, Lucy Wolley Dod, Guy Beringer, Michael Bennett, Patricia Robertson, Sara Carnegie, Stephen Mayson, James Ford and the TIPS Network, Nicola Bonucci.

My agent, Charlotte Merritt of Andrew Nurnberg Associates, and Nick Humphrey, editor at Profile Books, along with his first-class team – we would not be here without you both.

And most notably, to my immediate family and close friends. Sorry if I bored you with my enthusiasm. Thank you for looking after me.

REFERENCES

Preface

1   Rothstein, B., 2011, 'Anti-corruption: The indirect "big bang" approach', *Review of International Political Economy*, 18(2), pp. 228–50.

Introduction

1   Platt, E., and Parker, G., 17 October 2020, 'UK credit rating downgraded by Moody's', *Financial Times*.

2   Ernst & Young, 2012, *UK Bribery Digest: Fraud Investigation and Dispute Services*, Edition 1, London: Ernst & Young LLP.

3   BBC News, 18 November 2011, 'Court clerk Munir Patel jailed for taking bribes', available at: www.bbc.co.uk/news

4   Ernst & Young, 2013a, *UK Bribery Digest*, Edition 2, London: Ernst & Young LLP.

5   Ernst & Young, 2013b, *UK Bribery Digest*, Edition 3, London: Ernst & Young LLP.

6   Vannucci, A. and Porta, D., 1999, *Corrupt Exchanges: Actors, Resources and Mechanisms of Political Corruption*, New York: Aldine de Gruyter.

7   Lord, N., Doig, A., Levi, M., van Wingerde, K. and Benson, K., 2020, 'Implementing a divergent response? The UK approach to bribery in international and domestic contexts', *Public Money & Management*, 40(5), pp. 349–59.

8   Andresen, M. S. and Button, M., 2019, 'The profile and detection of bribery in Norway and England & Wales: A comparative study', *European Journal of Criminology*, 16(1), pp. 18–40, Table 1.

9   Home Office, 2024, *Economic Crime Survey*, London: Home Office.

10   Ernst & Young, 2018 and 2019, *UK Bribery Digest*, Editions 12 & 13, London: Ernst & Young LLP.

1. Peculiarly British: The Small Print on What We Mean by Corruption

1   For example, Heywood, P. M., 2017, 'Rethinking corruption: Hocus-pocus, locus and focus', *Slavonic and East European Review*, 95(1), pp. 21–48.

2   Pozsgai-Alvarez, J. and Pastor Sanz, I., 2021, 'Mapping the (anti-)corruption field: Key topics and changing trends, 1968–2020', *Journal of Computational Social Science*, 4(2), pp. 851–81.

3   Johansen, E., 1990, *Political Corruption: Scope and Resources: An Annotated Bibliography*, New York: Garland Publishing.

4   Dobson Phillips, R., Dávid-Barrett, E. and Barrington, R., 2025, 'Defining corruption in context', *Perspectives on Politics*, pp. 1–15.

5   An excellent summary of the theoretical debates can be found in Picci, L., 2024, *Rethinking Corruption: Reasons Behind the Failure of Anti-Corruption Efforts*, Cambridge: Cambridge University Press.

6   Dobson Phillips et al., 2025, op. cit.

7   Nye, J. S., 1967, 'Corruption and political development: A cost–benefit analysis', *American Political Science Review*, 61(2), pp. 417–27.

8   Noonan, J. T., 1987, *Bribes*, Berkeley: Univ of California Press; Picci, 2024, op. cit.

9   Heywood, P., 1997, 'Political corruption: Problems and perspectives', *Political Studies*, 45(3), pp. 417–35; Philp, M., 1997, 'Defining political corruption', *Political Studies*, 45(3), pp. 436–62.

10 Kaufmann, D. and Vicente, P. C., 2011, 'Legal corruption', *Economics & Politics*, 23(2), pp. 195–219.

11 Lessig, L., 2013, '"Institutional corruption" defined', *The Journal of Law, Medicine & Ethics*, 41(3), pp. 553–5; Thompson, D. F., 2018, 'Theories of institutional corruption', *Annual Review of Political Science*, 21(1), pp. 495–513.

12 Williams, W., 2020, *Windrush Lessons Learned Review*, London: House of Commons, p. 7.

13 Lessig, 2013, op. cit.

14 Johnston, M., 2005, *Syndromes of Corruption: Wealth, Power, and Democracy*, Cambridge: Cambridge University Press.

15 Ibid., Appendix A, p. 221.

16 Ibid., pp. 60–88.

17 Dincer, O. and Johnston, M., 2025, *Corruption in America: A Fifty-Ring Circus*, Cambridge: Cambridge University Press.

18 For example, Vergara, C., 2020, *Systemic Corruption: Constitutional Ideas for an Anti-Oligarchic Republic*, Princeton: Princeton University Press.

19 Mungiu-Pippidi, A., 2015, *The Quest for Good Governance: How Societies Develop Control of Corruption*, Cambridge: Cambridge University Press.

20 Schama, S., 26 April 2025, 'Trump's war on knowledge', *Financial Times*.

21 BBC Radio 4, 7 May 2023, *Desert Island Discs*.

2. Two Baronesses and Other Stories: Applying the Theory to Real-life Cases

1 Russell, B., 1938, *Power: A New Social Analysis*, London: George Allen & Unwin.

3. How We Got Here: A Brief Recap of the Past 600 years

1 Charteris-Black, J., 2011, *Politicians and Rhetoric: The Persuasive Power of Metaphor*, Basingstoke: Palgrave Macmillan, p. 54.

2 Rothstein, B., 2011, 'Anti-corruption: The indirect "big bang" approach', *Review of International Political Economy*, 18(2), pp. 228–250.

3 Kroeze, R., Vitória, A. and Geltner, G. (eds.), 2018, *Anticorruption in History: From Antiquity to the Modern Era*, Oxford: Oxford University Press; see therein Watts, John, J., 'The Problem of the Personal: Tackling Corruption in Later Medieval England, 1250–1550', Chapter 6.

4 Shipley, T. and Barrington, R. (eds.), 2022, 'A Bibliography for UK Corruption Studies', CSC Working Paper No. 14, Falmer: University of Sussex.

5 Doig, A., 1984, *Corruption and Misconduct in Contemporary British Politics*, Harmondsworth: Penguin Books.

6 Jones, P., 2023, *Corrupt Britain: Public Ethics in Practice and Thought Since the Magna Carta*, Cham: Palgrave Macmillan.

7 Chibnall, S. and Saunders, P., 1977, 'Worlds apart: Notes on the social reality of corruption', *The British Journal of Sociology*, 28(2), pp. 138–54; Jones, P., 2012, 'Rethinking corruption in post-1950 urban Britain: The Poulson affair, 1972–1976', *Urban History*, 39(3), pp. 510–28; Jones, P.,

2019, 'Urban governance and its disorders: Corruption in the cities', *International Journal of Regional and Local History*, 14(2), pp. 55–61.

8   O'Connell, D., 20 August 2006, 'BAE cashes in on £40bn Arab jet deal', *The Sunday Times*.

9   An excellent summary of this passage of history is available in: *The Bribery Act 2010: Post-legislative Scrutiny*, London: House of Lords, 2019.

10   Standards in Public Life (The Nolan Report), 1995, London: HMSO.

11   Wearmouth, R., 4 November 2021, 'Britain could "slip into being a corrupt country", ethics chief warns amid Tory sleaze row', *Daily Mirror*.

12   Evans, J., 2023, *Upholding Standards in Public Life: A Keynote Speech by Lord Evans*, London: Institute for Government.

13   Knights, M., 2021, *Trust and Distrust: Corruption in Office in Britain and its Empire, 1600–1850*, Oxford: Oxford University Press.

14   Cawood, I. and Crook, T., 2022, *The Many Lives of Corruption: The Reform of Public Life in Modern Britain, c. 1750–1950*, Manchester: Manchester University Press

4. Tone from the Top: Political Corruption

1   Transparency International UK, 2 December 2022, 'Analysis finds dozens of potential Ministerial Code breaches were not investigated', available at: www.transparency.org.uk

2   For example, Geoghegan, P., 2020, *Democracy for Sale: Dark Money and Dirty Politics*, London: Bloomsbury Publishing; and Cave, T. and Rowell, A., 2014, *A Quiet Word: Lobbying, Crony Capitalism and Broken Politics in Britain*, London: Penguin.

3   Cave, T., January 2012, *Written Evidence Submitted by Tamasin Cave, SpinWatch*, London: Political and Constitutional Reform Committee, available at: www.parliament.uk; Transparency International UK, 2015, *Accountable Influence: Bringing Lobbying Out of the Shadows*, available at: www.archive.transparency.org.uk

4   Dunn, W., 3 July 2024, 'Revealed: the 103 professional lobbyists standing in the 2024 general election', *New Statesman*.

5   Barrington, R., 25 November 2021, 'There is more corruption and corruption risk in and around this government than any British

government since 1945', LSE British Politics Blog, available at: https://blogs.lse.ac.uk/politicsandpolicy/government-corruption

6   Blick, A. and Hennessy, P., 2019, *Good Chaps No More? Safeguarding the Constitution in Stressful Times*, London: The Constitution Society, p. 5.

7   Oborne, P., 2020, *The Assault on Truth: Boris Johnson, Donald Trump and the Emergence of a New Moral Barbarism*, London: Simon & Schuster; see also Oborne, P., 18 November 2019, 'How the media let Boris Johnson get away with his deceit', *Guardian*.

8   Hastings, M., 24 June 2019, 'I was Boris Johnson's boss: he is utterly unfit to be prime minister', *Guardian*.

9   Blick and Hennessy, 2019, op. cit., p. 7.

10   Major, J., 19 June 2025, *Speech at the Institute for Government Conference*, available at: www.johnmajorarchive.org.uk

11   London Playbook, 19 June 2025, available at: www.politico.eu/newsletter/london-playbook

12   Heren, K., 15 October 2022, 'Tory government is "most corrupt for at least a century", says Gordon Brown as he unveils sweeping reforms', available at: www.lbc.co.uk

13   Committee of Public Accounts, 2022, *Government's Contracts with Randox Laboratories Ltd*, HC 28, Session 2022–23, London: House of Commons, p. 5.

14   Hine, D. and Peele, G., 2016, *The Regulation of Standards in British Public Life*, Manchester: Manchester University Press, pp. 1–2.

15   *Financial Times*, 1 August 2021, 'The Conservatives and the whiff of chumocracy', available at: www.ft.com

16   Waterson, J., 24 August 2022, 'Emily Maitlis says "active Tory party agent" shaping BBC news output', *Guardian*.

17   Verity, A., 13 November 2023, 'Cameron's return revives memories of Greensill finance scandal', available at: www.bbc.co.uk/news

18   Bowers, J., 25 October 2024, 'Starmer's ethical scorecard so far', *Prospect Magazine*.

19   Kingstone, K., 12 December 2025, 'The Anti-Corruption Strategy: where are the commitments on political integrity?' *Spotlight on Corruption*, available at: www.spotlightcorruption.org

20   Dávid-Barrett, E., 5 May 2022, 'Is the UK sliding into state capture?' The Constitution Society, available at: www.consoc.org.uk

21 Hine, D. and Peele, G., 2016, 'The Regulation of Standards in British Public Life: Doing the Right Thing?' in Hine and Peele, 2016, op. cit., p. 1.

22 Dávid-Barrett, 2022, op. cit.

5. Former Glories: Monarchy and Empire

1 openDemocracy, 9 September 2021, 'Concerns raised over top Tory donors bankrolling Prince Charles' charity', available at: www. opendemocracy.net; *Financial Times*, 1 August 2021, op. cit.

2 Scott, J. C., 1969, 'The analysis of corruption in developing nations', *Comparative Studies in Society and History*, 11(3), pp. 315–41.

3 Kroeze, R., Dalmau, P. and Monier, F., 2021, 'Introduction: Corruption, Empire and Colonialism in the Modern Era: Towards a Global Perspective', in Kroeze, R., Dalmau, P. and Monier, F. (eds.), *Corruption, Empire and Colonialism in the Modern Era*, Palgrave Studies in Comparative Global History, Singapore: Palgrave Macmillan.

4 Knights, M., 2021, *Trust and Distrust: Corruption in Office in Britain and its Empire, 1600–1850*, Oxford: Oxford University Press, Chapter 2.

5 Cawood, I. and Crook, T., 2022, 'Epilogue: The British Way in Corruption', in Cawood and Crook (eds.), 2022, op. cit., p. 287.

6 Finn, M. C., 2019. 'Material turns in British history: II. Corruption: imperial power, princely politics and gifts gone rogue', *Transactions of the Royal Historical Society*, 29, pp. 1–25.

7 Rotberg, R. I., ed. M. F. Shore, 1988, *The Founder: Cecil Rhodes and the Pursuit of Power*, Oxford: Oxford University Press, p. 70.

8 Ibid., p. 187.

9 Gandhi, M., ed. Louis Fischer, 2002, *The Essential Gandhi: An Anthology of His Writings on His Life, Work, and Ideas*, New York: Vintage, p. 144.

10 Angeles, L. and Neanidis, K. C., 2015, 'The persistent effect of colonialism on corruption', *Economica*, 82(326), pp. 319–49.

11 Macpherson, W., 1999, *The Stephen Lawrence Inquiry*, Cm. 4262, London: HMSO.

12 Casey, L., 2025, *National Audit on Group-Based Child Sexual Exploitation and Abuse*, London: Home Office.

13 Barr, A. and Serra, D., 2010, 'Corruption and culture: An experimental analysis', *Journal of Public Economics*, 94(11–12), pp. 862–9.

6. The Private Sector Paradox: Is it, or Isn't it?

1 Kay, J., 31 October 2025, 'What exactly are we paying for? The UK's legacy of privatising utilities', *Financial Times*.

2 Wood, G., 2003, *Edison's Eve: A Magical History of the Quest for Mechanical Life*, New York: Anchor Books.

3 Campbell, D., 14 March 2025, 'What were the Lansley reforms and how did they create NHS England?', *Guardian*.

4 Muirhead, C., 19 January 2025, 'Children's homes run by private equity rake in millions', *This is Money*, available at: www.thisismoney.co.uk

5 Bach-Mortensen, A. M., Goodair, B. and Barlow, J., 2022, 'Outsourcing and children's social care: A longitudinal analysis of inspection outcomes among English children's homes and local authorities', *Social Science & Medicine*, 313, p. 115323.

6 Robinson, M., 5 September 2017, 'How Macquarie bank left Thames Water with extra £2bn debt', available at: www.bbc.co.uk/news; Healy, E., 29 April 2025, 'Macquarie "very proud" of Thames Water ownership', *Financial Times*; Macquarie Group Limited, August 2023, *Thames Water – Factsheet: Upgrading London's Water and Wastewater Infrastructure*, Sydney: Macquarie Group Limited, available at: www.macquarie.com

7 Sri-Pathma, V. and Labiak, M., 28 May 2025, 'Thames Water fined £122.7m in biggest ever penalty', available at: www.bbc.co.uk/news

8 Croft, J., 12 January 2022, 'UK government's "VIP lane" for PPE suppliers was unlawful, High Court rules', *Financial Times*.

9 Goodrich, S. (ed), 2024, *Behind the Masks: Corruption Red Flags in COVID-19 Public Procurement*, London: Transparency International UK.

10 Dávid-Barrett, E., Fazekas, M., Hellmann, O., Márk, L. and McCorley, C., 2020, 'Controlling corruption in development aid: New evidence from contract-level data', *Studies in Comparative International Development*, 55(4), pp. 481–515.

11 Hayman, G., 9 September 2024, 'Was UK's COVID PPE procurement even worse than we thought? New analysis raises more red flags',

London: Open Contracting Partnership, available at: www.open-contracting.org

12   Williams, M., 8 September 2021, 'Record profits for Tory donor's firm that won huge PPE contracts', openDemocracy, available at: www.opendemocracy.net; Burke, D., and Bright, S., 21 September 2023, 'Tory donor whose firm got £160million in Covid contracts handed top Government trade job', *Mirror*.

13   Good Law Project, 23 February 2024, 'How to build a thriving business: Sell the government £551m of useless PPE', available at: www.goodlawproject.org

14   Smith, B., 11 March 2022, 'Seven billion items of pandemic PPE "not fit for purpose"', *Civil Service World*.

15   National Audit Office, 26 November 2020, press release: Investigation into government procurement during the COVID-19 pandemic, available at: www.nao.org.uk

16   Committee on Standards in Public Life, June 2014, *Ethical Standards for Providers of Public Services*, London: Committee on Standards in Public Life.

17   Committee on Standards in Public Life, May 2018, *The Continuing Importance of Ethical Standards for Public Service Providers*, London: Committee on Standards in Public Life, p. 7.

18   Hayman, 9 September 2024, op. cit.

19   Baker, A., 2010, 'Restraining regulatory capture? Anglo-America, crisis politics and trajectories of change in global financial governance', *International Affairs*, 86(3), pp. 647–63.

20   Home Office, 2024, op. cit.

21   BBC Radio *File on 4*, 17 January 2023, 'Catastrophe at the Academy,' available at: www.bbc.co.uk/programmes.

22   Chartered Institute of Building, September 2013, *A Report Exploring Corruption in the UK Construction Industry*, Ascot: Chartered Institute of Building.

23   Gee, J., Button, M., Hock, B. and Shepherd, D. W. J., 2021, *Fraud and Corruption in the Construction Sector*, London: Crowe UK.

24   Chartered Institute of Building, 2013, op. cit.

25   Kersley, A., 28 February 2025, 'Collapsing balconies, West Ham tickets

and a council that got very cosy with developers', available at: www.
the-londoner.co.uk.

7. Men in Suits: The Old and New Establishment

1   Lammy, D., 21 May 2024, *Kleptocracy Speech*, London: Institute for
Public Policy Research.

2   Markson, T., 4 July 2023, 'Blob? What blob? Sunak rejects criticism of
civil service', available at: www.civilserviceworld.com

3   Truss, L., 10 December 2024, *The Prime Minister Versus the Blob:
Documentary*, produced by Palladium Pictures for the *Wall Street
Journal*, available at: www.elizabethtruss.com

4   Truss, L., 20 February 2025, speech to CPAC 2025, available at: www.
elizabethtruss.com

5   Jones, O., 2014, *The Establishment: And How They Get Away With It*,
London: Allen Lane.

6   Warren, M. E., 2006, 'Political corruption as duplicitous exclusion', *PS:
Political Science & Politics*, 39(4), pp. 803–7.

7   Kaltwasser, C. R., Taggart, P. A., Espejo, P. O. and Ostiguy, P. (eds.),
2017, *The Oxford Handbook of Populism*, Oxford: Oxford University
Press.

8   Foreign, Commonwealth and Development Office, 3 March 2022,
Designation: Igor Ivanovich Shuvalov (RUS0265), *UK Sanctions List*,
available at: https://search-uk-sanctions-list.service.gov.uk/
designations/RUS0265/Individual

9   Transparency International UK, 31 January 2018, 'Unexplained Wealth
Orders in use: Here's at least 5 cases the police should consider today!',
London: Transparency International UK, available at: https://archive.
transparency.org.uk/uwo-consider-today

10 *Financial Times*, 7 April 2025, 'Letter from Charlie Geffen: It's entirely
right Big Law avoids a fight with the administration', available at: www.
ft.com

11 Siddons, E. and Pegg, D., 17 April 2025, 'Queen Elizabeth's lawyer
helped manage millions for alleged war criminal Rifaat al-Assad', *The
Bureau of Investigative Journalism*, available at: https://www.
thebureauinvestigates.com

12 Coughtrie, S. and ARTICLE 19, 2022, *'London Calling': The Issue of*

    Legal Intimidation and SLAPPs Against Media Emanating from the United Kingdom, London: Foreign Policy Centre.

13 Heathershaw, J., Prelec, T. and Mayne, T., 2024, *Indulging Kleptocracy: British Service Providers, Postcommunist Elites, and the Enabling of Corruption*, Oxford: Oxford University Press.

14 Cowdock, B., 2022, *Bell Pottinger and Reputation Laundering in South Africa*, in Barrington, R., Dávid-Barrett, E., Power, S. and Hough, D., (eds.), 2022, *Understanding Corruption: How Corruption Works in Practice*, Newcastle: Agenda Publishing, p. 197.

15 Amersi, A., 1 September 2022, 'I'm a Tory Party donor – here's what you don't know about cash for access', *The London Economic*, available at: https://www.thelondoneconomic.com/opinion

16 Pickard, J., Kinder, T. and Thomas, D., 3 March 2022, 'Boris Johnson under pressure to sack Tory fundraiser over Russia links', available at: www.ft.com; Elliott, K., 3 March 2022, 'The 6 Russian oligarchs who donated £2m to Tory party since Boris became PM', *Express*.

17 Pickering, H. and Gouglas, A., 28 February 2023, 'Most special advisers become lobbyists after leaving government – new research', *The Conversation*.

18 Shone, E., 6 March 2025, 'Dozens of Tory spads become lobbyists amid "unenforceable" revolving door rules', available at: https://www.opendemocracy.net

19 Transparency International UK, 31 January 2018, op. cit.

20 HM Government, 2025, *National Security Strategy 2025: Security for the British People in a Dangerous World*, CP 1338, London: HM Government, para 20.

8. Men in Uniform: Police, Prisons and Borders

1   Transparency International, 2013, *Global Corruption Barometer 2013*, Berlin: Transparency International, available at: www.transparency.org/en/gcb

2   Zotzmann, K., 2025, *Codes of Corruption: A Critical Realist Discourse Analysis of Illicit Transactions*, Abingdon: Taylor & Francis.

3   Bisoyi, S., 14 November 2025, 'CBI files FIR, takes over Odisha police recruitment scam case', *Indian Express*.

4   Holmes, R., 6 December 2016, 'The secret prison corruption epidemic

the government doesn't want you to know about', BuzzFeed News, available at: https://www.BuzzFeed.com; Barrington, R., Silverman, J. and Hutton, M., 2021, 'Corruption in UK prisons: A critical evaluation of the evidence base', *Prison Service Journal*, 252, pp. 46–57.

5   House of Commons Justice Committee, 19 March 2019, 'Prison population 2022: planning for the future', Sixteenth Report of Session 2017–19, London: House of Commons.

6   Prisoners' Advice Service, 28 October 2025, 'Number of prison and probation staff dismissed for misconduct doubles', available at: https://www.prisonersadvice.org.uk

7   Kotecha, S., 14 November 2024, 'Prison officers deal drugs and ask inmates for sex, BBC told', available at: www.bbc.co.uk/news

8   Ibid.

9   Taylor, M., 27 October 2023, 'Barlinnie boss calls for new law to punish corrupt prison officers', *Holyrood News*, available at: www.holyrood.com/news

10   Kotecha, 2024, op. cit.

11   BBC News, 18 July 2011, 'Downview sex case prison governor jailed', available at: www.bbc.co.uk/news

12   Prisons and Probation Ombudsman, 2025, *Investigation into the Failing of Medomsley Detention Centre between 1961 and 1987*, London: Prisons and Probation Ombudsman.

13   Cadbury, R., 29 January 2024, 'Written Question 11799: Prison Officers: Dismissal', available at: www.parliament.uk

14   Kotecha, 2024, op. cit.; see also https://www.gov.uk/government/statistics/
hm-prison-and-probation-service-workforce-quarterly-march-2025

15   Gregory, R. and Macaulay, M., 2023, Chapter 5: Integrity and Misconduct in Public Office, in *Handbook of Public Administration Reform*, Cheltenham: Edward Elgar Publishing, pp. 77–89.

16   For example, Inside Time: www.insidetime.org

17   Issah, H., 14 November 2014, 'Inside UK prisons: Shocking reports of corruption and misconduct among officers', available at: https://swipein.co.uk/inside-uk-prisons-shocking-reports-of-corruption-and-misconduct-among-officers; Shipley, D., 15 November 2024, 'How corrupt are Britain's prisons?', *Spectator*.

18 Podmore, J., 2012, *Out of Sight, Out of Mind: Why Britain's Prisons Are Failing*, Hull: Biteback Publishing, p. 88.

19 Kotecha, 2024, op. cit.

20 HM Prison and Probation Service, 2020, *HMPPS Business Strategy: Shaping Our Future*, London: HM Prison and Probation Service.

21 insidetime, 11 November 2025, 'Disciplinary investigations into MoJ staff rise by 70%', available at: www.insidetime.org

22 Sources for statistics and references in this section can be found at Barrington, R., and Fouladvand, S., 5 September 2024, *Corruption, Human Trafficking and UK Borders*, Centre on Migration, Policy and Society (COMPAS) Blog, available at: www.compas.ox.ac.uk

23 Jancsics, D., 2019, 'Law enforcement corruption along the U.S. borders', *Security Journal*, 32(3), pp. 237–56.

24 UNDP, 30 September 2021, *Corruption and Contemporary Forms of Slavery: Examining Relationships and Addressing Policy Gaps*, New York: UNDP.

25 Haenlein, C., 25 April 2024, *Organised Crime and the UK Border: Tackling Criminal Innovation at the Frontline*, London: RUSI.

26 Warren, J., 14 March 2024, 'Met Police's corrupt police officer hotline is rolled out nationally', available at: www.bbc.co.uk/news

27 Webb, S. and Burrows, J., 2009, *Organised Immigration Crime: A Post-conviction Study*, Home Office Research Report 15, London: Home Office, p. 5.

28 For example, Clarkson, W., 2020, *Line of Duty – The Real Story of British Police Corruption*, London: John Blake Publishing; Gillard, M., 2019, *Legacy: Gangsters, Corruption and the London Olympics*, London: Bloomsbury Publishing.

29 BBC News, 7 October 2022, 'Met Police creates anti-corruption unit to "root out" criminal officers', available at: www.bbc.co.uk/news

30 *The Economist*, 3 April 2025, 'State capture is a growing threat. Reversing it is hard', pp. 50–51.

31 Holmes, L., 2014, 'Police Corruption and Misconduct in Central and Eastern Europe', in William B. Simons (ed.), *East European Faces of Law and Society: Values and Practices*, Leiden: Brill Nijhoff, pp. 151–74.

32 Leveson, Lord Justice, 2012, *An Inquiry into the Culture, Practices and Ethics of the Press*, HC 780-II, London: HMSO, p. 933 s.7.1.

33 Available at: https://archive.org/details/OperationTiberius

34 Harper, T., 11 January 2014, 'The corruption of Britain: UK's key institutions infiltrated by criminals', *Independent*.

35 See also Cox, B., Shirley, J. and Short, M., 1977, *The Fall of Scotland Yard*, London: Penguin.

36 De Simone, D., 14 November 2023, 'Senior Stephen Lawrence officer Ray Adams was corrupt, says secret Met report', available at: www.bbc.co.uk/news

37 Ellison, M., 2014, *The Stephen Lawrence Independent Review: Possible Corruption and the Role of Undercover Policing in the Stephen Lawrence Case – Summary of Findings*, HC 1094, London: HMSO.

38 Ibid., paras 2c and 2d.

39 Daniel Morgan Independent Panel, 2021, *The Report of the Daniel Morgan Independent Panel*, vols. I–III. HC 11-I/II/III, London: HMSO.

40 Available at: https://www.met.police.uk/police-forces/metropolitan-police/areas/notices/daniel-morgan-independent-panel-report

41 Casey, L., 2023, *An Examination of the Metropolitan Police Service: Final Report*, London: Metropolitan Police Service, p. 284.

42 Undercover Policing Inquiry, available at: https://www.ucpi.org.uk; see also https://www.spycops.co.uk/the-story and https://campaignopposingpolicesurveillance.com

43 Casey, L., March 2023, *Baroness Casey Review: Press Notice*, London: Metropolitan Police Service, available at: https://www.met.police.uk

44 Ibid., p. 7.

45 Criminal Cases Review Commission, n.d. *Police Misconduct: DS Ridgewell*, available at: https://ccrc.gov.uk/police-misconduct-ds-ridgewell

46 Independent Police Complaints Commission, 2012, *Corruption in the Police Service in England and Wales: Second Report – a Report Based on the IPCC's experience from 2008 to 2011*, HC 784, London: HMSO.

47 Independent Office for Police Conduct, 8 October 2025, 'Gross misconduct proven against ex-Warwickshire detective who formed inappropriate relationship', available at: https://www.policeconduct.gov.uk

48 Greater Manchester Police, 19 April 2024, 'Serving police officer jailed

after being found guilty of corruption charges', available at: https://www.gmp.police.uk/news

49   Independent Police Complaints Commission, 2012, *The Abuse of Police Powers to Perpetrate Sexual Violence*, London: IPCC, Foreword.

50   Independent Office for Police Conduct, 2024, *Learning the Lessons Issue 44: Corruption*, London: IOPC, p. 11.

51   Casey, 2023, op. cit., p. 279.

52   Independent Office for Police Conduct, 2024, op. cit., p. 36.

9. Two Sides of the Coin: The Influencing Sectors

1   Persson, A., Rothstein, B. and Teorell, J., 2013, 'Why anticorruption reforms fail – systemic corruption as a collective action problem', *Governance*, 26(3), pp. 449–71.

2   Cheeseman, N. and Peiffer, C., 2025, 'Opening the door to anti-system leaders? Anti-corruption campaigns and the global rise of populism', *European Journal of Political Research*, 64(1), pp. 134–55.

3   BBC Radio 4, 26 July 2023, *Reflections: Kenneth Clarke*, Series 1 Episode 1, available at: https://www.bbc.co.uk/programmes

4   Hilton, A., 25 February 2016, 'Stay or Go?', *Evening Standard*.

5   Leveson, Lord Justice, 2012, op. cit., p. 1748.

6   Savage, M., 26 April 2025, 'Gordon Brown makes criminal complaint against Rupert Murdoch's media empire', *Guardian*.

7   See in particular the BBC's Local Democracy Reporting Service, available at: https://www.bbc.co.uk/lnp/ldrs

8   Fukuyama, F., 2021, 'Making the internet safe for democracy', *Journal of Democracy*, 32(2), pp. 37, 44.

9   Asomah, J. Y., Dim, E. E., Li, Y. and Cheng, H., 2024, 'What factors are associated with public corruption perception? Evidence from Canada', *Journal of Financial Crime*, 31(3), pp. 524–44.

10   Media Matters, 26 February 2024, 'A guide to the MAGA media universe', available at: www.mediamatters.org

11   Nation Cymru, 13 February 2022, 'Concern Anglesey second home hotspot is being used to create "shell companies"', available at: https://nation.cymru

12   BBC News, 22 July 2010, updated 5 August 2013, 'Timeline: Ian Tomlinson's death', available at: www.bbc.co.uk/news

13 Duncan, P. and Lord, N., 2024, 'Fit and proper? Analyzing the potential for illicit activity through English Premier League club ownership structures', *Sport in Society*, pp. 1–21.

14 Harwood-Baynes, M., 5 November 2021, 'Azeem Rafiq: Yorkshire Cricket chairman resigns as he accuses club board of refusing to accept racism claims', available at: https://news.sky.com

15 United Nations Office on Drugs and Crime, 9 December 2021, *Global Report on Corruption in Sport*, Vienna: UNODC, p. 35.

16 Barrington, R. (ed.), 2010, *Corruption in the UK: Part One – National Opinion Survey*, London: Transparency International UK.

17 Hough, D. 2025, *Foul Play*, Newcastle: Agenda Publishing, p. 120.

18 Proverbs 17:23.

19 Independent Inquiry into Child Sexual Abuse (2022), *The Report of the Independent Inquiry into Child Sexual Abuse*, HC 720, London: HMSO.

20 Culbertson, A., 27 May 2024, 'Nigel Farage called out for "blanket accusation" as he says "growing number" of Muslims "loathe" British values', available at: https://news.sky.com

21 Charity Commission, 2023, *Charities and Their Relationship with the Public: Trust in Charities 2023*, London: Charity Commission for England and Wales.

22 Summary of *The Times*' reporting on this: Weakley, K., 9 February 2018, 'Oxfam accused of covering up use of prostitutes by aid workers', available at: https://www.civilsociety.co.uk/news

23 BBC News, 11 February 2018, 'Oxfam Haiti sex claims: Charity "failed in moral leadership"', available at: www.bbc.co.uk/news

24 openDemocracy, 14 June 2019, 'The tangled web of Tory leadership candidates and climate science denial', available at: https://www.opendemocracy.net

25 Kiely, E., Gore, D'A. and Farley, F., 10 September 2024, *A Guide to Project 2025*, available at: https://www.factcheck.org

26 Griffiths, S., 24 September 2024, 'The changing think tank environment', available at: https://consoc.org.uk; Monbiot, G., 16 September 2025, 'Trussed up', available at: https://www.monbiot.com

27 Matthews, D., 10 November 2022, 'Universities silent as UK

government seeks to close Confucius Institutes', available at: https://
sciencebusiness.net

28 Cooley, A., Prelec, T., Heathershaw, J. and Mayne, T. (2021), *Paying for a World Class Affiliation: Reputation Laundering in the University Sector of Open Societies*, Washington, DC: National Endowment for Democracy.

10. Life Beyond London: Local Government

1 This story is drawn from Berriman, A., 2015. *Squibs: The 1830 Chichester Election Campaign*, New Chichester papers no. 7, Chichester: University of Chichester.

2 Jones, P., 2013, *From Virtue to Venality: Corruption in the City*, Manchester: Manchester University Press, pp. 116–17; see also Jones, P., 2022, 'Civic Corruption in the Twentieth Century: The Case of Belfast and Glasgow, c. 1920–70', in Cawood and Crook (eds.), 2022, op cit., pp. 259–78.

3 Caller, M., 2021, *Liverpool City Council Best Value Inspection: December 2020–March 2021*, London: Ministry of Housing, Communities and Local Government.

4 Drury, C., 28 March 2025, 'You did what you were told: Inside Liverpool City Council's collapse', *Independent*.

5 BBC News, 23 April 2015, 'Tower Hamlets election fraud mayor Lutfur Rahman removed from office', available at: www.bbc.co.uk/news; see also Richard Mawrey QC's Judgment: Erlam & Ors v Rahman & Anor [2015] EWHC 1215 (QB).

6 Bond, D., 13 May 2022, 'Lutfur Rahman: Inside the shock return of Tower Hamlets' divisive mayor', *Evening Standard*.

7 Mawrey Judgment, para 250.

8 Ibid., paras 247–8.

9 Ibid., paras 504–7.

10 Ibid., paras 464–8.

11 Ibid., para 475.

12 Bromley-Derry, K., Binjal, S., Jenkins, J. and Simpkins, P., 2024, *Best Value Inspection of the London Borough of Tower Hamlets*, London: Ministry of Housing, Communities and Local Government, Conclusion section 10.

13   Clark, N., 21 January 2026, 'Government may tighten grip on east London council', available at: www.bbc.co.uk/news

14   Mawrey Judgment, para 474.

15   Timmins, N., 7 February 2011, 'Scrapping audit body risks "independence"', *Financial Times*.

16   Dávid-Barrett, E., Barrington, R. and Maxwell, N. (eds.), 2013, *Corruption in UK Local Government: The Mounting Risks*, London: Transparency International UK.

17   Thomas, H., 6 September 2023, 'Local government audit is a serious mess', *Financial Times*.

18   Department for Communities and Local Government News Story, 12 August 2010, 'Eric Pickles "shows us the money": Departmental books are opened to an army of armchair auditors', available at: https://www.gov.uk/government/news/eric-pickles-shows-us-the-money-as-departmental-books-are-opened-to-an-army-of-armchair-auditors

19   Worthy, B., 27 September 2023, 'Who's watching local government?', UK in a Changing Europe, available at: https://ukandeu.ac.uk

20   Stride, G. and Walker, A., November 2023, *The Changing Role of the Monitoring Officer*, London: Local Government Information Unit.

21   Ministry of Housing, Communities and Local Government, 2020, op. cit.

22   Williams, J., 7 January 2025, 'UK officials recommend probe into Houchen's Teesworks project', *Financial Times*.

23   Department for Levelling Up, Housing and Communities, 7 June 2023, *Terms of Reference: Independent Review into the Tees Valley Combined Authority's Oversight of the South Tees Development Corporation and Teesworks Joint Venture*, London: DLUHC.

24   Ministry of Housing, Communities and Local Government, 2020, op. cit.

25   Dávid-Barrett, Barrington, and Maxwell (eds.), 2013, op. cit.

26   Silva, R., 8 July 2024, 'Our corrupt planning system needs rebuilding', *The Times*.

27   Kiely, M., July 2024, letter to *The Times*, apparently unpublished but available on LinkedIn *sub* Mike Kiely; see also Waite, R., 9 July 2024, 'Ex-PM adviser's swipe at "corruption" in planning system sparks backlash', *Architects' Journal*.

28   Klitgaard, R., 1988, *Controlling Corruption*, Berkeley: University of California Press.

29   Goodrich, S. (ed.), 2020, *Permission Accomplished: Assessing Corruption Risks in Local Government Planning*, London: Transparency International UK.

30   Holly Watt, H., Newell, C. and Bryant, B., 10 March 2013, 'Councillors for hire who give firms planning advice', *Daily Telegraph*.

31   Tower Hamlets Borough Council, 25 January 2018, *Non-Executive Report of the Standards (Advisory) Committee*, available at: https://towerhamlets.moderngov.co.uk

32   Goodrich (ed.), 2020, op. cit.

33   Ministry of Housing, Communities and Local Government, 2020, op. cit., p. 21.

34   Jones, A., 2021, 'Combatting corruption and collusion in UK public procurement: Proposals for post-Brexit reform', *Modern Law Review*, 84(4), pp. 667–707.

35   Home Office, 6 February 2025, *Serious and Organised Crime Local Profiles: A Guide*, London: Home Office.

11. The Nations: Life Far Beyond London

1   Jones, P., 2022, 'Civic Corruption in the Twentieth Century: The Case of Belfast and Glasgow, c. 1920–70', in Cawood and Crook, 2022, op. cit., pp. 259–78.

2   Mungiu-Pippidi, A., 2013, 'Becoming Denmark: Historical designs of corruption control', *Social Research: An International Quarterly*, 80(4), pp. 1259–86 – borrowing from Francis Fukuyama.

3   Veenendaal, W., 2019, 'How smallness fosters clientelism: A case study of Malta', *Political Studies*, 67(4), pp. 1034–52.

4   Openshaw, P., 6 November 2025, *Inquiry into the Retirement of the Former Commissioner of Police: Final Report*, Gibraltar: Government of Gibraltar.

5   Goodrich, S., 19 January 2025, 'Grossly improper: How Gibraltar's Chief Minister interfered in a criminal investigation', available at: www.transparency.org.uk

6   Goodrich, S. (ed.), 2025, *Power Politics: Emerging Insights Into Climate Lobbying in Scotland*, London: Transparency International UK

7   https://www.copfs.gov.uk/crime-info/bribery-and-corruption/bribery-prosecutions-in-scotland

8   The Construction Index, 19 June 2015, 'Four jailed over Edinburgh council corruption', available at: https://www.theconstructionindex.co.uk

9   Construction Management, 30 April 2012, 'Council official sacked after contractor reports attempted bribe', available at: https://constructionmanagement.co.uk

10 The Edinburgh Tram Inquiry, 2023, *Lord Hardie's Report*, Edinburgh: The Edinburgh Tram Inquiry.

11 *Daily Record*, 2 September 2012. 'Revealed: 145 cops reported for alleged corruption … but just six prosecuted', available at: https://www.dailyrecord.co.uk/news

12 Ibid.

13 BBC 1 *Disclosure*, 27 September 2022, 'The Great Ferries Scandal', available at: www.bbc.co.uk/programmes

14 Smith, B., 22 September 2023, *Procurement of Vessels 801 (MV Glen Sannox) and 802. Allegations of Fraud. Report to Caledonian Maritime Assets Limited*, Edinburgh: Caledonian Maritime Assets Limited.

15 Williams, M., 30 November 2022, 'Anger as £130m of taxpayers' money "lost" by Scot gov-run shipyard', *Herald*.

16 Matthews, A. and Vladev, L., 16 October 2023, 'National Museum Wales: Payment of £325k to ex-chief questioned', available at: www.bbc.co.uk/news

17 Audit Wales, 2023, *Governance Arrangements Relating to the Employment Dispute at Amgueddfa Cymru – National Museum Wales*, Cardiff: Audit Wales.

18 Welsh Government, 13 July 2023, *National Museum Wales: Tailored Review*, Cardiff: Welsh Government; Public Accounts and Public Administration Committee, June 2024, *Scrutiny of Accounts: Amgueddfa Cymru 2021–22*, Cardiff: Welsh Parliament.

19 Lewis, G., 27 February 2024, 'Vaughan Gething cleared of code breach over £200k donation', available at: www.bbc.co.uk/news

20 YouGov, 2024, 'Should there be a limit on donations made to political parties by individuals?', London: YouGov, available at: https://yougov.co.uk

21 Evans, N., April 2023, *Prosiect Pawb: Key Findings*, available at: https://www.partyof.wales/prosiect_pawb

22 Cagurangan, M-V., 11 March 2023, 'Panuelo bares rampant bribery; several FSM officials in cahoots with China', available at: https://www.pacificislandtimes.com

23 Silke, A., 2000, 'Drink, drugs, and rock'n'roll: Financing loyalist terrorism in Northern Ireland – Part two', *Studies in Conflict & Terrorism*, 23(2), pp. 107–27.

24 Jupp, J. and Garrod, M. (2019), 'Legacies of the Troubles: The links between organized crime and terrorism in Northern Ireland', *Studies in Conflict & Terrorism*, 45(5–6), pp. 389–428.

25 Department of Finance (Northern Ireland), 2020, *The Report of the Independent Public Inquiry into the Non-domestic Renewable Heat Incentive (RHI) Scheme*, vols 1–3, Belfast: Department of Finance (RHI Inquiry Report, 2020).

26 RHI Inquiry Report, 2020, vol. 3 para 58.3 section 38.

27 Ibid., para 54.63.

28 Reports available at: https://www.niauditoffice.gov.uk

12. Fruitless Inquiries: The Vacuum at the Heart of Public Inquiries

1 See also Building Control Independent Panel, 15 July 2025, *Guidance: Problem Statement for the Building Control Independent Panel*, London: Ministry of Housing, Communities and Local Government.

2 The Edinburgh Tram Inquiry, 2023, op. cit.

3 Department of Finance (Northern Ireland), 2020, op. cit.

4 Independent Inquiry into Child Sexual Abuse (2022), op. cit.

5 Casey, 2025, op. cit.

6 Abbasi, K., 2024, 'Infected blood scandal: British medicine's worst moment', *BMJ* 2024; 385: q1235.

7 Infected Blood Inquiry, 2024, *Infected Blood Inquiry: The Report*, HC 569-I-7, London: HMSO.

8 https://www.ucpi.org.uk

9 https://covid19.public-inquiry.uk

10 https://www.postofficehorizoninquiry.org.uk

11 James, J., 1 November 2017, 'The patronising disposition of unaccountable power': *A Report to Ensure the Pain and Suffering of the*

Hillsborough Families Is not Repeated, HC 511, London: House of Commons.

12 Tees Valley Review, 23 January 2024, *Independent Review Report: South Tees Development Corporation and Teesworks Joint Venture*, London: Department for Levelling Up, Housing and Communities.

13 Tobin, S., 6 September 2022, 'Osofsky calls for reform of disclosure rules', *Law Society Gazette*.

14 Covid Counter Fraud Commissioner, December 2025, *Pursuing Recoveries and Preventing Reoccurrence: Final Report of the Covid Counter Fraud Commissioner*, CP 1462, London: HM Treasury.

13. Seven Threats to the Body Politic: How Things Might Go Badly Wrong

1 Marquette, H. and Peiffer, C., 2018, 'Grappling with the "real politics" of systemic corruption: Theoretical debates versus "real-world" functions', *Governance*, 31(3), pp. 499–514.

2 Bauhr, M., 2012, 'Need or greed corruption?', in Holmberg, S. and Rothstein, B. (eds.), *Good Government*, Cheltenham: Edward Elgar Publishing.

3 Literature reviewed in Campbell, L., 2016, 'Corruption by Organised Crime' – A Matter of Definition?, *Current Legal Problems*, vol. 69, issue 1, pp. 115–41.

4 NCA, April 2020, *Annual Plan 2020–2021: Leading the UK's Fight to Cut Serious and Organised Crime*, London: National Crime Agency.

5 Available at: https://archive.org/details/OperationTiberius

6 Fieschi, C. and Heywood, P., 2004, 'Trust, cynicism and populist anti-politics', *Journal of Political Ideologies*, 9(3), pp. 289–309.

7 NCA, 2025, *National Strategic Assessment 2025 of Serious and Organised Crime*, London: National Crime Agency.

8 https://globalinitiative.net/analysis/ocindex-2023

9 Vannucci, A., 2024, 'Mani pulite ("clean hands")', in De Sousa, L. and Coroado, S. (eds.), *Elgar Encyclopedia of Corruption and Society*, Cheltenham: Edward Elgar Publishing, pp. 176–9.

10 Vannucci, A., 1997, 'Politicians and Godfathers: Mafia and Political Corruption in Italy', in della Porta, D. and Meny, Y. (eds.), *Democracy*

and Corruption in Europe*, London: Frances Pinter Publishers,
pp. 50–64.

11   Haberly, D. and Wójcik, D., 2022, *Sticky Power: Global Financial Networks in the World Economy*, Oxford: Oxford University Press; see also Haberly, D., Garrod, G. and Barrington, R., 2024, 'From Secrecy to Scrutiny: A New Map of Illicit Global Financial Networks and Regulation', CSC Working Paper No. 18, Falmer: Centre for the Study of Corruption, University of Sussex.

12   See https://www.nationalcrimeagency.gov.uk/threats-2025/ nsa-illicit-finance-2025

13   HM Government, December 2025, *UK Anti-Corruption Strategy 2025*, *CP1454*, London: Home Office, para 54.

14   Intelligence and Security Committee of Parliament, 21 July 2020, *Russia*, HC 632, London: HMSO.

15   Bennett, O. and Shalchi, A., 6 April 2022, *Economic Crime in the UK: A Multi-billion-pound problem*, CBP 9013, London: House of Commons Library.

16   Uslaner, E. M., 2015, 'The Consequences of Corruption', in Heywood, P. (ed.), *Routledge Handbook of Political Corruption*, Abingdon: Routledge, pp. 198–211.

17   Rothstein, B. and Uslaner, E. M., 2005, 'All for all: Equality, corruption, and social trust', *World Politics*, 58(1), pp. 41–72.

18   Cheeseman, N. and Peiffer, C., 2025, 'Opening the door to anti-system leaders? Anti-corruption campaigns and the global rise of populism', *European Journal of Political Research*, 64(1), pp. 134–55.

19   Newburn, T., 2016, 'Social Disadvantage, Crime, and Punishment', in Hartley, D. and Platt, L. (eds.), *Social Advantage and Disadvantage*, Oxford: Oxford University Press, pp. 322–40.

20   https://taxpolicy.org.uk/2023/01/29/ three-wrong-takes-on-the-zahawi-affair

21   Magnus, L., 29 January 2023, *Letter from Sir Laurie Magnus to the Prime Minister, 29 January 2023*, London: Prime Minister's Office, 10 Downing Street.

22   Taggart, P., 2018, 'Populism and "Unpolitics"', in Fitzi, G., Mackert, J. and Turner, B. (eds.), *Populism and the Crisis of Democracy: Volume 1: Concepts and Theory*, Abingdon: Routledge, pp. 79–87.

23   Geoghegan, P., 5 January 2019, 'Revealed: the dirty secrets of the DUP's "dark money" Brexit donor', available at: www.opendemocracy.net.

24   Dunning, S. and Kwong, A., September 2022, *An Investigation of China's Confucius Institutes in the UK*, London: The Henry Jackson Society.

25   Intelligence and Security Committee of Parliament, 13 July 2023, *China*, HC 1605, London: HMSO, para 10.

26   Zakaria, F., 1997, 'The rise of illiberal democracy', *Foreign Affairs*, 76, p. 22.

27   House of Lords, 6 March 2025, 'Iranian State Threats', *House of Lords Hansard*, vol. 844, no. 105, col. 365.

28   Tidy, J., 31 January 2026, 'I mocked the Saudi leader on YouTube – then my phone was hacked and I was beaten up in London', available at: www.bbc.co.uk/news

29   Murphy, S., 14 July 2019, 'Reporter who Boris Johnson conspired to have beaten up demands apology,' available at: www.theguardian.com

30   Dávid-Barrett, L., 5 May 2022, 'Is the UK sliding into state capture?', *The Constitution Society*, available at: www.consoc.org.uk

14. Dull-but-Important: The UK's Special Powers

1   For more details on whistleblowing reforms needed in the UK see the NGO Protect: https://protect-advice.org.uk

2   Barrington, R. and Dávid-Barrett, E., 2023, 'Advocacy groups', in *Elgar Concise Encyclopedia of Corruption Law*, Cheltenham: Edward Elgar Publishing, pp. 12–15.

3   Bingham, T. H., 2011, *The Rule of Law*, London: Penguin.

4   Stott, D., 13 January 2021, 'Ministerial influence in judicial appointments – taking back control?' UK Constitutional Law Blog, available at: https://ukconstitutionallaw.org

5   https://worldjusticeproject.org/rule-of-law-index/global/2024/historical

6   Amin, L., 2020, 'Art of Darkness: How the government is undermining freedom of information', London: openDemocracy, pp. 6–7.

7   https://www.corruptionrisk.org/about

8   https://openaccess.transparency.org.uk

9   The National Archives, 2024, *Annual Report and Accounts 2023–24*, HC 71, London: The National Archives.

10 Evans, J., 11 November 2020, *The Hugh Kay Lecture: Are We in a Post-Nolan Age?*, speech delivered at the Institute of Business Ethics.

11 Evans, J., 17 October 2023, *Upholding Standards in Public Life: A Keynote Speech by Lord Evans*, London: Institute for Government.

12 Heywood, P. M. and Rose, J., 2015, 'Curbing Corruption or Promoting Integrity? Probing the Hidden Conceptual Challenge', in Hardi, P., Heywood, P. and Torsello, D. (eds.), *Debates of Corruption and Integrity: Perspectives from Europe and the US*, London: Palgrave Macmillan, pp. 102–19.

13 Major, J., 20 May 1995, 'Mr Major's Doorstep Comments on the Nolan Report', doorstep comments made in south-east Cambridgeshire, 20 May, available at: https://johnmajorarchive.org.uk

14 Committee on Standards in Public Life, 1995, *Standards in Public Life: First Report of the Committee on Standards in Public Life*, Cm 2850-I, London: HMSO, paras 18–19.

15 Culbertson, A., 6 June 2021, 'Boris Johnson's anti-corruption tsar resigns over Partygate and will vote for PM to go', available at: www.news.sky.com

16 Committee on Standards in Public Life, 2021, *Upholding Standards in Public Life: Final Report of the Standards Matter 2 Review*, London: Committee on Standards in Public Life.

17 Jones, P., 2016, *From Virtue to Venality*, Manchester: Manchester University Press, p. 116.

15. The Blindfold Orchestra: Who Is in Charge?

1 Maxwell, N., Cowdock, B. and Barrington, R. (eds.), 2016, *Corruption Laws: A Non-Lawyers' Guide to Laws and Offences in the UK Relating to Corrupt Behaviour*, London: Transparency International UK, Annex 1, pp. 64–5.

2 Independent Commission for Aid Impact Information Note, March 2020, *Mapping the UK's Approach to Tackling Corruption and Illicit Flows*, London: Independent Commission for Aid Impact, Annex A.

3 Bociga, D., Bellotti, E. and Lord, N., 2025, 'The network architecture of anti-money laundering: Strategic and tactical (dis)connections in the UK's policy, supervision, and enforcement landscape', *British Journal of Criminology*, p. 101ff.

References

4   DFID, 2006, *Combating International Corruption: UK Action Plan for 2006/07*, London: Department for International Development (DFID).

5   Cameron, D., 3 December 2017, *Corruption: More than a Cancer: Transparency International UK Annual Lecture*, London: Transparency International UK.

6   Gordon, A., 27 June 2017, 'What we know about corruption in the 2018 and 2022 World Cup bids', available at: https://www.vice.com

7   Institutional arrangements are laid out in UK's UNCAC submission of 2019: HM Government, 2019, *Country Review Report of the United Kingdom: United Nations Convention against Corruption*, London: HM Government.

8   Barrington, R., Franca e Ribeiro, A. and Garrod, G. (eds.), 2022, 'Resourcing UK Law Enforcement to Tackle Grand Corruption and Kleptocracy', CSC Working Paper No. 13, Falmer: Centre for the Study of Corruption, University of Sussex.

9   Ernst & Young, 2020, *UK Bribery Digest,* Edition 14, accessed 20 May 2021, London: Ernst & Young LLP.

10 Heathershaw, J. and Mayne, T., 2023, 'Explaining suspicious wealth: Legal enablers, transnational kleptocracy, and the failure of the UK's Unexplained Wealth Orders', *Journal of International Relations and Development*, 26(2), pp. 301–23.

11 Evans, J., 8 July 2018, 'HMRC doubles fines for money laundering', *Financial Times*.

12 Barrington, Franca e Ribeiro and Garrod (eds.), 2022, op. cit.

13 United Nations Office on Drugs and Crime, 2012, *Jakarta Statement on Principles for Anti-Corruption Agencies*, Jakarta: UNODC, available at: www.unodc.org

16. Look Away Now: Learnings and How to Fix Things

1   Major, J., 19 June 2025, *Keynote Speech. The Nolan Principles at 30: What Does the Future Hold for Standards in Public Life?*, Institute for Government, available at: https://www.instituteforgovernment.org.uk

2   Heywood, P. M., 2018, 'Combating corruption in the twenty-first century: New approaches', *Daedalus*, 147(3), pp. 83–97; Hough, D., 2017, 'International approaches to tackling corruption: What works and what doesn't?', *Frontiers of Law in China*, 12(3), pp. 339–54; Kaufmann, D.,

29 November 2012, 'Rethinking the fight against corruption', Brookings, available at: https://www.brookings.edu/articles
3   Kuris, G., 2015, 'Watchdogs or guard dogs: Do anti-corruption agencies need strong teeth?', *Policy and Society*, 34(2), pp. 125–35.
4   Pasculli, L., 2019, 'Seeds of systemic corruption in the post-Brexit UK', *Journal of Financial Crime*, 26(3), pp. 705–18.

SELECTED BIBLIOGRAPHY

Abbasi, K., 2024, 'Infected blood scandal: British medicine's worst moment', *BMJ* 2024;385: q1235.

Andresen, M. S. and Button, M., 2019, 'The profile and detection of bribery in Norway and England & Wales: A comparative study', *European Journal of Criminology*, 16(1), pp. 18–40.

Angeles, L. and Neanidis, K. C., 2015, 'The persistent effect of colonialism on corruption', *Economica*, 82(326), pp. 319–49.

Asomah, J. Y., Dim, E. E., Li, Y. and Cheng, H., 2024, 'What factors are associated with public corruption perception? Evidence from Canada', *Journal of Financial Crime*, 31(3), pp. 524–44.

Bach-Mortensen, A. M., Goodair, B. and Barlow, J., 2022, 'Outsourcing and children's social care: A longitudinal analysis of inspection outcomes among English children's homes and local authorities', *Social Science & Medicine*, 313, p. 115323.

Baker, A., 2010, 'Restraining regulatory capture? Anglo-America, crisis politics and trajectories of change in global financial governance', *International Affairs*, 86(3), pp. 647–63.

Barr, A. and Serra, D., 2010, 'Corruption and culture: An experimental analysis', *Journal of Public Economics*, 94(11–12), pp. 862–9.

Barrington, R. (ed.), 2010, *Corruption in the UK: Part One – National Opinion Survey*, London: Transparency International UK.

Barrington, R., Silverman, J. and Hutton, M., 2021, 'Corruption in UK prisons: A critical evaluation of the evidence base', *Prison Service Journal*, 252, pp. 46–57.

Barrington, R., Franca e Ribeiro, A. and Garrod, G. (eds.), 2022. *Resourcing UK Law Enforcement to Tackle Grand Corruption and Kleptocracy*, CSC

Working Paper No. 13, Falmer: Centre for the Study of Corruption, University of Sussex.

Barrington, R., Dávid-Barrett, E., Power, S. and Hough, D. (eds.), 2022, *Understanding Corruption: How Corruption Works in Practice*, Newcastle: Agenda Publishing.

Barrington, R. and Dávid-Barrett, E., 2023, 'Advocacy groups', in *Elgar Concise Encyclopedia of Corruption Law*, Cheltenham: Edward Elgar Publishing.

Barrington, R., Dávid-Barrett, E., Dobson Phillips, R. and Garrod, G. (eds.), 2023, *Dictionary of Corruption*, Newcastle: Agenda Publishing.

Bauhr, M., 2012, 'Need or greed corruption?', in Holmberg, S. and Rothstein, B. (eds.), *Good Government*, Cheltenham: Edward Elgar Publishing.

Berriman, A., 2015, *Squibs: The 1830 Chichester Election Campaign*, New Chichester papers no. 7, Chichester: University of Chichester.

Bingham, T. H., 2011, *The Rule of Law*, London: Penguin.

Blick, A. and Hennessy, P., 2019, *Good Chaps No More? Safeguarding the Constitution in Stressful Times*, London: The Constitution Society.

Bociga, D., Bellotti, E. and Lord, N., 2025, 'The network architecture of anti-money laundering: Strategic and tactical (dis)connections in the UK's policy, supervision, and enforcement landscape', *British Journal of Criminology*, pp. 101ff.

Campbell, L., 2016, 'Corruption by Organised Crime – A Matter of Definition?', *Current Legal Problems*, vol. 69, issue 1, pp. 115–41.

Cave, T. and Rowell, A., 2014, *A Quiet Word: Lobbying, Crony Capitalism and Broken Politics in Britain*, London: Penguin.

Cawood, I. and Crook, T. (eds.), *The Many Lives of Corruption: The Reform of Public Life in Modern Britain, c. 1750–1950*, Manchester: Manchester University Press.

Charteris-Black, J., 2011, *Politicians and Rhetoric: The Persuasive Power of Metaphor*, Basingstoke: Palgrave Macmillan.

Cheeseman, N. and Peiffer, C., 2025, 'Opening the door to anti-system leaders? Anti-corruption campaigns and the global rise of populism', *European Journal of Political Research*, 64(1), pp. 134–55.

Chibnall, S. and Saunders, P., 1977, 'Worlds apart: Notes on the social reality of corruption', *The British Journal of Sociology*, 28(2), pp. 138–54.

Clarkson, W., 2020, *Line of Duty – The Real Story of British Police Corruption*, London: John Blake Publishing.

Cooley, A., Prelec, T., Heathershaw, J. and Mayne, T. (2021), *Paying for a World Class Affiliation: Reputation Laundering in the University Sector of Open Societies*, Washington, DC: National Endowment for Democracy.

Cowdock, B., 2022, *Bell Pottinger and Reputation Laundering in South Africa*, in Barrington, R., Dávid-Barrett, E., Power, S. and Hough, D. (eds.), *Understanding Corruption: How Corruption Works in Practice*, Newcastle: Agenda Publishing.

Cox, B., Shirley, J. and Short, M., 1977, *The Fall of Scotland Yard*, London: Penguin.

Dávid-Barrett, E., Barrington, R. and Maxwell, N. (eds.), 2013, *Corruption in UK Local Government: The Mounting Risks*, London: Transparency International UK.

Dávid-Barrett, E., Fazekas, M., Hellmann O., Márk, L. and McCorley, C., 2020, 'Controlling corruption in development aid: New evidence from contract-level data', *Studies in Comparative International Development*, 55(4), pp. 481–515.

Dincer, O. and Johnston, M., 2025, *Corruption in America: A Fifty-Ring Circus*, Cambridge: Cambridge University Press.

Dobson Phillips, R., Dávid-Barrett, E. and Barrington, R., 2025, 'Defining Corruption in Context', *Perspectives on Politics*, pp. 1–15.

Doig, A., 1984, *Corruption and Misconduct in Contemporary British Politics*, Harmondsworth: Penguin Books.

Duncan, P. and Lord, N., 2024, 'Fit and proper? Analyzing the potential for illicit activity through English Premier League club ownership structures', *Sport in Society*, pp. 1–21.

Fieschi, C. and Heywood, P., 2004, 'Trust, cynicism and populist anti-politics', *Journal of Political Ideologies*, 9(3), pp. 289–309.

Finn, M. C., 2019, 'Material turns in British history: II. Corruption: imperial power, princely politics and gifts gone rogue', *Transactions of the Royal Historical Society*, 29, pp. 1–25.

Fukuyama, F., 2021, 'Making the internet safe for democracy', *Journal of Democracy*, 32(2), pp. 37–44.

Gee, J., Button, M., Hock, B. and Shepherd, D. W. J., 2021, *Fraud and Corruption in the Construction Sector*, London: Crowe UK.

Geoghegan, P., 2020, *Democracy for Sale: Dark Money and Dirty Politics*, London: Bloomsbury Publishing.

Gillard, M., 2019, *Legacy: Gangsters, Corruption and the London Olympics*, London: Bloomsbury Publishing.

Goodrich, S. (ed.), 2020, *Permission Accomplished: Assessing Corruption Risks in Local Government Planning*, London: Transparency International UK.

Goodrich, S. (ed.), 2024, *Behind the Masks: Corruption Red Flags in COVID-19 Public Procurement*, London: Transparency International UK.

Gregory, R. and Macaulay, M., 2023, 'Integrity and Misconduct in Public Office', in *Handbook of Public Administration Reform*, Cheltenham: Edward Elgar Publishing.

Haberly, D. and Wójcik, D., 2022, *Sticky Power: Global Financial Networks in the World Economy*, Oxford: Oxford University Press.

Haberly, D., Garrod, G. and Barrington, R., 2024, 'From Secrecy to Scrutiny: A New Map of Illicit Global Financial Networks and Regulation', CSC Working Paper No. 18, Falmer: Centre for the Study of Corruption, University of Sussex.

Harper, T., 2022. *Broken Yard: The Fall of the Metropolitan Police*, London: Biteback Publishing.

Heathershaw, J., Prelec, T. and Mayne, T., 2021, *Indulging Kleptocracy: British Service Providers, Postcommunist Elites, and the Enabling of Corruption*, Oxford: Oxford University Press.

Heathershaw, J. and Mayne, T., 2023, 'Explaining suspicious wealth: Legal enablers, transnational kleptocracy, and the failure of the UK's Unexplained Wealth Orders', *Journal of International Relations and Development*, 26(2), pp. 301–23.

Heidenheimer, A. J., Johnston, M. and LeVine, V. T. (eds.), 2024, *Political Corruption: A Handbook*, Abingdon: Routledge.

Heywood, P. M. (ed.), 2015, *Routledge Handbook of Political Corruption*, Abingdon: Routledge.

Heywood, P. M., 2017, 'Rethinking corruption: Hocus-pocus, locus and focus', *Slavonic and East European Review*, 95(1), pp. 21–48.

Heywood, P. M., 2018, 'Combating corruption in the twenty-first century: New approaches', *Daedalus*, 147(3), pp. 83–97.

Heywood, P. M. and Rose, J., 2015, 'Curbing corruption or promoting integrity? Probing the hidden conceptual challenge', in Hardi, P., Heywood, P. and Torsello, D. (eds.), *Debates of Corruption and Integrity: Perspectives from Europe and the US*, London: Palgrave Macmillan UK.

Hine, D. and Peele, G., 2016, *The Regulation of Standards in British Public Life*, Manchester: Manchester University Press.

Holmes, L., 2014, 'Police corruption and misconduct in Central and Eastern Europe', in William B. Simons (ed.), *East European Faces of Law and Society: Values and Practices*, Leiden: Brill Nijhoff, pp. 151–74.

Hough, D., 2017, 'International approaches to tackling corruption: What works and what doesn't?', *Frontiers of Law in China*, 12(3), pp. 339–54.

Hough, D. 2025, *Foul Play*, Agenda Publishing: Newcastle, p. 120.

Jancsics, D., 2019, 'Law enforcement corruption along the U.S. borders', *Security Journal*, 32(3), pp. 237–56.

Johansen, E., 1990, *Political Corruption: Scope and Resources: An Annotated Bibliography*, New York: Garland Publishing.

Johnston, M., 2005, *Syndromes of Corruption: Wealth, Power, and Democracy*, Cambridge: Cambridge University Press.

Jones, A., 2021, 'Combatting corruption and collusion in UK public procurement: Proposals for post-Brexit reform', *Modern Law Review*, 84(4), pp. 667–707.

Jones, O., 2014, *The Establishment: And How They Get Away With It*, London: Allen Lane.

Jones, P., 2012, 'Rethinking corruption in post-1950 urban Britain: The Poulson affair, 1972–1976', *Urban History*, 39(3), pp. 510–28.

Jones, P., 2013, *From Virtue to Venality: Corruption in the City*, Manchester: Manchester University Press.

Jones, P., 2019, 'Urban governance and its disorders: Corruption in the cities', *International Journal of Regional and Local History*, 14(2), pp. 55–61.

Jones, P., 2022. 'Civic Corruption in the Twentieth Century: The Case of Belfast and Glasgow, c. 1920–70', in Cawood, I. and Crook, T. (eds.), *The Many Lives of Corruption: The Reform of Public Life in Modern Britain, 1750–1950*, Manchester: Manchester University Press.

Jones, P., 2023, *Corrupt Britain: Public Ethics in Practice and Thought Since the Magna Carta*, Cham: Palgrave Macmillan.

Jupp, J. and Garrod, M., 2019, 'Legacies of the Troubles: The links between organized crime and terrorism in Northern Ireland', *Studies in Conflict & Terrorism*, 45(5–6), pp. 389–428.

Kaltwasser, C. R., Taggart, P. A., Espejo, P. O. and Ostiguy, P. (eds.), 2017, *The Oxford Handbook of Populism*, Oxford: Oxford University Press.

Kaufmann, D. and Vicente, P. C., 2011, 'Legal corruption', *Economics & Politics*, 23(2), pp. 195–219.

Klitgaard, R., 1988, *Controlling Corruption*, Berkeley: University of California Press.

Knights, M., 2021, *Trust and Distrust: Corruption in Office in Britain and its Empire, 1600–1850*, Oxford: Oxford University Press.

Kroeze, R., Vitória, A. and Geltner, G. (eds.), 2018, *Anticorruption in History: From Antiquity to the Modern Era*, Oxford: Oxford University Press.

Kroeze, R., Dalmau, P. and Monier, F. (eds.), 2021, *Corruption, Empire and Colonialism in the Modern Era*, Palgrave Studies in Comparative Global History, Singapore: Palgrave Macmillan.

Kuris, G., 2015, 'Watchdogs or guard dogs: Do anti-corruption agencies need strong teeth?', *Policy and Society*, 34(2), pp. 125–35.

Lessig, L., 2013, '"Institutional corruption" defined', *The Journal of Law, Medicine & Ethics*, 41(3), pp. 553–5

Lord, N., Doig, A., Levi, M., van Wingerde, K. and Benson, K., 2020, 'Implementing a divergent response? The UK approach to bribery in international and domestic contexts', *Public Money & Management*, 40(5), pp. 349–59.

Marquette, H. and Peiffer, C., 2018, 'Grappling with the "real politics" of systemic corruption: Theoretical debates versus "real-world" functions', *Governance*, 31(3), pp. 499–514.

Maxwell, N., Cowdock, B. and Barrington, R. (eds.), 2016, *Corruption Laws: A Non-lawyers' Guide to Laws and Offences in the UK Relating to Corrupt Behaviour*, London: Transparency International UK.

Mungiu-Pippidi, A., 2013, 'Becoming Denmark: Historical designs of corruption control', *Social Research: An International Quarterly*, 80(4), pp. 1259–86.

Selected Bibliography

Mungiu-Pippidi, A., 2015, *The Quest for Good Governance: How Societies Develop Control of Corruption*, Cambridge: Cambridge University Press.

Newburn, T., 2016, 'Social Disadvantage, Crime, and Punishment', in Hartley, D. and Platt, L. (eds.), *Social Advantage and Disadvantage*, Oxford: Oxford University Press.

Noonan, J. T., 1987, *Bribes*, Berkeley: University of California Press.

Nye, J. S., 1967, 'Corruption and political development: A cost–benefit analysis', *American Political Science Review*, 61(2), pp. 417–27.

Oborne, P., 2020, *The Assault on Truth: Boris Johnson, Donald Trump and the Emergence of a New Moral Barbarism*, London: Simon & Schuster.

Pasculli, L., 2019, 'Seeds of systemic corruption in the post-Brexit UK', *Journal of Financial Crime*, 26(3), pp. 705–18.

Persson, A., Rothstein, B. and Teorell, J., 2013, 'Why anticorruption reforms fail – systemic corruption as a collective action problem', *Governance*, 26(3), pp. 449–71.

Philp, M., 1997, 'Defining political corruption', *Political Studies*, 45(3), pp. 436–62.

Picci, L., 2024, *Rethinking Corruption: Reasons Behind the Failure of Anti-Corruption Efforts*, Cambridge: Cambridge University Press.

Podmore, J., 2012, *Out of Sight, Out of Mind: Why Britain's Prisons Are Failing*, Hull: Biteback Publishing.

Pozsgai-Alvarez, J. and Pastor Sanz, I., 2021, 'Mapping the (anti-) corruption field: Key topics and changing trends, 1968–2020', *Journal of Computational Social Science*, 4(2), pp. 851–81.

Rotberg, R. I., 1988, *The Founder: Cecil Rhodes and the Pursuit of Power*, Oxford: Oxford University Press.

Rothstein, B., 2011, 'Anti-corruption: The indirect "big bang" approach', *Review of International Political Economy*, 18(2), pp. 228–50.

Rothstein, B. and Uslaner, E. M., 2005, 'All for all: Equality, corruption, and social trust', *World Politics*, 58(1), pp. 41–72.

Russell, B., 1938, *Power: A New Social Analysis*, London: George Allen & Unwin.

Scott, J. C., 1969, 'The analysis of corruption in developing nations', *Comparative Studies in Society and History*, 11(3), pp. 315–41.

Shipley, T. and Barrington, R. (eds.), 2022, 'A Bibliography for UK

Corruption Studies', CSC Working Paper No. 14, Falmer: University of Sussex.

Silke, A., 2000, 'Drink, drugs, and rock'n'roll: Financing loyalist terrorism in Northern Ireland – Part two', *Studies in Conflict & Terrorism*, 23(2), pp. 107–27.

Taggart, P., 2018, 'Populism and "Unpolitics"', in Fitzi, G., Mackert, J. and Turner, B. (eds.), *Populism and the Crisis of Democracy: Volume 1: Concepts and Theory*, Abingdon: Routledge.

Thompson, D. F., 2018, 'Theories of institutional corruption', *Annual Review of Political Science*, 21(1), pp. 495–513.

Uslaner, E. M., 2015, 'The Consequences of Corruption', in Heywood, P. (ed.), *Routledge Handbook of Political Corruption*, Abingdon: Routledge.

Vannucci, A., 1997, 'Politicians and Godfathers: Mafia and Political Corruption in Italy', in della Porta, D. and Meny, Y. (eds.), *Democracy and Corruption in Europe*, London: Frances Pinter Publishers.

Vannucci, A., 2024, 'Mani pulite ("clean hands")', in De Sousa, L. and Coroado, S. (eds.), *Elgar Encyclopedia of Corruption and Society*, Cheltenham: Edward Elgar Publishing.

Vannucci, A. and Porta, D., 1999, *Corrupt Exchanges: Actors, Resources and Mechanisms of Political Corruption*, New York: Aldine de Gruyter.

Veenendaal, W., 2019, 'How smallness fosters clientelism: A case study of Malta', *Political Studies*, 67(4), pp. 1034–52.

Vergara, C., 2020, *Systemic Corruption: Constitutional Ideas for an Anti-Oligarchic Republic*, Princeton: Princeton University Press.

Warren, M. E., 2006, 'Political corruption as duplicitous exclusion', *PS: Political Science & Politics*, 39(4), pp. 803–7.

Watts, John, J., 2018. 'The Problem of the Personal: Tackling Corruption in Later Medieval England, 1250–1550', in Kroeze, R., Vitória, A. and Geltner, G. (eds.), *Anticorruption in History: From Antiquity to the Modern Era*, Oxford: Oxford University Press.

Zakaria, F., 1997, 'The rise of illiberal democracy', *Foreign Affairs*, 76, p. 22.

Zotzmann, K., 2025, *Codes of Corruption: A Critical Realist Discourse Analysis of Illicit Transactions*, Abingdon: Taylor & Francis.